D1288962

TINKER
IN TELEVISION
FROM GENERAL SARNOFF TO GENERAL ELECTRIC

■

Grant Tinker and Bud Rukeyser

SIMON & SCHUSTER
NEW YORK LONDON TORONTO SYDNEY TOKYO SINGAPORE

SIMON & SCHUSTER
Rockefeller Center
1230 Avenue of the Americas
New York, New York 10020

SIMON & SCHUSTER and colophon are registered trademarks
of Simon & Schuster Inc.
Designed by H. J. Kim & P. L. Koay
Manufactured in the United States of America

1   3   5   7   9   10   8   6   4   2

Library of Congress Cataloging-in-Publication Data
Tinker, Grant.
Tinker in television: from General Sarnoff to General Electric/
Grant Tinker and Bud Rukeyser.
p.   cm.
1. Tinker, Grant.   2. Television broadcasting—United States
—Biography.   3. Executives—United States—Biography.
4. National Broadcasting Company, Inc.   5. MTM
Enterprises.   I. Rukeyser, Bud.   II. Title.
PN1992.4.T55A3   1994
791.45′0232′092—dc20   94-25865
[B]   CIP
ISBN: 0-671-75940-X

In gratitude to all the talented people who have made coming to work each day so rewarding—and to the wonderful people who have made it so nice to come home.

G.A.T.

For Phyllis, Jill, and Trish.

B.R.

Those who recognize its romantic and mystical aspects have a better chance of running the business of it successfully, because the two are intertwined.

—Bob Costas, on *Later . . . with Bob Costas*
(he was talking about baseball)

ACKNOWLEDGMENTS

This is not an as-told-to book. It's Grant's book—his experiences, views, insights, even indictments—all of which I have helped organize and structure, and to which I have contributed a great deal of history and information about network television. Grant and I worked closely together during his third and final hitch at NBC, and he asked me to join him on this new project. The authors of most books about television have been either broadcast journalists, writing about news, or print reporters covering the broadcast beat; Grant's book was to be the first to look at forty-plus years of network television from the inside out, and from the top down.

Most of the research was completed during a year I spent at Columbia University as a senior fellow at the Freedom Forum Media Studies Center, and I'm grateful beyond measure to Ev Dennis, the Center's director, for taking me in. He, then–Associate Director Jane Coleman, and their staff—in particular Lisa DeLisle, Wendy Boyd, and my research assistant, Chanan Beizer—provided bountiful resources and support. Fellow fellows Henry Graff, Jim Hoge, Bernie Kalb, Kati Marton, Richard Bernstein, and Pat Garry provided wise counsel and some great lunches.

A book like this owes its life to the people who contributed facts, reminiscences, ideas, and encouragement—and to some who did much more. We owe special thanks to Becky Saletan, our editor; to Jay Acton and Stu Miller, our agents; to Doreen Behnke, for turning out hours of transcribed tapes and countless pages of copy; and to Ken Auletta and Peter Kaplan, two friends who know plenty about writing and editing books and generously shared their knowledge with two guys who didn't.

Many broadcasting colleagues helped with anecdotes, fact-checking, and moral support: Bill Alexander, Alan Baker, Curt Block, Steve Bochco, Patricia Brown, Allan Burns, Bob Butler, Tony Cervini, Cory Dunham, Tom Ervin, Stu Erwin, Cathy Gay, Gary David Goldberg, Maury Goodman, Peter Grad, Stu Gray, Larry Grossman, Bob Jacobs, Jerry Jaffe, Rob Kaplan, Jay Kriegel, Bob Lewine, Melissa Ludlum, Patty Matson, Gene McGuire, Howard Monderer, Bas O'Hagan, Bruce Paltrow, Fred Paxton, Ancil Payne, Jay Sandrich, Herb Schlosser, Irwin Segelstein, Michael Silver, Frank Stanton, Ray Timothy, George Vradenberg, Bob Walsh, and some who prefer anonymity.

Financial and ratings data were provided by Wertheim, Schroder; John Reidy at Smith Barney; Rich MacDonald at Wasserstein & Perella; Susan Kempler at Morgan Stanley; Geoff Foisie and Steve Coe at *Broadcasting* magazine; and Jack Loftus, Diane Buono, and JoAnn LaVerde at Nielsen.

Friends from the press—in particular Verne Gay at *Newsday,* Neil Hickey and Roger Youman at *TV Guide,* and Don West at *Broadcasting*—went out of their way to help us, and Alison Soler at the King School and Mary Farrington at Dartmouth dug into their archives to supply information about Grant's alma maters.

Finally, I'd like to thank my co-writer for his friendship and for letting me in on this caper. In thirty years at NBC, I reported directly to the last four CEOs and learned something from each about what makes network television a different kind of business. The lasting lesson of the Grant Tinker story is that the surest way to succeed in this particular business is to aim at something higher than the bottom line.

                                                        B.R.

On a spring day in 1981, sitting in my MTM office in Studio City, California, minding my own business, I took a call from Paul Ziffren, the distinguished and influential West Coast attorney. Paul was a courtly man, and he spent a couple of minutes proving it before getting to the reason for his call: "As I'm sure you know," he said, "Thornton Bradshaw has left the presidency of Arco to become the new chairman of RCA. He's got all sorts of difficult problems to deal with, and one of them is NBC. That's a world Brad doesn't know a lot about, so he's been sitting down with some people around town to get a sense of the company and its problems. You've worked at NBC and you also deal with them now. Brad wonders if you'd be willing to have lunch and share some of your views."

Would I ever! I had worked for NBC twice, once in the early fifties and again in the sixties. For several years I'd been watching with growing dismay the deterioration of a company for which I still had a great deal of affection. NBC was in turmoil; it had slipped from its perennial second-place-with-honor to a dismal third, had only one regular series in the top twenty, employee morale was terrible, and the press had written the company off.

Although NBC had changed in many ways during the fifteen years since my second tour of duty, to me it would always be, somehow, the family I'd first joined in 1949. I deplored what had happened to the company and had some strong opinions about what was wrong with it. I told Paul I'd be delighted to meet Thornton Bradshaw, and we arranged a lunch date for later that week.

We met at Perino's, a rather snooty Wilshire Boulevard restaurant that was well off my beaten path. I liked Bradshaw instantly. Pipe-smoking and tweedy, obviously intelligent, he had an avuncular, old-shoe quality that put me immediately at ease. Paul was there to make the introductions and get the conversation started, but he wasn't needed for long. Brad started asking a number of frank and leading questions, and I gave him exceedingly candid answers. I wasn't just voluble; *I knew everything*. And since Bradshaw had played no role in the NBC decline, I had no hesitation in telling him exactly what I thought. My principal theme was the way the company (and, for that matter, ABC and CBS) behaved toward creative people. It was a song that could have been sung to Bradshaw by almost anyone in the business of supplying programs to the networks.

I explained that the primary responsibility of program executives is to select and buy the shows their network wishes to broadcast. Decisions about which to choose are based largely on judgments about the experience and creative ability of the producers: Do they have a vision of their project that can be translated into a successful network program? Does the work they've done in the past indicate they can select and attract the writers, actors, and directors necessary to produce good television? But, I went on, there have always been far too many network executives who overstep their selecting and buying function and attempt to "produce the producers." With little or no creative credentials, they impose their judgments on the very people they've retained to produce their shows. The frequent result of their meddling and mandating is damage to the ultimate product. NBC, I told Bradshaw, was at the time the worst offender. As a result, the most coveted creative people, exactly the ones the network desperately needed to help it out of third place, were avoiding NBC because of its stifling oversupervision of program production.

This argument was entirely valid, although it was self-serving to a degree. If I could make the producers' case with Bradshaw, I'd serve my own cause at MTM at the same time. For that matter, if I could get him to make some changes at NBC, I'd be doing the entire production community a giant favor.

While I was waxing so wise about the dangers of network interference in the creative process, I also got in some good licks about the foolish and disrespectful way the networks treated programs once they were on the air. Too often shows were canceled and discarded long before they had sufficient time to find their audiences. Or nervous network executives moved programs from night to night, time period to time period, in the desperate and almost always futile hope that viewers would somehow find them. Even as I spoke, MTM's *Hill Street Blues* was a victim of such behavior. In the few months it had been on the schedule, always with anemic Nielsen shares, NBC had moved it back and forth from 10 o'clock Thursday to 10 o'clock Saturday to 9 o'clock Tuesday. Even the cult that loved it from the beginning had trouble finding it. Clearly, the larger potential audience for *Hill Street* was going to need time and stable scheduling in order to get comfortable with its complexity and innovative style. Until NBC stopped jerking it around, I was convinced, there was no way to find out how large the potential was. At that moment, *Hill Street* was languishing in ninetieth place (out of 106 network programs), right behind an ABC show called *Those Amazing Animals*.

So Bradshaw got an earful, unquestionably far more than he had bargained for. But he had asked for it. I had been on the production company side of the fence, tilting at network windmills, for more than a dozen years, and my hapless interviewer paid a price that day for each and every year. He was a patient and attentive listener, though, and I don't think we got out of Perino's in under three hours. As I drove back to my office, I told myself I had gone on far too long. Even so, I wasn't unhappy to have unburdened myself to someone who might actually be able to change some things.

Three weeks later, with that lunch a receding memory, I received a second phone call, this time from Brad directly. "I wanted to thank you for your time and for some exceedingly interesting insights," he said. "They gave me a lot to think about. Now I have some new questions, and I wonder if I could impose on you once more. I'm here at Arco, cleaning out my office. Could you possibly come downtown tomorrow and join me for lunch in my dining room?" I could and I would and I did.

Twenty years in Los Angeles and I was still a stranger to downtown. Just making my way to the fiftieth floor of the Arco Tower was an adventure, but I finally found Bradshaw pawing around among a career's worth of oil business memories. Over appetizers in the executive dining room, he reviewed our earlier meeting, and as the entrée went south, he wondered aloud whether NBC was even salvageable, whether the boat had already sunk. My response must have been on the positive side, because then and there he sprang the trap:

"I don't suppose you'd consider coming back to help."

I wrongly assumed he was talking about the top programming post in Burbank, president of the Entertainment division, the job NBC president Fred Silverman had recently given Brandon Tartikoff. I quickly declined, concealing my surprise that he would even think the assignment would interest me.

"No, I mean coming back to run the whole company. Is that a ridiculous thought?"

"As a matter of fact, it isn't," I heard myself say.

Up to that moment, I had been in the no-lose, ego-satisfying role of guest expert, giving lots of advice while bearing absolutely no responsibility. Along with every television producer past and present, I had occasionally expressed the thought that anyone—certainly I—could run a network better than the idiots who were doing it. This was usually said as a throwaway line at a staff meeting, and, in that context, "the network" meant the Hollywood-based program departments. But Brad was talking about running all of NBC: the television network, the radio networks, the News and Sports divisions, and the array of television and radio stations the company owned in cities across the country—thousands of people and myriad corporate duties. I thanked him for the offer, but pointed out that I liked living in California and he was talking about a job in New York.

"Do the job from here," Brad countered. "You could move the people you need from New York to Burbank."

That showed Brad's unfamiliarity with how the company and the business worked, and I told him I didn't think NBC could be run from Burbank. Almost all of its entertainment programs were commissioned from that production outpost, but the *business* of the company was conducted in New York, where most of its divisions were necessarily headquartered. The functions they represented could not be properly supervised on a long-distance basis. But to his surprise (and, on reflection, my own amazement), I heard myself say, "I'll do it."

Go figure. In one short sentence, I had made a commitment to leave California, where the livin' was easy, and a situation that was completely under my control, with good profits and high prestige. I was running a production company that I had started and built, one that not very arguably was the best in the business, supplying shows that plenty of people would have killed for. Yet I had just said I would give all that up to become once again a salaried employee, based in a city I didn't like, and this time charged with the responsibility of resurrecting a company that was the industry laughingstock.

In hindsight, it was a decision I never should have made. The eventual cost to me was incalculable, but I remember the thinking that got me there. It had been eleven years since my wife, Mary Tyler Moore, and I had started MTM on the strength of a single thirteen-episode commitment. *Mary Tyler Moore* had succeeded beyond our wildest dreams, the first of a series of acclaimed shows to carry our logo. We had been able to attract an inordinate share of the most talented practitioners available to television, and the programs they created would be celebrated for years to come.

Yet it was hard for me to imagine matching those cherished MTM experiences and associations in the future, let alone surpassing them. And our success had changed the nature of the company. Where once I had been closely involved in everything that went on, now we were larger and somehow more impersonal. My own role had changed from hands-on to eyes-on. The psychic income was sharply down and, while coming to work each day was hardly a chore, the thrill was largely gone.

At the same time, the prospect of returning to NBC was a powerful magnet. I had a wonderful memory of what it used to be, and a terrible impression of what it had become. Fred Silverman was justly renowned for the programming wonders he had previously performed at both CBS and ABC, but as president of NBC, he seemed to be fruitlessly spinning his wheels. Today he's a prolific producer, able and successful, but then he was in a frantic, almost manic, period. He hadn't been able to repeat the magic he'd managed at CBS and ABC; everything he tried went wrong and NBC was sinking fast.

Whenever I'd go over to NBC's Burbank headquarters—MTM had only recently begun doing shows for them—the good memories from the sixties would reemerge. Brandon's office was my old office, and some of the people I had worked with were still there. The whole town was aware of what was happening to NBC, but as a loyal alumnus I felt its failure more than most. I never thought of it as a company owned by shareholders. To me, it was a bunch of people, many of them friends, who were floundering. So when Brad popped the question and I said yes, I wasn't thinking about RCA shareholder values or other corporate concerns.

Back in 1949, I had entered the company at the bottom; now I was being asked to come back at the top. And not just to run it, but to save it. The seductive image was of a man on a white horse riding to the rescue of old friends.

It was months later, at an RCA board meeting (one of oh-so-many over the next five years), that I realized what a serious miscalculation I'd made. I walked into the paneled boardroom on the fifty-third floor of 30 Rockefeller Plaza on a day of black clouds and drenching rain. Sitting around the table were captains of industry in suits that matched the color of the New York sky. Mostly, they wanted to talk about NBC and why we still hadn't turned it around, so I found myself the center of unwanted attention.

That was when it finally dawned on me: I was busting my ass not for the people downstairs at NBC, but for the gray suits sitting around that table and the shareholders they represented. That scenario was far less romantic, far less noble, and far less attractive than the one I had fantasized. Had I originally viewed Bradshaw's appeal in that context and, more emphatically, had I been able to foresee that five years later General Electric would gobble up the fruits of our restoration labors, I surely would have turned him down.

But on that sunny June afternoon, the challenge Bradshaw offered was irresistible. And my crusade delusion even extended to a grand gesture about remuneration. The minute I was back in my MTM office, Paul Ziffren was on the phone. "Brad's embarrassed," he began. "He never even asked how much you wanted." Later, it would occur to me that Paul was really offering, in his decent, understated fashion, to make the deal for me. He probably would have made a great one, too, perhaps including some sort of percentage interest in NBC's ultimate success. Instead, I told him—and this really shows how far down the path of righteousness I was—"I'm not doing this for money. I just think I can do it and I *want* to do it."

Paul was persistent: "I've got to tell Brad something." "Okay," I said. "I've read NBC was paying Fred Silverman a million dollars a year. Tell Brad I'll do it for $500,000."

And that's what I did.

Leaving a job in which I was doing well in order to try something entirely new has been a lifelong habit. The thought of planning a career path never crossed my mind, so what looks in retrospect like a carefully organized pattern of résumé-building was really a series of separate, sometimes accidental opportunities. "Why not?" has always been my substitute for long-range planning.

That was certainly the case during my growing-up years. I wasn't exactly aimless; I just wasn't required to do a lot of forward thinking. My father was a very organized, rational guy, and the household he headed was a reflection of him. He worked for the same lumber company all his adult life (eventually as president), and never moved from the Stamford, Connecticut, house in which I grew up until we kids had all left home. My mother's death at fifty-eight left him a widower for more than two decades.

I was bracketed by two sisters, Phyllis and Joan. We didn't interact much, except at dinnertime. They did girl things, and I spent most of my time out and about, usually playing whatever sport was in season. We all got along pretty well, but we had very little in common other than our parents. Even in my teens, when I discovered other girls, I only tolerated my sisters.

Today, most of our contact is by phone. Both of them have been better at keeping up the sibling relationship than their inattentive brother. Joan now lives in Florida and Phyllis remains in Connecticut, where she culls the Stamford *Advocate* for news that might interest me. Periodically she cheers me up by calling to read me the obituary of one of my childhood friends.

My early years were entirely unremarkable. I had parents who were decent and responsible and, to the extent the Depression permitted, generous providers. My mother always valued education, probably because she left Vassar during her freshman year to get married and never finished college. At about the same time, she became deaf, which in turn fostered her lifelong love of books. All through my high school years, she was a stickler about getting me to do my homework. I can remember many nights sitting in my room at 11 o'clock, staring at the same page of homework I'd been looking at since right after dinner.

Like most of my other life decisions, my choice of a college was haphazard. My dad never went beyond high school, so all his alumni loyalties were centered on the U.S. Army. He had served during World War I in the Fighting 69th and was wounded at Chateau Thierry. Every year he attended the reunion of the Rainbow Division at the Seventh Regiment Armory in New York, and sometimes he'd take me to West Point to watch Army play football. But because we lived in Connecticut, it was more convenient to drive to the Yale Bowl, even though Dad had no ties there, old school or otherwise. For some reason we frequently wound up at the Dartmouth game, usually played in New Haven in those days. Practically everyone in the place was an Old Blue, which naturally caused me to root for Dartmouth. Somewhere along the way it just became understood that I'd be going to college in Hanover, New Hampshire. Very scientific.

By the time I graduated from high school in June 1943, World War II was well underway. I had already been accepted for pilot training in the Air Corps, and I was gung-ho to fly. The problem was that I couldn't be called up until my eighteenth birthday in January. To fill in the six-month gap, I applied to Dartmouth and was immediately accepted, no great civilian trick in 1943. I boarded the overnight train at Stamford, got off at White River Junction with two modest suitcases, and made my way over to Hanover, which I'd never even visited. As soon as the various registration details had been dealt with, I headed for the baseball field.

I had been baseball captain at the King School in Stamford, a boys' school so small that almost everybody was on one team or another, and many of us played everything. I had batted around .450 that spring and thought I was pretty hot stuff. That thought lasted until the first day of practice at Dartmouth, when it became immediately apparent that I was in a new league. I was a seventeen-year-old kid in the midst of a bunch of older Marine Corps and Navy guys in the V12 program. To me they looked and played like the New York Yankees. I spent the summer as an unutilized utility infielder.

Exactly one week after my eighteenth birthday I was inducted into the Air Corps at Fort Devens in Massachusetts. I spent the next two years being transferred all over the country as a PAC, a pre-aviation cadet, along with thousands of other guys my age who had arrived in the program a year too late. Dick Van Dyke, I would learn twenty years later, was among them. I was shunted from Massachusetts to North Carolina to Indiana to Illinois to West Virginia to Alabama and to several bases in Texas, doing scut work, K.P., and guard duty, and getting a little training but never flying.

When the war ended, I was stationed (stalled is more like it) in Big Spring, Texas. The Air Corps gave us the choice between an honorable discharge or signing up for three more years, with the guarantee that we'd become pilots. I'd been so eager to fly for so long that I actually considered the prospect seriously before coming to my senses. Young guys in the postwar period were expected to move expeditiously to whatever educational level they could manage, and then get on as quickly as possible with the business of earning a living. Flying planes when there was no war to fight fell into the category of unacceptable delay.

So, in February 1946 I went back to Dartmouth. Between the months I'd already put in and some academic work I'd done in the Air Corps, I got credit for a complete freshman year. Tuition was only $450 a year then, but it was an amount my father would have had trouble handling. The G.I. Bill paid my tuition plus $60 a month, and I bused trays at the Hanover Inn for my meals.

After the humbling experience of my freshman season, I realized baseball wasn't an option, so I switched to tennis. During the Depression, my dad and some neighbors had built a tennis court in the field next to our house to use on weekends. It was a clay court, and my job as a kid was maintaining it—brushing, rolling, and putting down the lines. It was a pain-in-the-ass job, but my reward came on Saturdays and Sundays when someone would hit with me. If one of the men didn't show up, I'd even get a chance to play, so I got into tennis at a very early age. Considering that I've played the game for over fifty years, it's amazing that I never got to be a real "A" player. And now, some recent surgery to replace my right knee has ended my court career.

At Dartmouth I wasn't good enough to play singles, but made the team as the doubles partner of Bob Jordan, who's now a very fine artist living in New Jersey. We did reasonably well competitively, keeping in mind that Dartmouth was not exactly in the major league of college tennis. The weather was chilly, the season short, and we spent the spring hitting indoors. The Dartmouth facilities were a step up from the court my dad built, but no threat to UCLA or the University of Miami. Along with the tennis, I was a garden variety journeyman jock, playing touch football and softball in the fraternity leagues. Alpha Delta Phi, my house, was probably better known for athletics than for turning out Rhodes scholars, and I also did my share of helping to empty the kegs of beer that were a Saturday night fixture in the A.D. basement. Perhaps in recognition of this contribution, I was elected president of the fraternity in my senior year.

My academic record was extremely average, and I had to work hard to get it that high. Even with the help of Music Appreciation and other taxing courses, I maintained only a 2.6 average. I was an English major and spent countless hours in Baker Library trying without much success to equal the marks many classmates seemed to get without effort. But I did learn to work.

In the summer of 1947 I drove to California with my best friend, Harry Tremaine. We used his car, because I had not yet acquired the remarkable '36 Ford convertible that sat outside in the New Hampshire snow and ice most of my senior year, performing flawlessly whenever called on. Harry and I had each saved a few bucks, though no one ever spent less on a cross-country vacation than we did that summer.

It was my first time in California and I loved it. Just loved it. For a kid whose entire life experience had been New England–bound, Southern California was beguilingly casual and informal. While the phrase *laid back* was still uncoined, the concept had already taken hold. The world had not yet discovered this sunny paradise, come west to enjoy it, and overpopulated away its charms. When Harry and I finally exhausted our meager funds, we motored nonstop back to Connecticut. One of us drove while the other slept, and we made it home in something like forty-two hours. But a seed had been planted, and I began to realize that being an Easterner didn't have to be forever.

Back at Dartmouth, everyone had to write a senior thesis, and I chose Richard Brinsley Sheridan, the Irish dramatist who lived from 1751 to 1816 and produced three great comedies: *The Rivals, The School for Scandal,* and *The Critic.* He wrote them while in his twenties and then turned to a life in politics, thus assuring that his body of work would be small enough to be easily handled by a student researcher in the twentieth century. What's more, his wit, his ability to involve the audience quickly, his gift for dialogue, and his sharply drawn characters gave me a standard by which to judge literate comedy designed for a mass audience. Sheridan's style was very close to that of the best three-camera comedies on television, the kind on which MTM would later be founded. To me, he was a creative forerunner of Jim Brooks and Allan Burns and all the other world-class multiple-camera comedy writers. If Richard Brinsley Sheridan were alive today, he'd be winning Emmys.

Writing the thesis turned out to be easier than finding employment. Dartmouth, at least back in the late 1940s, was conscientious about helping each of its seniors land a job after graduation. Representatives from some of America's most prestigious companies came on campus to interview prospective employees. Despite the pleas of my placement counselor, I never saw any of them, simply because I had already decided what I wanted to do. I was going to go to New York, get a job in publishing, and live happily ever after.

The picture I had of publishing was based on nothing more than the love of reading I'd inherited from my mother, and not on any knowledge whatsoever of the business. I saw myself sitting in an office all day, reading, making judgments, working with authors, and commissioning worthy projects. I learned how unrealistic this was when I started knocking on doors. I knew absolutely no one in the business and was surprised to discover that none of New York's publishing houses gave a rat's ass that I wanted to work for them.

After several weeks of coming up dry in the big city, I got a call from my placement counselor back in Hanover, who was still irritated by my refusal to interview with Minnesota Mining or

American Sugar. He wasn't surprised to learn that I was striking out. At that stage, I was resigned to the realization that I wasn't going to be a publishing mogul and, in fact, was becoming a little desperate about finding any work at all. So I responded eagerly to a suggestion I might have dismissed out of hand three weeks earlier.

"I've heard NBC might be starting a training program," he said. "Maybe you ought to go by there for an interview."

Late one February morning in 1949, I took the elevator to the seventh floor of the RCA Building to make my assault on the NBC personnel department. All I knew about NBC was that it broadcast many of the programs I had grown up with. The radio in our Stamford living room was often tuned to NBC's New York flagship station, then WEAF, where I could listen with my father and sisters to *Fibber McGee and Molly, Bob Hope, Edgar Bergen and Charlie McCarthy, Mr. District Attorney, The Aldrich Family, The Great Gildersleeve,* and an array of serials that were part of every kid's life. I didn't know that NBC had been the most powerful company in radio ever since RCA's David Sarnoff founded it in 1926, and that I was arriving just as the streak was ending. CBS's William Paley had picked off Jack Benny from the NBC schedule in late 1948 and in the following months was to take Red Skelton, George Burns and Gracie Allen, and Edgar Bergen. By the end of 1949, CBS would have twelve of the top fifteen shows and NBC's era of radio dominance would be finished.

In 1949, network radio itself was in its final years at center stage, its successor just off in the wings. Nearly 40 million American homes owned at least one radio, while only 940 *thousand* had a TV set.

Several years earlier, NBC had sent TV sets to the homes of New York's most influential advertising executives. The idea was to get them excited about the new medium and to start a ripple of enthusiasm among their affluent friends and neighbors. It worked pretty well with the Madison Avenue big shots who lived in Connecticut, Westchester, and Long Island, but it was a dismal failure in Manhattan. Skyscrapers caused NBC's signal from the Empire State Building to bounce all over town, and ad agency honchos on the Upper East Side were getting an unwatchable jumble of ghosts, distortion, and snow.

O. B. Hanson, who had been NBC's chief engineer since the founding of the company, wrote a memo to president Niles Trammell explaining that there was no way to deliver a clear over-the-air signal to viewers in Manhattan. He asked Trammell's permission to approach the telephone company about sending the network's programs to its New York City viewers over the phone lines. Trammell rejected the idea on the spot. We're broadcasters, he said, and the whole idea of broadcasting is over-the-air transmission. So ended the prospect of what might have been a watershed alliance: NBC and AT&T combining to deliver the first cable programs to American viewers.

In 1948, RCA had commissioned a study designed to assess the prospects of television and the part it might play in NBC's future. One of America's leading management consulting firms spent several months conducting interviews and produced a fat tome, replete with footnotes, that provided the definitive answer: Television, while an interesting technological development, would never replace radio as NBC's main business. Sometimes it pays not to know these things.

Three weeks and several interviews after my initial appointment, I was scheduled for one final audition with thirty-two-year-old Charles E. Denny, recently hired as NBC's executive vice president, following his service as chairman of the Federal Communications Commission. Mr. Denny was unavailable, so instead I had a very pleasant meeting with his scholarly young assistant, David Adams, who must have stamped me "approved." Adams would remain in high-level posts at NBC throughout his working life, giving valued advice and counsel to an array of CEOs.

I went home to Stamford to sweat out the result. The call finally came. I was being hired as NBC's first executive trainee for one year, at $3,000. If I lived up to expectations, I would earn a real job within the company.

For the next few months I was shuttled from department to department, learning a little about everything from music rights to sound effects. The training program had very little structure, but NBC continued to hire more eager young guys, several of whom went on to enjoy long careers in broadcasting: Rick Kelly stayed at NBC for more than forty years and ran the corporate events unit, Jack Kiermaier became a senior executive at CBS, Don Hyatt produced award-winning public affairs programs for NBC, and Pat Harrington was an NBC time salesman before he went on to become a successful comedian and actor.

Harrington, who was funny long before he was paid to be, once pulled a legendary hoax on his NBC colleagues. He located an actor who looked a lot like RCA chairman General David Sarnoff and had him burst unannounced into the weekly sales meeting. "Carry on, gentlemen," the poseur said reassuringly to the awe-struck gathering. "Periodically I like to visit every part of the RCA family, and today I'm interested in how NBC sells its pro-grams. Please just go about your business and pretend I'm not even in the room."

For the next fifteen minutes or so, the sales staff went stiffly through the motions, never able to forget for a second that their careers were in the hands of that imposing fellow sitting silently in the back. Finally, the General spoke up. "I'm curious," he said, as every head in the room spun around, "why you people even bother to print a rate card, since you seem to make entirely different deals with every advertiser." No one wanted to risk saying the wrong thing, so there was silence.

After letting the question hang for a long moment, Pat Har-rington cleared his throat. "Look, General," he said, as the re-lieved group turned his way. "We're much too busy to play questions and answers. Why don't you just get your ass back up to the fifty-third floor and let us run the fucking network."

NBC finally ran out of departments for its first management trainee, and I was assigned to the Night Operations unit. I be-came the junior person in a four-man group whose job was to operate the NBC Radio Network after everyone else had gone home. The boss was a young fellow named Bob Wogan, who was to remain an NBC Radio stalwart for more than four decades. We came in at 5 P.M. and left at 1 A.M., when the network went off the air, and we were also the weekend staff.

Our little unit rattled around in offices on the second floor of the RCA Building, where scores of radio people worked during more normal business hours. Radio City Music Hall was right across 50th Street from our offices, and on warm nights in that pre-air-conditioning era, the windows to the Rockettes' dressing room would frequently be left open. To four young guys at NBC, it was a nice fringe benefit—better than most of the shows we were broadcasting.

Because we were a network staff in microcosm, we got involved in everything. We'd field all the calls that came in from the public, track down missing announcers and see that they'd be in the right studio at the right time, make sure the band from the St. Francis Hotel in San Francisco got on the air at midnight, and deal with the occasional little emergency. Often I'd deliver the Teletyped messages that came in during the night to the sixth-floor office suite of Joe McConnell, NBC's president, the same space I'd be occupying as chairman some thirty years later.

At about this time, the winter of 1949, I met Ruth Byerly, who was to become my first wife, ultimately the mother of my daughter and three sons, and the first of three wonderful women in my life. She was the date one evening of a Connecticut friend, John de Garmo, who had just begun what would become a very successful career in advertising. Though I had a date of my own that Saturday night, I was immediately attracted to Ruth. I called John on Monday to learn more about her and to inquire whether he'd mind if I asked her out. I ignored his obvious reluctance, forcing him to respond unenthusiastically, "No, of course not." I called Ruth that day, and we got together by the end of the week.

Ruth was a graduate of Finch, slightly younger than I, and already an entrepreneur. She had opened a shop in Norwalk specializing in baby clothes and accoutrements, and that, given my own lowly status at NBC, impressed me. But I was more impressed by Ruth herself. She was bright, attractive, and had a great sense of humor. We had a lot in common, and she was fun to be with. I was still commuting to New York from Stamford, and Ruth lived in nearby Wilton, making it easy for us to see each other. Our fairly speedy courtship was driven by what was then conventional behavior for young folks: finish college, find a job, get married. The sequence was usually managed as though everyone were going to a fire.

Ruth and I were married March 1, 1950, and promptly accomplished the next expected activity by producing son number one, Mark, in January of the next year. Michael followed in 1952,

Jodie in 1954, and John appeared in 1958, by which time I was working at McCann-Erickson. The creative head of the agency was a much-respected man named Jack Tinker (no relation). I persuaded Ruth that a desirable result of naming our son John was that he'd be called Jack. I'm partial to a final "k" in front of Tinker. It just sounds strong and right to me, at least for sons, though my parents obviously didn't share that opinion. And wouldn't you know, John never did become Jack.

After about eleven months on the night shift at NBC Radio, I knew it was time to stop rehearsing and get a real job. I was married by now, and Mark was on the way. I told the NBC personnel department that I needed to find a permanent assignment or I would have to look elsewhere. They came up with the exalted title of "operations manager of the radio network," gave me my own secretary, a fourth-floor office with a window that overlooked the Rockefeller Center skating rink, and a 10 percent raise, to $3,300 a year. Still, I felt it was a job I didn't deserve. I had scant knowledge of how the business worked and less experience than the people I was now supervising. I figured I was the beneficiary of NBC's need to give one of its trainees a responsible job so that the program would appear to be working.

After I'd been at it for a little while, a tough, hard-drinking Irishman named Bud Barry came over from Young & Rubicam to head up NBC Radio's network programming. Late one afternoon he asked me to join him for a drink. Afternoon became evening and the drink turned into many drinks, our palship growing as the Scotch went down. It was almost 10 o'clock when Bud walked me over to Grand Central Station to get my train to Connecticut. We stopped at the newsstand, each of us simulating sobriety. All pretense ended when I dropped my newspaper to the marble floor. I remember muttering, "Oh, fuck it," as I proceeded to kick the *World-Telegram* across the concourse of the station. This sophisticated performance impressed Barry, because as we parted, he said, "You seem okay to me. I'm going to take a chance and leave you where you are." Not so fast, I reacted ungratefully. "I'm good at my job and I should be getting more money." He said he'd sleep on it, which was clearly a good idea. A couple of days later, he called to say he was giving me a "huge" raise, building it up so much I was convinced I was going to be rich. Huge turned out to be $600 a year, taking me all the way to $3,900.

For the next year or so I worked under Barry at NBC Radio, making little impact on the world of broadcasting but learning every day and meeting lots of people. One of those I met was Bob Wamboldt, who had left NBC to become third-in-command at Radio Free Europe (RFE). He asked me to drop by their offices on 57th Street, off Sixth Avenue, and I went, although without any particular interest. I perked up when Bob and a couple of his colleagues told me about RFE's plans to open a facility similar to the one already in operation in Munich, which was broadcasting into six Iron Curtain countries. The new origination point was to be Istanbul, and they wanted to send me there. The job had a kind of romantic, save-the-world sound that appealed to me, even though at that point I couldn't have located Istanbul on a map. I responded to it with the first flick of what I would come to recognize as career-long job restlessness. In this case, the decision was made easier when they offered me $8,000 a year, twice what I was getting at NBC. I went home to Connecticut, talked to Ruth about it, and we agreed it would be a worthwhile adventure.

Radio Free Europe was funded not so secretly by the CIA, though nobody talked about it. There were international anxieties, particularly among the intelligence community, in those early "cold war" days. Some of them seem almost paranoid in retrospect, but at the time, the memory of war was still fresh. I was too unsophisticated in such matters to understand why, if the Voice of America could acknowledge its government underwriting, Radio Free Europe couldn't.

RFE's New York office was a Babel of foreign accents, with most of the staff working at the various "desks" that created and produced the programming broadcast into the six target countries. Each desk had a counterpart in Munich, and only a handful in either location were Americans. I worked there for almost a year before I began to suspect there might never be an Istanbul RFE facility—and there never has been. Baby number two was not far off, and I decided I should get back to the real world.

One day in late 1952, while schlepping around midtown, I ran into John Moses, a man I'd done business with at NBC. John was a combination personal manager/promoter with a one-man office at 57th and Fifth, and he used to come to NBC to sell us people and programs. I had still been at the network when he brought us a brilliant young comedy team from a Boston radio station. Bob (Elliot) and Ray (Goulding) were an immediate hit on NBC, especially on radio. They did several years of early evening television shows, too, but the wonderfully funny characters they created, as well as the ridiculous situations they put them in, played best in the "theater of the mind" that radio allowed.

John was a well-liked and effective salesman, but followthrough was not his strong suit. He asked me to come to work for him, and I did. I think he paid me $250 a week, and the next two years were the best learning experience in all my business life. John took care of the personal management of a rather short list of clients. I spent my time trying to sell programs to network radio and local television, and then producing whatever shows we sold.

One day John pulled out of the files a sketchy idea for a radio program that had been given to him several years earlier by a man named Don Reid. The idea, maybe a page in length, was nothing more than a bare-bones suggestion for a quiz competition between colleges. When John asked my opinion, I told him without great enthusiasm that it probably could be a show, and that there was a guy I knew who might be worth talking to about it.

The guy was Allen Ludden, who was then doubling as program executive and on-air personality for WTIC, the NBC Radio affiliate in Hartford. He hosted a show called *Mind Your Manners,* a rather goody-two-shoes effort to teach kids how to behave. We carried it on Saturday mornings when I was at NBC, and Allen and I would occasionally have lunch when he was in New York. He was an inventive guy, full of ideas and energy.

I drove up to Hartford one very hot Sunday afternoon and we sat in his backyard and talked about the notion. Virtually on the spot, Allen created the show that was to become *College Quiz Bowl:* the two colleges, the remotes, the toss-up questions, the bonus questions, the general format. My contribution consisted largely of sitting there while he outlined an entire radio program, and then asking him if he wanted to be involved. He not only wanted to be involved, but within weeks he quit his job, moved his wife and three children to Dobbs Ferry, and began to commute to our Manhattan office.

To sell the show, we went to Jack Cleary, a blustery Irish guy Bud Barry had brought in as program director of NBC Radio. We made our pitch and Jack said, yeah, he'd give it a try. The sale was not quite that easy, but television was displacing radio as the dominant national medium, making network radio programming decisions increasingly less and less important and therefore much quicker.

The show originated out of a small NBC studio at 30 Rock, where our skeleton crew consisted of the announcer, Peter Roberts, and a director and an engineer in the control room. Allen was seated in the studio, talking to the two colleges by remote hookup. When one college pushed a button to answer the toss-up question, the other school's button became inoperative, an element Allen had worked out with the NBC engineers.

Although I had the title of producer, my most important function was to stand in front of Allen and keep score on a big blackboard. It was as bush league as all that. To complicate matters, I frequently butchered the fast-changing score. Time after time I would add incorrectly or give 25 points to the wrong team, and Allen, agonizing, had to ad lib until I got it right.

But the basic concept was sound and the competition was exciting, so the show survived. Part of the appeal lay in the attractive, enthusiastic undergraduates who made up the teams. And a lot of it came from the depth of their collective knowledge; the audience at home wondered, How can they know all this stuff? (In the quiz scandal abuses of the late fifties, a few unscrupulous producers and sponsors would try to guarantee that amazement by rigging their shows.)

In 1959, long after I had gone on to other things, Allen converted the radio show into a television program, *College Bowl*. It was sponsored by General Electric and ran on CBS and NBC for many years. Allen insisted on the TV show's most memorable production feature, the horizontal split screen to accommodate eight players, and then had to convince skeptical network technicians that it would actually work. Which it and the program certainly did. More than thirty years later, *College Bowl* still showed up on the Disney Channel. But Reid, Moses, and Cleary wound up as owners, while Allen, its real creator, had no piece of the show.

During our first few months on radio, we had no sponsors and little income. Allen was having trouble just feeding his family. Network radio was languishing, well on its way to the permanently diminished state brought about by television, and funds to underwrite programming were hard to come by. So I came up with an idea for a summer radio show that would cost the network virtually nothing. Again we called on Jack Cleary at NBC. Every Saturday night for twelve weeks, we told him, we'd get four different NBC radio affiliates to originate a half-hour each. They'll showcase their best local amateur talent, at their expense, and feed the two hours to the network. Each Saturday we'd pick a winner. On the thirteenth week, we'd bring the twelve winners to New York to compete for the grand prize in a big one-hour final show.

And that's exactly what we did. We flew out all over the country—to places as small as Lima or Zanesville, Ohio—to convince station managers and program directors what a wonderful opportunity we were giving them. The whole thing cost NBC a pittance, and *New Talent, U.S.A.* became a perfectly good summer replacement show, with Allen as host, on what was left of the NBC Radio Network.

Allen was a television natural, and a tireless one. For a time, we had him working three one-hour television shows a day, five days a week each, at three different locations. Fighting through Manhattan traffic to get to each studio on time was Allen's daily excitement, but he never missed a show.

We started in the morning with a local program on Channel 7, ABC's flagship station in New York, broadcast live from the Upper West Side from 8 to 9. Allen was the host; I was the producer. We had a weather girl, a lady from the Bronx Zoo who always brought an animal, various guests, and a lot of rip-and-read news. It was a very primitive forerunner of *Good Morning, America,* and Channel 7 didn't pay a penny for it.

The general manager, a man named John Mitchell, gave us the time, brokering it, in effect, and we and the station salesmen would try to sell the program to local advertisers. Our take was a percentage of whatever business was brought in, with the station keeping the lion's share. I don't know whether this practice was FCC-sanctioned, but those were frontier days for many television stations. They did what they had to do to survive. Down the road, when they became money machines, there would be time to live by the rules.

Our show opened the same way each morning. We had one camera outside the ground-floor studio, shooting east on 66th Street, toward Central Park. While our up-tempo, recorded theme music began to play, the camera would pick up whatever was happening on the block. Then, around the corner, Allen would appear, ostensibly coming from home, and we would stay with him as he walked right to camera and turned into the open doors of the studio.

One memorable day, Allen was waiting around the corner and didn't get his cue. Since our show was live, and we were committed to the outside camera, we had no choice but to stay with the street action until Allen appeared. The only thing moving on West 66th Street that morning was a dog trotting on the sidewalk, so that's what viewers saw. All was well until Fido squatted for a leisurely dump, an exercise we showed in its entirety as our theme music underscored the scene. It may have been a television first—possibly an only.

When each morning's show ended, Allen and I would return to the office, where I would spend most of the day. Allen would have to leave almost immediately to head over to WNBC-TV for the second of his three daily gigs, a one-hour program in which he played Ed McMahon to Norman Brokenshire from noon to 1 P.M. At 4 P.M., he'd be at Channel 11, WPIX, where he was the Dick Clark of their one-hour *Dance Time* show. He was running all the time, finally making a good living, and on his way to a successful performing and producing career.

Meanwhile, our office was a hand-to-mouth affair, and I was having an identity crisis. John had Bob and Ray doing a fifteen-minute TV program for NBC, plus radio, but there was little activity with our few other clients. I always had the gnawing feeling, as I boarded the train to Connecticut each evening, that what I was doing was quite trivial and had little future. Most of my fellow commuters had much more substantial careers, and I felt aimless by comparison.

By 1954, when the phone call came from McCann-Erickson, I was ready for a change. They offered me the post of director of program development and I grabbed it. Here was a chance to move into a structured organization that did something I wouldn't have to explain to my more conventionally employed peers. More important, I wouldn't have to explain it to myself.

As had been the case in radio, many network television programs were bought or packaged by sponsors, through their advertising agencies. The biggest agencies, which also bought the airtime from the networks, became major players in television programming. J. Walter Thompson, Young & Rubicam, BBD&O, Benton & Bowles, and a handful of others maintained television departments of considerable size, and worked directly on every aspect of their clients' shows. They selected or commissioned the programs, placed them on a network, and then supervised their production. In other words, they performed many of the functions later preempted by network Entertainment divisions. It was the heyday of advertiser/agency influence on America's television programming. That has a pejorative ring to it, but a strong argument can be made that prime-time schedules were better then.

They were certainly more eclectic. Network research departments were still absorbed with validating the strength of television vis-à-vis its radio and print competition, and hadn't yet begun to meddle in the distinctly inexact science of programming. Phrases like "audience flow" and "program compatibility" were only just entering the scheduling lexicon. While each network had a vice president in charge of programming, the people in those jobs had a great deal of advertiser help in selecting the shows the burgeoning television audience would see.

The fifties decade in television has often been called "the golden years," and in many ways it's an apt designation. The medium was fresh and innocent and, for viewers, almost magical. It was a time of true experimentation and evolution; creative people, many of them barely out of school, didn't yet know what this wondrous animal could or couldn't do—so they made up the rules as they went along.

It's probably apocryphal to say that the home audience in those early days would "watch the test pattern," but people with television sets certainly had healthy, forgiving curiosity about the new medium. It was radio with pictures, and thousands of families were getting their first sets every month, providing a constant supply of eager, neophyte viewers. It would be years before an appreciable segment of television homes could be considered selective in their viewing habits, much less sophisticated. Programmers were presenting their work to a grateful and ever-growing audience. Comedy abounded—from Sid Caesar to Jackie Gleason to Milton Berle to Lucy to Phil Silvers to Jimmy Durante and countless more. They weren't all funny all the time, but the collective batting average was high. Some of the most popular programs were in forms that have almost disappeared from prime time. There were always musical-variety shows— Perry Como, Andy Williams, Dinah Shore, and later, in the sixties, Judy Garland, Glen Campbell, and Dean Martin—and there were myriad weekly dramatic shows, most of them live.

Sometimes the work of such producers as Fred Coe, Martin Manulis, Herbert Brodkin, David Susskind, and George Schaefer was truly remarkable. There were weekly opportunities for talented directors—Arthur Penn, Sidney Lumet, John Frankenheimer, Fielder Cook, George Roy Hill, and many others on showcases like *Studio One, Playhouse 90, Kraft Television Theatre,* and *Philco Playhouse.* Out of television's pioneering efforts in live drama came writers and directors and actors who went on to create the best of the next generation's television shows and movies and plays.

My job at McCann was to stay on top of everything that was happening on the sponsor front, and I invented something that quickly made me a small star within the television department.

In that era, information about what the big companies were planning to do with their network properties was particularly important to every agency. If you were the first to find out that a certain sponsor was about to drop its interest in a popular program, one of your clients might well win the battle to buy in. Competition was fierce in this sellers' market, information was ammunition, and knowing something a few hours early often made the difference.

With the help of sources I developed at ABC, NBC, and CBS, I started a daily internal one-page publication at McCann that carried up-to-the-minute information on what was happening on the sponsor front at each network. I called it the "Five O'Clock Report" and even had stationery printed up with a little clock in the upper-left corner, the hands pointing to five.

Each day I'd make three calls, one to each of my network moles. Often I'd pick up a valuable tidbit, usually about network-advertiser interaction or opportunity, but even on the slow days there was almost always something of inside interest to pass along. I had a system that resulted in almost instantaneous communication, or as close to it as you could get in those pre-fax days. I'd dictate whatever I'd learned, my secretary would type it onto a stencil, and by five o'clock a mimeographed report would be sitting on the desk of every account executive at McCann. Each account guy could quickly check out what had happened that day and, when appropriate, contact his clients. By 5:30, before other potential sponsors even knew there was an opportunity, a McCann client might have bought half-sponsorship of a desirable show.

The thirty-year feeding frenzy to buy network advertising time was already well underway; demand far exceeded supply. So the Five O'Clock Report turned me into something of a hot-shot at McCann-Erickson. And I was in the right place at the right time. Television was becoming big business in the fifties, and for a would-be programmer, the big advertising agencies were where the action was.

I had been at McCann a couple of years when I went into therapy.

Ruth was pregnant with our third child, Jodie. I was working long hours and our marriage was in trouble. I came home dead tired every night after the train ride to Connecticut, and saw far too little of my kids. I was thirty years old and full of self-doubt. I was working hard to move ahead on the career front, but didn't feel ready for the responsibilities that would accompany a promotion, and doubted I'd be up to the task if and when a better opportunity was offered.

Even now, with many years' distance between me and my demons of that day, I can't easily articulate what was bothering me, and certainly not why. Just as problems that are normally manageable become overwhelming when considered at a sleepless 3 A.M., I surely overreacted to my own sense of foreboding. But at the time, it seemed all too real. At the core was a dread of being the focus of attention, as when speaking in public or presenting a recommendation or a plan—requisite activity at an advertising agency.

This is a common ailment, but it usually subsides with growth and experience. In my case, it got worse. I became more uneasy and more anxious, particularly as my professional progress made "hiding" impossible. I was not only shrinking from activities my colleagues had every reason to think would come easily to a guy doing exemplary work, but I had the extra burden of carrying around a secret I couldn't share with them. Acting one way while feeling another—all day, every day—was taking me to a dangerous stress level.

I had been trying to figure out what was wrong on my own,

with absolutely no success, when one day somebody told me that McCann's medical plan would pay 75 percent of therapy costs. I made an appointment with a consulting physician, who listened and recommended a psychiatrist, a little old woman from Vienna, with an office at 96th Street and Park Avenue.

At first I went twice a week, but as my anxieties grew, it became four times. I'd leave my office about six and take the Madison Avenue bus uptown. This was classic Freudian therapy, with the analyst sitting in a chair and me stretched out on the couch. Sometimes I was so tired I'd doze off right in the middle of a session. Or she'd ask me what I was thinking about, and I'd respond with something like, "I don't know. I'm not really thinking about anything," and she'd say "Go with that." It sounds inane, but it was helpful, and I kept going for about eighteen months. After each session, I'd cab up to 125th Street and get the train to Darien. I'd arrive home at about 9:30, hardly an improvement in the father/husband department, but if I hadn't had that wonderful old Austrian lady shrink to talk to, I'm not sure I wouldn't have gone off the high board.

Not long after I joined McCann-Erickson in 1954, the agency decided to put more resources and energy into television. In an effort to attract new clients with bigger television budgets, the agency hired some experienced (and expensive) executives with heavy broadcast backgrounds. We moved from 50 Rockefeller Plaza to new offices on Third Avenue, and they brought in a dapper veteran named Terry Clyne to run the whole broadcast department. He vowed that we'd become the first agency to bill $100 million in television and radio, which indeed we did. Today the number seems ridiculously small, but it was a first.

An additional layer of management was added to the television department, and I inherited a new boss, Lance Lindquist. He had been brought in by Clyne from a smaller agency, and he proved to be a good guy to work for, bright and with a good sense of humor. Clyne, on the other hand, was a tough, no-nonsense taskmaster, very difficult to be around. With Lindquist between us in the chain of command, I didn't have to deal with Clyne very often, but there were moments.

One afternoon he called and asked if I would come to his office, which was up in the building's stratosphere. When I got there, he was sitting at his desk, looking elegant as always in his

French-cuffed shirt. "I've got a problem," he said. "I've double-booked myself. There's a lady I'm supposed to have a drink with at the Berkshire Hotel, but I have to be somewhere else and I can't reach her. I wonder if you'd go over and buy her a drink, or buy her several."

My God, this is going to be exciting, I thought. One of Terry Clyne's women had to be some movie star in from California. I flew downstairs, zipped through my work, and set off to keep his 6 P.M. appointment. At the Berkshire, I was escorted to the table reserved for Mr. Clyne, where I was greeted by a woman whom the term *unattractive* doesn't begin to describe. The real reason why Clyne had delegated the assignment became painfully clear. My picture of Terry Clyne as a glamorous man-of-the-world was irrevocably altered, though he got high marks for craftiness.

For the time being, I was generally content at McCann. I was learning a lot and working long hours. I spent my day evaluating program submissions and opportunities and interacting with the agency's account executives whose clients had television interests. Then one day out of the blue, my secretary buzzed to say that an H. P. Warwick wanted to speak with me. I knew that Warwick was president and co-owner of Warwick and Legler, an advertising agency considerably smaller than McCann. We had never met, but he introduced himself in a strong, friendly voice, and got right to the point: "I've heard great things about you, and wonder if you'd come over to see me."

I couldn't imagine where or why he'd heard anything about me, much less "great things." But the call sounded promising and I agreed to pay him a visit. A day or two later I found myself in the gleaming new offices of Warwick and Legler in the gleaming new Seagram Building on Park Avenue. H. P. Warwick turned out to be short, stocky, smiling, and tough—a cross between Edmund Gwenn and "Two-Ton Tony" Galento. I liked him immediately, but there was a message between the lines of the cordiality: Don't mess with this guy.

H.P. made me feel at home, then he got right down to business. He explained that one of the agency's clients, Revlon, which had been tarnished in the recent quiz scandals, was concerned about its future television presence. A few quiz programs, including Revlon's *The $64,000 Question,* had become popular by trafficking in the incredibly deep knowledge certain contestants manifested on a variety of subjects. Incredible indeed! The contestants, it turned out, had been coached. When the scams were unmasked, the dishonest producers were identified and disgraced, and along with them a few sponsors who had sold a lot of product in the process. Revlon had been the chief beneficiary and, complicit with the producers, a principal villain. H.P. wanted me to get Revlon involved with quality programs that would still meet the company's marketing needs.

There were two Warwick sons at the agency. Bill was nominally head of the television department, such as it was, and he joined us in H.P.'s office. We hit it off immediately. I was offered a job on the spot. It sounded like a challenging step up and paid considerably more than I'd been making at McCann-Erickson. Second son John Warwick came in to sign off on the offer, and I indicated real interest before leaving.

Once again, my lifelong proclivity for moving on took over. I didn't attempt to bargain with McCann, simply told them I was leaving and phoned H.P. to say I'd accept. There were no hard feelings at McCann, and Lance Lindquist was particularly pleased that I'd improved my standing in the work world. In a matter of weeks, the transition was just a memory, and I quickly felt at home in my new situation.

Several months after I began work on the Revlon account, H.P. apparently decided I was doing a good enough job that he could tell me how I really got hired. It seems he had made a slight mistake. The McCann-Erickson executive he had "heard great things about" was not me but my boss, Lance Lindquist. Characteristically, H.P. had vaguely recalled a name, and his secretary, usually accurate at translating his inexact instructions, simply got the wrong guy on the phone.

By the time I learned this humbling news, I was immersed in Revlon matters. Thanks in large part to the big audiences they had reached through the now-discredited quiz shows, the company was in high gear. Their headquarters were at 666 Fifth Avenue, the awful-looking skyscraper known then as "the box the Seagram Building came in." I had been spending enough time there to be certain I would never want to be in the cosmetics business. Meetings with their advertising people were full of jargon, and I felt like a visitor to a foreign country, trying to learn a whole new language. It took several meetings before I figured out that a "shade promotion" was a marketing effort for a particular color of lipstick or nail polish.

The absolute ruler of the company was Charlie Revson, who seemed to me, on the few occasions I was in his Presence, to be cruel, smart, and totally focused. He was one of those absolutely confident people who don't know there are other people in the room, at least not living, feeling people. He trafficked in their ideas, rudely rejecting most and accepting some without recognizing authorship or expressing gratitude. The word *tyrant* comes to mind. My most repellent memory is of Revson, nattily suited, white silk tie against white shirt, French cuffs resting on the table, stopping to belch in the middle of a sentence, which he completed without apology.

Those meetings were no fun, but some of the television shows Revlon sponsored, through Warwick and Legler, were. One was *The Garry Moore Show,* produced by Bob Banner and broadcast live on CBS, Tuesdays from 10 to 11 P.M. It was one of a host of wonderful variety shows that proliferated in those early days, and the place where Carol Burnett began her illustrious television career.

The year I covered the show, its summer replacement was even better. *The Andy Williams Show,* solidly produced by Perry Lafferty and imaginatively directed by a young Canadian, Norman Jewison, ran for thirteen weeks. The art director was Gary Smith, who would later become a collector of Emmys as a producer of some of television's most honored specials, from Bette Midler to Baryshnikov. *The Andy Williams Show* was as good a musical-variety series, now an extinct breed, as there ever was. I was proud to be the "agency fink" assigned to cover it.

On Friday nights I went over to a tiny CBS studio on Vanderbilt Avenue, part of Grand Central Station, to represent Revlon at what would be the last gasp of Edward R. Murrow's *Person to Person.* The dress rehearsal consisted of short conversations with the "persons" waiting at their remote locations, and once it was established that the communications hardware was functioning properly, everyone had a break for a couple of hours.

Ed was approaching the end of his historic radio and television career by then, and he had a world-weary demeanor, an air of sadness, that I found appealing and heroic. On a number of occasions, he invited me to join him for a drink or two across the street at the Vanderbilt Hotel bar. Once the show was completed at 11 P.M., Ed would disappear into the night, and I'd catch the train to Darien.

My home life was hardly enhanced by the hours I kept or by my frequent absences. I had rediscovered California, and Bill Warwick and I found far too many excuses to head west, ostensibly in search of specials for Revlon to sponsor. The state of my marriage encouraged me to be away from home too much, and being away, on top of my long commuter hours, only hastened the deterioration.

Except for dealing with the driven people at Revlon, whose style always made me uncomfortable, my short stay at Warwick and Legler was fun, probably too much fun. Throughout my working life, anytime a job got to be too enjoyable, the Jonathan Edwards in me would kick in, an inner voice saying, "Get serious. Work is supposed to be work."

Eighteen months into my Warwick stay I was already in my characteristic time-to-move-on frame of mind when I got another phone call, this one from Ted Steele, a major presence at Benton & Bowles. B&B was a topflight advertising agency, particularly active in television for clients like Procter & Gamble, General Foods, and S.C. Johnson. Its television department, under a dynamo named Tom McDermott, had become one of the best. When McDermott left to run Four Star Television, his replacement, Ollie Barbour, found Tom's shoes a bit too large for comfort, and Steele thought of me. The offer was to join B&B as vice president in charge of programs, clearly a more challenging and better job than the one I had.

I was beginning to worry about my itinerant tendencies. Each time Ollie Barbour called, I resorted to every variety of stalling and shit-kicking. Finally, I got a call from the president of Benton & Bowles, Bob Lusk, whom I'd never met. Lusk said he'd like to have a drink with me and he named a nondescript bar on Third Avenue. He was six and a half feet tall, brimming with confidence, and immensely likable. It was not a long meeting.

"I understand you're having a little trouble deciding whether or not you want to come with us," he began.

I was in a negotiating mode. "Well, I'm not unhappy where I am. The problem—"

Glancing at his watch, Lusk broke in, "Listen, if you can't see that what we want you to do is a lot better opportunity than you have now, you may not be the right guy."

"I'll come," I said.

I never regretted doing so. Benton & Bowles had a topflight television department, filled with people who later in their careers were to have senior programming jobs at the networks, ad agencies, and Hollywood production companies—people like Irwin Segelstein, Freddy Bartholomew, Lew Wechsler, Lee Currlin, Merrill Grant, Alan Wagner, Phil Capice, and John Hamlin. *Variety* once called Benton & Bowles "the cradle of programmers," and, indeed, the group I inherited there left a considerable imprint on the television business. For the next twenty years or so, anyone needing a top program executive often looked first for a Benton & Bowles graduate.

I had barely gotten comfortable with new names and faces when Bob Lusk loomed in my doorway late one afternoon. He came in and closed the door. "Something's come up rather unexpectedly," he said. "Have you met Lee Rich yet?" I told him I hadn't, but knew he ran the media department.

"Right," Lusk said, "and he's very important to the agency. He's making it clear that unless he's given the responsibility for the program department as well as his own, he may have to consider leaving. We can't afford to lose him. Would you have a problem reporting to him?" And so I inherited Lee Rich as my boss. I didn't know much about media, and he didn't know much about programs, so our deficiencies turned out to be complementary.

Benton & Bowles had about a dozen shows that our clients bought outright, and an equal number they co-sponsored. In my first year there, 1959, I spent more nights at the Bel Air Hotel in Los Angeles than at home. As head of the department, Lee had to handle a lot more client contact than I did, which made his superimposition a blessing in disguise. I got to spend more time with the television shows and the people who made them.

In addition to other series, including *The Ann Sothern Show, The Danny Thomas Show, The Real McCoys, The Rifleman,* and *The Andy Griffith Show,* our clients sponsored a number of television specials, many of them documentaries, when they had out-of-the-ordinary marketing opportunities. One vivid example of just such an opportunity was the then-unprecedented endorsement by the American Dental Association (ADA) of Procter & Gamble's Crest toothpaste with fluoride. P&G invested heavily in a huge television effort to sock home that competitive advantage while they had it, and a couple of executive careers went into high gear as a corollary.

The Benton & Bowles account executive handling Crest was a young guy named Jack Bowen. His brand manager counterpart at P&G was John Smale. Together they leapt to the task of telling the world about Crest, the wonders of fluoride, and the ADA endorsement, coordinating the efforts of all of us who contributed. As they say on Madison Avenue, these guys sold a lot of toothpaste. I don't think anyone was surprised when, not that many years later, Bowen and Smale became chief executive officers of their respective companies.

It was during the Crest blitz that I got to know a heavyweight from the creative and production side of television, a man who would become a good and permanent friend. David Wolper had been making and selling documentary programs since the early fifties. At the time, when the medium was young, most of us learned and progressed within large, established organizations. That was a road Wolper was too impatient to travel. He was entrepreneurial and a bit of a nonconformist, and he chose to build and grow a company of his own. His primary interest was documentary films, an area in which he was so prolific that even today, almost two decades after he turned his attention to other forms, he is still the most productive documentarian television has known.

David's entry into broadcasting's big league was *The Race for Space,* which included Russian film footage no network could get. IBM took an option on the program, but even that powerful company was unable to knock down the high wall network News divisions had erected years earlier to keep the work of outside producers off their schedules. Efforts to get networks to carry news or public affairs programming not produced in-house had always been rebuffed. The rigid policy was part appropriate insurance of network standards—"we need to know the program is being done right"—and part exclusionary arrogance—"our News division can do it better."

Rejected by the networks, Wolper turned to station managers all over the country. He'd been selling them product for years and had many strong personal relationships. By phone and tireless travel, he called in enough markers to put together an ad hoc network of 125 stations to carry the program, which was sponsored by Shulton. With a somewhat younger Mike Wallace as host/narrator, the show attracted considerable attention.

The following year, Wolper bought Theodore H. White's *The Making of the President 1960,* and with the help of his sponsor, Xerox, managed to persuade ABC to carry the ninety-minute program. The Television Academy voted it Program of the Year. It would be a while before independent public affairs productions were really welcome at the networks, but the door had been opened. While I was at Benton & Bowles, we walked through that door several times with hour specials, bought to celebrate the virtues of brushing with Crest.

Many other celebrated Wolper documentaries followed, and he turned out a number of feature films as well. Probably his most famous credit is *Roots,* the historic miniseries that attracted one of the largest television audiences of all time. A few years later, he performed the same trick with *The Thorn Birds.* Wolper has also set standards by which to measure live extravaganzas, first with his stunning opening and closing ceremonies for the 1984 Summer Olympics in Los Angeles. Two years later he topped himself in New York, when he overcame daunting logistical challenges to produce the massive television show built around the restoration of the Statue of Liberty, culminating in a moving relighting of the torch she holds high.

It's surely apparent that I am a great fan of David Wolper, who always promises a lot and then delivers more than he promises. Over the past couple of decades, some of my most enjoyable times have been on trips to faraway places with David and his fabulous wife, Gloria. Together, they're a great team—perfectly matched opposites.

It was becoming painfully clear by now that my own marriage was no longer working. I had spent the fifties in single-minded devotion to several jobs in succession, which took its toll on the domestic front. Ruth, who had been a wonderful wife, was an even better mother, which was fortunate because after twelve years we would decide to pack in our marriage.

Couples usually part company either mad or sad, and we qualified for the second category. In the home where I grew up, divorce was a foreign word, not even remotely an option for my mother and father. That wasn't true of Ruth, but she was as old-fashioned as I. On a given workday, as agreed, I came out from the city, threw all my clothes into my car, and headed back to New York, where I had arranged to take over a friend's apartment. John was too young to know what was going on, and it fell to Ruth to explain my absence to the other three kids. I hadn't gone more than a couple of blocks before I had to pull over and bawl about the whole sorry situation.

A lot of years and many miles later, I can still conjure up that feeling. I regretted having failed as a husband, but that part only involved two adults. Leaving the kids provided the real pain; they were all young, they hadn't brought themselves into the world, and they didn't get a vote on the decision. No amount of alimony or child support assuages that kind of guilt, and one result is that I've been something of a soft touch as a father ever since. And indirectly and subtly, consciously or not, all my kids have let me know that they were hurt by my departure and resented my absence as they grew up. I'm sure their attitudes would have been even more severe had Ruth not been such a consummate and embracing mother. She not only filled in for me, but all the while she represented me to all the children as a good person. When she married again five years later, it was to a widower named Dick Fricke, who brought along four offspring of his own. The Fricke kids were lucky that their dad chose so wisely, as was I in picking such a winner to be the mother of my children.

Sheldon Leonard had spent most of the afternoon in my Benton & Bowles office, sounding, as he always does, like a Jersey City stevedore delivering the words of William Buckley. He was unhappy and upset because he and his partners, Danny Thomas and Carl Reiner, had thus far failed in their efforts to find the right lead actor for their new series.

Sheldon and Danny had no such problem with their earlier series together, *Make Room for Daddy,* a CBS hit from the day it premiered in 1953. That series, then in its eighth season and renamed *The Danny Thomas Show,* had been created as a vehicle for Danny, produced by Lou Edelman, and would remain a fixture on the CBS schedule for another three years.

The new project was the creation of Carl Reiner, who had written and produced a pilot starring himself and Barbara Britton. It hadn't sold, but Carl had holed up for the summer at Fire Island and written scripts for another dozen episodes. He and Sheldon then presented the program to Procter & Gamble through Benton & Bowles. P&G was the largest advertiser in television and when they talked, everybody listened. Any series that P&G wanted to sponsor was usually guaranteed to find a comfortable spot on a network schedule.

Based on the high caliber of Carl's scripts and the combined production auspices of Thomas/Leonard/Reiner, P&G had commissioned a pilot, which Sheldon was to direct. But even with sponsor interest and thirteen scripts already written, the project was moribund until the male lead was found. A dispirited Sheldon Leonard finally left my office to get ready for an evening at the theater.

He called the next morning in a much-improved mood. "I've

found our guy," he announced. The show he had seen was *Bye Bye Birdie* and its star, Dick Van Dyke, would be Rob Petrie.

Finding Laura Petrie proved equally difficult, and Leonard and Reiner were coming up empty. When Danny Thomas stuck his head in Sheldon's Hollywood office one afternoon, they shared their problem with him. A couple of years earlier, Danny's long-running show had read a number of young actresses for the part of his daughter. One in particular had acquitted herself well, but her pert look had cost her the job. "With that nose," Danny had said, "no one would believe she's my daughter."

Now, standing in the doorway of Sheldon Leonard's office, his memory hit the jackpot. "How about the girl with the three names?"

Bingo! Mary Tyler Moore became Mrs. Rob Petrie. Up to that point, Mary had worked mostly as a dancer and had relatively little acting experience. Her voice and her legs had been heard and seen on *Richard Diamond,* and she had danced her way across ovens and refrigerators as a little elf, Happy Hotpoint, in a series of appliance commercials.

Mary was a felicitous choice for the Laura role, one I knew nothing about until I went to Los Angeles to see the pilot being shot. Even on our first meeting, part of the immediate attraction I felt for Mary was her natural quality that made the role come alive, to say nothing of comedic skills I'm sure Carl and Sheldon never counted on. The other part was that she simply knocked my socks off.

Not long after, another career-changing moment presented itself by chance. Ruth and I, on one of our last social outings together, had gone to a party at the Old Greenwich home of Allen Dingwall, an advertising executive with General Foods. I did very little nonbusiness elbow rubbing with clients, but I liked Allen and he lived only a few miles down the road from Darien.

Among the guests was a man even less likely to show up for such a party. Mort Werner was someone I knew only slightly, but I knew a lot about him. Until recently, he had been head of television for Young & Rubicam, the large, exceedingly re-spected agency that was B&B's principal competition for Procter & Gamble and General Foods business. Y&R and B&B co-existed peacefully and cooperatively, because that's the way those big clients wanted it, and each agency was secure with its own assigned brands and products. In fact, so much business from the two corporate giants was represented on the television shows handled by the agencies that there was considerable interaction between them. Mort spent his days at Y&R much as we spent ours at B&B, and occasionally our paths would cross in Cincinnati and White Plains, the respective headquarters of P&G and General Foods.

Mort had just left Y&R to return to NBC as vice president in charge of programs. He had been there in the fifties when Pat Weaver was shaping the medium, introducing a variety of innovations, including early-morning and late-night programming and pioneering the concept of prime-time specials, which Weaver called "spectaculars." Mort had played an important part in the launching of the *Today* show.

I wandered into the backyard to take a break, and encountered him making his own temporary escape. Standing at the back fence, we started making pleasant party conversation about his new job. He motioned toward the house, saying he hadn't missed some of those people. "Producing the *Today* show was more fun," Mort said, "but this beats trips to Cincinnati and White Plains. You once worked for NBC, didn't you?" I told him that my first job right out of college had been with the NBC Radio Network. He asked if I'd ever thought about going back. The bulb now blinking, I replied that I guessed I had. "I'm in the market for some good help," he said. "Want to talk about it next week?"

I said I'd love to. Mort and I met once during the week, and I agreed to come to work at NBC as soon as I could properly excuse myself from Benton & Bowles. The idea of returning to 30 Rockefeller Plaza was very attractive to me, but the real appeal was the prospect of spending all day, every day, in the program business.

The Monday morning I reported for work on the fourth floor of the RCA Building, I found Mort on the phone. He motioned me to have a seat. Against the back of his couch stood several cardboard charts, the kind we all used for presentations, and another wave from Mort invited me to look them over. The selling task of this particular presentation was to make the point that Johnny Carson would be an ideal replacement for Jack Paar, who was giving up his role as host of *The Tonight Show*. Amid all the research data was one note of whimsy, the only memorable part of the whole pitch. Carson, one panel said, had had some failure up to that point in his television career, but had hosted *Who Do You Trust?,* a game show. Jack Paar, it went on, likewise had some failure in his pre-*Tonight* days, and had hosted something called *Bank on the Stars,* also a game show. With all that in common, the argument went, Carson surely would make a perfect successor to the departing Paar.

Off the phone, Mort told me he was due on the sixth floor later in the day to sell the notion to Bob Kintner, NBC's president. Others through the years have taken credit for selecting Johnny Carson, but I believe Mort Werner deserves it. For NBC, it would turn out to be a thirty-year good idea.

Mort had immediate work for me. NBC had sold DuPont a weekly hour, 10 to 11 on Sunday evenings, along with the promise to deliver first-class shows—everything from documentaries to serious drama. NBC News would handle the documentaries and the program department was to take care of the dramas. So far, nothing had been done from our end to keep that promise, and time was short. Mort wanted me to recruit enough talented producers to get the job done, and they were going to have to work fast.

The DuPont Show of the Week premiered September 17, 1961, and for three years was NBC's quality prime-time showcase. During that first year, I turned to such pros as Fielder Cook, Jerry Hellman, David Susskind, and Frank Schaffner to produce programs for us, most of them done live from NBC's Brooklyn studios. Even then, the Brooklyn facility was hardly state-of-the-art (although it continued in use for another three decades), but every one of the DuPont programs was more than presentable, and some were wonderful. DuPont was happy, or as happy as sponsors ever get, and Mort Werner was pleased.

Well before the last show aired that first season, I would be watching them at home in Studio City, California. Out of the blue, several months into my new adventure, Mort had asked how I'd feel about transferring to NBC's Burbank facility. He knew, of course, about my new relationship with Mary. We'd had dinner a couple of times when she came to New York to promote *The Dick Van Dyke Show* during its first season, and we had connected immediately. She had a great sense of fun (as the country was about to discover), but at the same time she was centered and sensible—and highly intelligent. There was no undue pretense to Mary; what you saw is what you got, what you heard is what she meant.

Mary had been married early, and was now divorced and living in a small house in Studio City with her very young son, Richie. Her parents lived no more than a block away, and right next door was her aunt Berte, who was the business manager at KNXT, the television station CBS owned in Los Angeles. As a high school kid Mary had spent a lot of time at the station doing minor jobs of various kinds. Television was no mystery to her; it always seemed to me to be in her blood.

Even without the considerable bonus of proximity to Mary, I would have jumped at the chance to work in Burbank. I've always felt most at home close to the programming action, even as far back as my first NBC Radio job in 1949. One of the many things I had learned then was how a national program service deals with a country divided into four time zones. Breaking news stories, as well as some specials and sports events, are transmitted to everyone simultaneously. But most of the network programming service is provided to each part of the country by a separate feed designed to accommodate how people live. Families on both coasts, who don't know or care how CBS does it, do know that *60 Minutes* will reliably turn up every Sunday at 7 P.M.

The major exception is the Central Time zone, where, since radio days, people have learned to live their viewing lives an hour earlier. Eight o'clock programs in New York and Los Angeles are seen at 7 in Chicago, and prime time ends at 10 P.M., not 11. Midwesterners have grown up with this anomaly, have long since adapted to it, and don't give it a second thought. Neither do broadcasters, but it once gave me a major problem.

When I moved to California to work as NBC's chief programmer in Burbank, Norman Felton, a very creative man, was running the television arm of MGM. His company was producing several first-class shows for us, one of which, *Mr. Novak,* had been created by its talented writer/producer, E. Jack Neuman. Prime time in those days began a half-hour earlier and *Mr. Novak,* about a high school teacher and his students, was broadcast from 7:30 to 8:30 P.M. on Tuesdays. The program, which starred James Franciscus and Dean Jagger, was a favorite of the critics, who applauded its positive values and the worthwhile stories it told to its primarily youthful audience.

In addition to being a good producer, Jack Neuman was a good citizen. He suggested to me that his popular program would be an ideal vehicle to impart to its young viewers some much-needed information about venereal disease. Since this was a subject rarely addressed in any forum available to the very group that could most benefit from it, I thought Neuman's idea was terrific. We would be doing a little prime-time good for a change, and NBC would get a few brownie points.

I encouraged Jack to go ahead with his plan, and he got so carried away that he turned out a story that took two episodes to tell. I was thrilled to read it and then upset to learn that Continuity Acceptance (the staff department later called Standards and Practices, which passed judgment on what was acceptable for broadcast) had turned thumbs down. They felt the subject matter was inappropriate for *Mr. Novak*'s early time period.

From my Burbank post I argued with them, but the network bureaucracy was immovable. I knew I'd have to make this sale in New York. I flew east, filled with that wonderful combination of high dudgeon and firm resolve that marks the true believer. Since my cause was so just, I bypassed all other executive levels and took it directly to Walter Scott, the head of the network.

Walter was a good and fair man, but not famous for risk-taking. He also possessed by far the bluest nose in NBC's management, so I knew that getting him to see it my way would wipe out anyone else's objections. As was his unfailing habit, Walter listened attentively to my fervent and well-rehearsed pitch. First came a warm smile of encouragement, then a progressively pained look as I got into the details of what I was asking him to do.

"We'll never have a better opportunity to use one of our programs to inform young people," I began. (Warm smile from Walter.) "The prevalence of venereal disease among teenagers [warm smile starts to fade] is skyrocketing, and Jack Neuman wants to do a two-parter about it on *Mr. Novak*." (Frown appears.)

Ever polite, Walter asked if we couldn't do some sort of show with similar information not at 7:30 but at 10 P.M., when viewers were more accustomed to "adult" themes. I explained that the audience we were trying to reach with this particular theme was exactly the young audience that watched *Mr. Novak*. We'd miss the target if we went to a later time period.

Walter pressed his lips together and shook his patrician head. "We just can't do it," he said.

I lost my cool. "For God's sake, Walter, why not?"

"Because, Grant, they'll be eating in Chicago."

After I had been on the new job for several months, Mort rearranged the staff, and I was promoted to West Coast head of programs. By then, Mary and I had decided to marry. I was not yet legally divorced, and that formality was now dispatched with a speed that surprised me. Ruth and I reached agreement on alimony and support matters in a manner that yet again displayed her fairness and common sense. Alabama offered instant divorces, so one afternoon I flew to Montgomery, and the next morning a local lawyer walked me through the courthouse procedure, which was completed by lunchtime. It was a rather insignificant way to end a significant part of my life.

Mary and I wanted our wedding to be as low-key as possible, and with the kind help of Danny Thomas we were able to arrange just that. On June 1, the two of us flew to Las Vegas and were at the Dunes Hotel by 11 A.M. A suite that actually belonged to a furrier had been put at our disposal, and several racks of ermine fur coats and jackets hung in the bedroom. We were married in the white on white (but furless) living room by Judge David Zenoff, who was a friend of Danny's. By two o'clock we were back on a plane for Los Angeles, and when we landed we went directly to the Bel Air Hotel, which had been my home away from home for several years. We anticipated a couple of days to ourselves, since Mort Werner had urged me to take some kind of honeymoon. However, the next morning, rather early, the phone rang. It was Mort. "I'm sorry to bother you, but there's a pilot that's available to see, if you can make it this morning." I wasn't thrilled, but there didn't seem to be much choice. "Okay, I'll see it and let you know what I think," I said, assuming he was in New York, as he had been the day before.

"No problem," he said, "I'm here at the hotel. I'll meet you in the lobby in a couple of minutes."

That was typical of Mort in two ways. He loved to move mysteriously and quickly and was on and off airplanes the way most people make trips to the market. His beat was almost exclusively New York and Los Angeles, but somehow he managed to get to San Francisco and Acapulco almost as much. The airlines had something called the triangular fare—three cities for the price of two—and Mort took full advantage of it. He delighted in turning up wherever you didn't expect him to be.

He also hated to make judgments and decisions on his own, and seldom did. He was a master of the noncommittal opinion. At the end of the pilot screening of *Profiles in Courage* in 1964, a roomful of people turned to where Mort was sitting in the last row. Everyone was waiting to hear what the head programmer thought. "It has a real theatrical quality," he managed. He much preferred having someone around to share the responsibility or, better yet, even to determine the course of action for him. During my time at NBC in the sixties, I was his principal security blanket at such moments; after I left, Herb Schlosser got the duty.

Mort's phone call effectively ended the honeymoon, not that Mary and I didn't have jobs to get on with. From an ex–Benton & Bowles colleague of mine, a wonderful man named Murray Bolen, we bought a house up in the hills above Studio City, and, with Mary's son, Richie, we soon moved in. Work for Mary meant a trip to Hollywood over Laurel Canyon to the *Van Dyke* show; for me it was a straight shot to NBC in Burbank.

Those were certainly the best days of a marriage that ultimately lasted almost eighteen years. Richie had started school and was typically rambunctious. In spite of a demanding daily work schedule, Mary was a loving and attentive mother to a boy who might otherwise have been overwhelmed by all the activity around him. He was a kid for whom words like innocent, naive, and ingenuous all applied.

Richie's presence in the house pretty much domesticated us, and we were only too happy to put in satisfying workdays and stay home most nights. It's fair to say I never took the place of Richie's own father, who had liberal visitation privileges, which he exercised frequently until he ultimately moved to northern California. Dick Meeker was into the outdoors, and Richie liked to go fishing with his dad.

Laura Petrie had emerged as a real factor in the *Van Dyke* show; Mary was doing good work in a good show and enjoying it immensely. She spent her days on the Desilu-Cahuenga lot. I was putting in longer hours at NBC in Burbank, where Mort Werner's laid-back style permitted me authority and responsibility as the West Coast *grand fromage* in programming. The bulk of my time was devoted to program development, largely meetings with many of the best creative people available to television.

From the start of the 1962–63 season, three months after Mary and I were married, I was the most faithful audience member of *The Dick Van Dyke Show*. I attended the Tuesday night filming of nearly every episode, leaving my NBC office in Burbank and driving over the hill to the Desilu-Cahuenga Studios in Hollywood. My usual vantage point was the cubicle of the show's camera coordinator, above and behind the audience bleachers. Frequently, I'd be looking down on the imposing and proprietary presence of Sheldon Leonard. Sheldon was used to being in charge, but in this case, he properly deferred to Carl Reiner, who ran the *Van Dyke* show as writer/creator and executive producer. The ensemble cast and director John Rich (in later years, it was frequently Jerry Paris) made up the rest of his team, along with Bill Persky and Sam Denoff, the young writers who supplied many of the scripts and soon came on staff as writer/producers.

Sometimes I'd wander around a bit, and more than once I noticed a distinctive, seemingly shy young man skulking on the periphery of the action. Years later I would recall that image and realize it had been communications-mogul-to-be Barry Diller, then a neophyte at the William Morris talent agency. There are stories about Barry reading all the agency's files to soak up as much industry knowledge as he possibly could. The *Van Dyke* show was a William Morris package, and Barry's presence was no doubt part of his self-education process.

In television's first couple of decades, many more episodes of a series were produced and broadcast each season. The mix, always dictated by economic factors, started in the fifties with thirty-nine originals and thirteen repeats and eventually went to the present low of twenty-two originals, even more repeats, plus a few preemptions. As time went on, it took producers and production companies much longer to accumulate enough episodes to enter the big-money syndication market. The *Van Dyke* show piled up 158 episodes in just five seasons; a few years later, it would take *Mary Tyler Moore* seven seasons to turn out 168 originals.

The production process of *The Dick Van Dyke Show* was typical of the multiple-camera genre, shot in front of an audience. It's a form I've always found particularly appealing, and is peculiar to television—really the medium's most natural and indigenous production technique. Originally, it involved three film cameras, and some of us older folk still refer to the process as "three-camera comedy." Today, it's more often taped, using four cameras, allowing the director more coverage choices and speedier postproduction.

What's being shot is a little play, and the audience is essential to the technique, both for their audible reactions and for motivating the performers. Much of television's best and most enduring comedy has been shot this way, from even before the original *I Love Lucy* through *Van Dyke* and *Mary* to *Family Ties, Cheers, Seinfeld,* and many, many others.

Multiple-camera audience comedy allows the participants, especially the actors, to keep hours far more civilized than the normal Hollywood shooting schedule. It's usually a five-day week, beginning Monday morning and ending Friday evening. Some shows work Wednesday through Tuesday, taking the weekend off. The *Van Dyke* show was on that schedule.

Day one begins with a reading of the new script, with the actors, producers, writers, director, and a few other members of the production team seated around a large table. From that reading on, the show evolves throughout the five days, a constant process of change and refinement as the participants delete what doesn't work and keep and improve what does. Usually by the first afternoon the production is "on its feet," the actors carrying scripts and the director starting to choreograph their moves.

Late on the third day there's usually a formal run-through, done primarily for the writer/producers. It's really their last chance to fix whatever is wrong, and if the show is in good shape, everyone gets to go home at a decent hour. If not, rewriting can extend into the wee hours.

On the morning of the fourth day, the actors get the revised pages, which are sometimes wholly new, and the director sets about camera blocking with technicians who work only the last two days. Finally, at the taping or filming late on the fifth day, everyone reaps the rewards of a hard week's work. The actors get psychic income from the response of the audience, the rest of the company and crew have the satisfying and special-to-show-business experience of seeing the results of their work, and the company producing the show has another episode in the bank. Under the firm but benign guidance of Carl Reiner, the extended family that worked so closely on the *Van Dyke* show was happy, relaxed, and productive.

As good as the show was, it was actually canceled by CBS at the end of its first season—almost before my weekly vigil had begun. The series premiered October 3, 1961, in the Tuesday, 8 to 8:30 P.M. time slot, was moved in January to Wednesdays at 9:30, and was notably missing from the fall schedule CBS announced in early 1962.

The days of sponsor-owned programs had been winding down for some time, and a major transition was taking place in the structure of the business. Production costs were at a point where few advertisers could continue to justify the risk of having too many eggs in a one-show basket. If the show didn't work, the money was down the drain. Spreading commercial minutes throughout a number of programs was to become the safe and sensible way for advertisers to spend their network dollars.

That development held twin benefits for ABC, CBS, and NBC: It would mean the end of advertiser influence on program content, and it would give the networks a new way to make money. Instead of simply selling time slots so major advertisers could broadcast their own shows, now they would sell the programs, too. That meant buying programs directly from producers and then reselling them, at marked-up prices, to advertisers. Instead of one revenue stream, they would have two.

The 1959 Congressional investigation into the quiz scandals clinched it. The rigging of shows had been perpetrated largely on programs produced by advertisers, which gave the networks a heaven-sent opportunity to put a public-service face on the program grab. Hereafter, went their self-righteous rationale, we'll take full responsibility for the programs we broadcast, by producing or buying them ourselves.

This left series like *The Dick Van Dyke Show*, which had been completely underwritten by Procter & Gamble, much more vulnerable to cancellation in the network scheduling process. CBS, having no ownership stake in the show, announced a 1962–63 schedule that did not include *Van Dyke*. Setting aside the issue of ownership, CBS was guilty of a network sin that is still being committed today. Lackluster first-year rating results were given greater weight than overwhelmingly positive critical reaction. Instead of basing their decision on their creative judgment of the show itself, as network executives are paid to do, CBS had opted to read the Nielsen numbers and then just give up.

CBS in that era was Jim Aubrey, the smart, tough "Smiling Cobra" who was absolute ruler of the television network. Aubrey loved to exercise his power, which frequently edged over into bullying. In the case of the *Van Dyke* cancellation, he was thumbing his nose at one of CBS's biggest customers (P&G) and at three people (Danny Thomas, Sheldon Leonard, and Carl Reiner) who together constituted one of the network's most valued production resources. Although the *Van Dyke* ratings during its first season left plenty of room for improvement, P&G was much more sanguine about the show than Aubrey was. But as he no doubt anticipated, the giant advertiser was characteristically too polite to use its corporate clout to seek a reversal.

Not so Sheldon Leonard, who had invested too much time and talent in what he knew was a superior television program to accept Aubrey's consignment to oblivion. He flew to Cincinnati and beseeched the P&G executives to stay with the show. Always reluctant to go to war with a network, P&G agreed to underwrite half the program if he could find a co-sponsor for the other half.

Sheldon made some calls and flew on to New York. There he met with Nick Keesley, a major player at Lennen and Newell, the ad agency that represented, among other large television advertisers, P. Lorillard. Nick was short, bald, perpetually tanned, and very direct. As soon as Sheldon explained why he had come, Nick got up from his desk and took him by the arm. "The Lorillard people are having a meeting right now. Come with me and you can talk to them yourself."

Off they went. Keesley introduced Leonard to a tableful of tobacco executives, and Sheldon, before sitting down, removed his gold wristwatch and placed it in front of him. "This won't take long," he told them. "I want to talk to you about a television show." He made a forceful and articulate pitch, put his watch back on, stood up, and departed for another ad agency, where he was scheduled to make the same plea. As he waited outside the conference room for his entrance cue, the receptionist handed him a telephone. It was Nick Keesley with news that would make Sheldon's second sales call unnecessary: Lorillard would happily spring for half the sponsorship. Now the show was fully sold and even Jim Aubrey wasn't up to challenging two such important customers at the same time. *The Dick Van Dyke Show* was put back on the fall schedule, where it won that year's Emmy for Outstanding Program in the Field of Humor and became a five-year hit for CBS.

Compared to the population explosion that happened later at all three networks, NBC Burbank had a tiny programming staff. When I arrived in 1962, there was one guy in development and I quickly transferred him. To me, program development *was* the job, and I wanted to do it myself. (By the eighties, network program departments would be grandly renamed "Entertainment divisions," bloated in size, with managers of Comedy Development reporting to directors of Comedy Development, who in turn would report to vice presidents of Comedy Development.) I had just six people to cover all the shows already on the air, and they simply didn't have time for the kind of oversupervision network people have since become famous for—but that was the whole idea. The mission was to get good producers and let them produce. At Burbank, we made term deals with David Dortort, who had done *Bonanza* for NBC; Bob Finkel, a great variety show producer; Sheldon Leonard, who came up with *I Spy* (and a star named Bill Cosby); and Norman Felton, who had a string of successes for NBC: *Dr. Kildare, The Lieutenant, The Eleventh Hour,* and *The Man from U.N.C.L.E.*

For years, producers have complained about aggressive network interference in their creative work, maintaining that nothing good comes out of a committee. Networks take the position that they're the customer and should have a say in the process. I've been on both sides of the fence, several times, and this one is an easy call to make.

Start with the fact that most network executives have never even worked in any meaningful capacity on a television program, much less produced one. There are a tiny number of exceptions, and I've found them to be among the most restrained and constructive in dealing with producers. A fine example would be Perry Lafferty, who had some excellent producer credits before he became West Coast head of programs for CBS in 1966. A couple of years later, I would have many opportunities to see Perry in action, dealing knowledgeably and easily with people who produced programs for CBS. He spoke their language, understood their problems, and had their respect.

Very few network executives without direct producing experience make a positive contribution to the process. One who does is CBS's erstwhile program chief, Jeff Sagansky, who has always read well, and has good character and story instincts. Most important, Jeff offers his notes and suggestions with the appropriate diffidence of a creative partner, not a boss.

Over the years, network executives in general have become infamous for confusing their role with that of the producer. As buyers, they unquestionably have the right to the final say. Unfortunately, all too often they exercise it. This self-defeating sin is usually committed by the younger, more arrogant networkers. Veteran practitioners often have learned to be helpful, not dictatorial; that's how they survived to become veterans.

For the people who make the shows, the producer–program executive relationship is a slippery slope. Someone whose hands are full simply meeting the relentless demands of supplying programs to a network schedule has very little time left over for fending off—or accommodating—supervision from the network. If the phenomenon weren't so distracting and time-consuming, it would be funny. The young network overseers come fully equipped with all the jargon and none of the skills and smarts born of real experience. Heaven only knows how many potentially successful television shows have gone down the tubes because their producers were obliged to act on bad network advice.

The best course of action for a producer is this: Make the show you want to make, the one that follows your vision, the one you have some passion for. Almost invariably, that show will be far better than the one that tries to accommodate too many network cooks. Obviously, this plan would be easier to follow if the networks took *their* best course of action: Don't try to produce the producers; you've employed them because you think they know how to make programs. Be ready to help if asked, otherwise get out of the way.

It has always seemed obvious to me that success in television programming comes about in two stages: First, the producer fashions a good show, and then the network places it in *one* time period and leaves it there. The goal is for new viewers to find it and for those who have already seen it to return to it. Then, all the promotion and word-of-mouth work in its favor. If the audience can't easily locate a program early in its life, it will never have the opportunity to see it several times, decide it's good, and make it a viewing habit. The show will almost surely fail. Most people won't work very hard to search for a show they've watched only once.

What network executives who select and buy and schedule programs are paid to do—what should be at the top of their job descriptions—is to make crucial judgments about those programs *after* they're on the air. If a show is slow to attract sufficient audience, and virtually all new shows are, it is at that point that the hardest judgment must be made. Is it the show that was expected? Is it well made? *Is it good?* If it is not what was bought, not as good as anticipated, and shows little or no promise of improvement, get rid of it. But if it is living up to its promise, bite the bullet and settle in for a long, disheartening wait. Many hugely successful television shows have been well into a second season before being discovered by an audience of appreciable size.

Keeping the faith sounds easy, but it isn't. In reality, the toughest challenge for the network program executive is to make gutsy, sometimes lonely calls about keeping or canceling programs. Often that entails ignoring ratings, research, and the conventional wisdom of colleagues or even of superiors with the ability to terminate programmers who make bad calls. Trusting visceral reactions, following instincts, separates the programming men from the boys (and now, the women from the girls). Throughout the history of television, there have been far too many boys.

There are abundant examples of programs that finally achieved success only after inordinate patience by the carrying network. Unfortunately, there has been a raft of worthwhile efforts that were not accorded the same degree of patience. No one can know how many of them might have worked, all because network decision-makers lacked the courage of what should have been their convictions and took what they thought was the safe course—cancellation.

I was always invited to New York meetings as the guest expert from the West Coast, Mr. Showbiz. On one of these trips, Walter Scott, the head of the network, asked me to take a look at a pilot John Mitchell had sneaked him from Columbia's television production company, Screen Gems. In the screening room, Walter, who had no show business orientation at all, said, "Grant, I have to give John Mitchell an answer by close of business today. Should we buy this or not?" We looked at it together, after which I told him it was a one-joke premise and NBC should pass. John Mitchell promptly took it to ABC, where *Bewitched* became a major hit for eight seasons. Mr. Showbiz, indeed.

It was during this same period that I learned one hard truth of the business: There is never enough time to read all the scripts and presentations that come flooding in. My nights and weekends became concentrated reading sessions, my only distraction from an otherwise idyllic way of life. Mary understood how the television business worked and had no problem with my never-ending homework, although she was such a quick study with lines she seldom had assignments of her own.

My Burbank job meant a great deal of travel to New York, and I'd often take the red-eye, leaving Los Angeles late at night and arriving at the crack of dawn. I'd go straight to the hotel, shower and change, and be the first guy at 30 Rock. Then I'd put in a long day, sitting in on sixth-floor meetings with Bob Sarnoff and Bob Kintner, and operations meetings with Walter Scott, Don Durgin, and Mort Werner. People were stunned at my stamina. They didn't know I had some pharmaceutical assistance.

My internist in California was someone I didn't see very often, because I was healthy. For a reason I've forgotten, he had prescribed some pills, "greenies," that were for diet control. I later discovered that he handed them out like little candies to everybody. The damn things scared me, because taking just one would keep me three feet off the ground all day. Even at nine o'clock at night, I'd still be feeling high, so the only time I'd take one would be at the hotel in New York after an all-night flight. The day would just fly by. My Superman number eventually so disquieted me that I simply discontinued the pills and pretty much gave up the red-eye. The good doctor may well have been ingesting too much of his own medicine; he finally crashed and burned, abandoned his practice, and disappeared.

From Studio City, Mary, Richie, and I moved "up" to Encino. For one school year, when Ruth was having trouble controlling our oldest son, Mark, he came out from Connecticut to live with us. That was fine with Mary, who had no problem relating to my kids at any stage of our marriage. Not that there weren't periods when one or more of the kids, hers or mine, were sufficiently screwed up to require remedial action, or at least action that was supposed to be remedial. There were several years when three out of the five—Michael, Jodie, and Richie—attended the Orme School in Arizona, a combination ranch and school where they rode horses and ate dust and hit the books at least enough to graduate. It was almost more reform school than boarding school.

Somehow, all five of our "mutual" kids made it through what I think were particularly difficult years for young people—the late sixties and early seventies. My four negotiated their rough patches and all turned out solid and well, thanks largely to the good influence and tireless efforts of their mother. Richie took longer to "find himself," and Mary never gave up on him.

My practice, while I was head of programming in Burbank, was to get in my car and visit NBC's program suppliers. That was more time-consuming and less efficient than making them come to my office, but it was not simply a courtesy. Visits to the offices of people like Sheldon Leonard, Norman Felton at MGM, or Jennings Lang at Universal gave me a chance to get to know the writers and producers they would involve, and were somehow less formal and more productive than meetings that took place on my turf. Today, it's a rare event when a network programmer even gets out of his chair, much less leaves the building.

One afternoon, I was scheduled to see Bill Dozier, who ran Screen Gems. It meant a trip to Beachwood Drive in Hollywood, where parking was always a problem. There was a large paved lot next to the Screen Gems building that was always filled to capacity with the cars of their employees. I called Dozier that morning, and said, "Listen, if I'm going to schlep all the way over there to hear about some turkeys you'll tell me are shows, the least you can do is have Bonnie make sure there's a space reserved in your parking lot." Bonnie was Bill's long-serving and wonderful secretary. The other well-known member of his office entourage was his faithful poodle, Mac, who went everywhere Bill went. At Christmas, Bill would send Mac to various offices around the building, mouth-delivering gifts to staff members, as directed. The dog was human, only smarter.

"I'll see to it myself, dear boy," said Dozier. "Your arrival will be anticipated."

In keeping with my lifelong compulsive punctuality, I left early, drove south on Beachwood, and turned into the parking lot. I was astonished to find both rows of spaces, normally filled with dozens of cars, starkly empty. And then, to my horror, I spotted a seemingly endless white banner, easily forty feet long, hanging from the side of the building. Its huge red letters proclaimed: THIS SPACE RESERVED FOR MR. TINKER. It was vintage Dozier, and the joke wasn't over. From every window, clusters of Screen Gems people stood watching, grinning, and applauding as I made the very long walk from my car to the front door. I tried to carry it off with a bit of panache, but I didn't come close.

Bill Dozier was too independent to be everyone's favorite guy. He did things his way and you could take it or leave it. He could be utterly charming, unless he felt like being an SOB. Some people liked him either way; I was one of those. However he behaved, his wonderful wife, Ann Rutherford, has always been loved by all.

Dozier spent a lot of years doing movies and television, both as producer and studio executive. While much of the product he generated was serious and tasteful, some of it reflected his highly developed sense of humor. Probably his most celebrated project was the wildly popular television series, *Batman*.

Toward the end of his life, he pretty much kept to himself in the Malibu beach house he and Ann loved. She would come "uptown" to their Beverly Hills home for a couple of days a week, but Bill became more and more hermitlike as he moved into his eighties. He was something of a contradiction—a self-reliant man who relied completely on his peerless wife.

Bill finally wore out and suddenly we learned he was gone. Funeral services were announced. Ann would later explain that he had left explicit instructions: She was to schedule services at

10:30 A.M. in Beverly Hills, "convenient to where most of our friends live, and at an hour when those going to work will only have to make a short stop on their way to the office." He also choreographed the entire event, right down to the music.

The result had a few characteristic Dozier touches. The music Bill had chosen was upbeat, mostly show tunes. Bill's son, Bob, and his old friend, producer Fred de Cordova, were among the eulogists. But the departed had seen to it that no one stayed on too long, most especially not himself. As the pallbearers accompanied the closed casket slowly up the aisle, and the last piece of music boomed from the speakers, we mourners were treated to an exuberant rendition of "Take Me Out to the Ball Game." It was Bill Dozier's way of saying "fuck you" to the Grim Reaper and "don't cry for me" to the rest of us.

I was on my way to a meeting with Bob Kintner, an event that one NBC executive compared to waking up, tied to a tree, in front of a firing squad.

Kintner was president of NBC and everything about him was intimidating, even his sixth-floor office in the RCA Building. Shaped like a giant shoebox, it was painted a watery green and decorated with drab, standard-issue company furniture. The desk was placed in the far-left corner, forcing his summoned executives to make a thirty-foot trek to reach him, all the while being stared at from behind cloudy corrective lenses by a pair of rheumy eyes.

Kintner's voice was a raspy growl, he was stone deaf in his right ear, and his fleshy face bore an impassive look that covered every emotion from boredom to fury. When he was distracted, which was often, the ash from his cigarette would fall into the folds of his rumpled suit jacket, which he never removed, and eventually to the floor. The lethal triple play of chain-smoking, near blindness, and heavy drinking made ashtrays superfluous. As he talked on the phone, he would swivel his chair on the plastic sheet underneath, dropping ashes all the while. By late afternoon, he had created a ground cover of ash all around him, a daily source of fascination for his staff.

For some reason, perhaps because he didn't see me every day, I enjoyed special standing with Kintner. For all his bad habits, he treated me with respect and I felt admiration and affection for him. Entertainment programming was the part of the business he knew least about, and programmers were to him a different and interesting breed. Whenever I came into New York from Burbank, every three weeks or so, I was included in his daily staff meetings, and sometimes, as now, he would invite me up for a one-on-one visit to talk about programs.

The good news was that the president of NBC valued my opinions; the bad news was that these invitations usually came toward the end of the day, when it was almost certain he'd be well into the vodka. This could mean slurred speech, inattentive vagueness, or total incoherence. The suspenseful part was that I never knew how I'd find him, which made a late-afternoon summons an adventure in anxiety.

I got off the elevator on the sixth floor and walked down the corridor into Kintner's outer office, where his secretaries sat. "Go right in," Muriel Mead said. "He's expecting you." I pushed open the door and looked in. At the other end of his office, as usual, the square of hard plastic under his desk was almost invisible under its blanket of ashes, as was much of his suit jacket. As I started across the room, Bob pushed back his chair with characteristic clumsiness. My eye was on him as I moved forward, and to my horror I saw one of the rear wheels of his chair roll off the edge of the plastic sheet. He was trying to rise; instead, he lost his balance and began to fall backward.

Without breaking stride, I executed a perfect hook slide, my momentum carrying me smoothly below his chair. That placed me under his backside at the precise moment he would have crashed to the floor. Almost supine, I managed to wrestle the runaway wheel back onto the platform and push the chair upright. The whole scene, certainly for me, played in extreme slow motion. When it was over, my leader was safely reseated at his desk, unaware that I had saved his life—in fact, oblivious to the whole event. I brushed an accumulation of ashes from my trouser legs and took a chair as though nothing had happened.

Bob Kintner was remarkable. As hard of hearing, half-blind, and alcohol-impaired as he was, he maintained a clear vision of what he wanted NBC to be, the ability to communicate it to the entire company, and the follow-through to get it done. That's not a bad definition of leadership. He had taken a company that was a perennial also-ran to CBS, spent hardly any time worrying about entertainment programming—about which he cared very little—and devoted his energies toward building the best News division in broadcasting—about which he cared a lot.

He had spent years as a newspaper reporter and columnist and worked quickly to change the conventional wisdom about the place of news in the network television picture. He gave NBC News priority status and plenty of airtime. Disputes between News and Entertainment executives were invariably resolved in favor of News. He gave Chet Huntley and David Brinkley their own prime-time programs, encouraged News to break into the schedule anytime they felt it was important, and instituted the "CBS Plus 30" rule.

CBS Plus 30 simply meant that whenever CBS and NBC News were on the air covering the same breaking event, NBC was to continue its coverage at least a half-hour after CBS went back to regular programming. The result was exactly what Kintner had anticipated: audiences, advertisers, affiliates, and the press came to regard NBC News as the leader, and ratings and reputation followed. In the summer of 1964, NBC's competitive advantage over CBS at the Republican Convention was so great that CBS News, dreading the prospect of a repeat performance when the Democrats met, replaced Walter Cronkite with Robert Trout and Roger Mudd. The new anchor team fared no better against Huntley and Brinkley than Cronkite had.

Kintner saw NBC News as the jewel in the network crown, not as a profit center. The way to manage network television was for the Entertainment arm to bring in sufficient dollars to fund a first-rate News division. News was unique; day in, day out, it was the only part of the schedule that was produced in-house. Each news program had NBC's name on it, and each one said something about what kind of company NBC was.

The CBS array of successful situation comedies kept them comfortably ahead of NBC in the weekly ratings race, but NBC, under Kintner, was demonstrating that a network could reach for something more than ratings. Jim Aubrey, then overseeing CBS's Nielsen-leading entertainment schedule, believed in interrupting it as seldom as possible. Most weeks on CBS looked exactly like the week before. Kintner went in a totally different direction.

He was an event-oriented broadcaster, and hardly a week went by on NBC without some kind of promotable program: a news hour produced by Fred Freed, Reuven Frank, Lou Hazam, Shad Northshield, or another of the talented documentary producers News chief Bill McAndrew had on staff, or perhaps a live drama or musical-variety special that would get people talking. These programs were frequently in color, as an increasing percentage of NBC's regular schedule was coming to be, even though few homes had color receivers and both other networks were broadcasting mostly in black-and-white.

RCA, NBC's parent, urgently wanted to put an RCA color set into every living room in America and was happy to underwrite the extra cost of producing programs in color. That gave NBC another edge, which Kintner was quick to exploit. NBC announced an all-color prime-time schedule in 1965, based on research showing that owners of new color sets would watch almost anything presented in color. The ratings advantage became so apparent that both other networks quickly followed suit, but once again NBC had been the leader.

I learned a lot from Bob Kintner, even though his style was nothing I ever wanted to emulate. He was a past master at management by intimidation. Most executives went to his office only when summoned, heard him out, and then fled. If his instructions weren't entirely clear, as was often the case, the prudent course was to make an educated guess about what he really wanted rather than initiate another meeting.

Kintner once sent a scrawled note to David Adams, NBC's longtime senior executive vice president and éminence grise. The price Adams paid for having a brilliant mind and the ability to think and speak in fully formed paragraphs was that Kintner kept him by his side most of the day. Usually, as on this occasion, it was late afternoon before Adams could make his getaway and start attacking his own work. He looked at the note and couldn't begin to decipher it. Dreading the prospect of a trip down the hall to tell his only-possibly sober boss that his handwriting was illegible, he opted to pass the message around the table at his own staff meeting, hoping that someone might have the Rosetta stone in his pocket.

No one did, but several minutes of intense scrutiny led to a majority decision that the note read: "David: Let's push the girl with the fan." The problem was that no one knew what the hell that meant. Adams was at the point of surrender when he looked again and the bulb went on. It didn't say "fan," it said "hair." "Let's push the girl with the hair." Adams knew immediately what his marching orders were. Kintner, never good at remembering anyone's name, was telling him to see that a major public relations effort was made on behalf of Liz Trotta, then an NBC News correspondent, who did in fact have a particularly full head of hair.

By 1966, Kintner had managed to get himself fired by new RCA chief Bob Sarnoff for various alcohol-related transgressions (including, most memorably, showing up smashed at a meeting of the NBC Affiliate Board in Acapulco). His old pal Lyndon Johnson offered him a job at the White House, and the rest of us at NBC moved up a notch.

I became vice president in charge of programs, the job I'd always aspired to, and signed a new five-year contract for $80,000 a year ("more money than you ever imagined you'd make in your life," my new boss, Don Durgin, suggested). I was preparing to move back to New York, when Mary was offered a job there, as well.

David Merrick had given her the lead in *Breakfast at Tiffany's,* a musical adaptation of Truman Capote's novel that Abe Burrows was going to direct on Broadway. Mary had finished her memorable five-year run as Laura Petrie on the *Van Dyke* show. She had made a multipicture deal with Universal, out of which had come one good movie, *Thoroughly Modern Millie,* with Julie Andrews, and a couple of forgettable ones. She begged out of the last in order to come east for *Breakfast at Tiffany's.* Everyone associated with the show was a first-rate talent: Bob Merrill wrote the music, Oliver Smith designed the scenery, Michael Kidd staged the musical numbers, and Richard Chamberlain was the male lead. *Breakfast at Tiffany's* looked like a can't-miss project that would keep Mary in New York for a long time.

We would need a place to live, and it occurred to me that Kintner had an apartment at 63rd and Fifth that he'd no longer be needing. I had never been in it, but the location was great. I phoned him and inquired whether the place was available. His reply was enthusiastic, even effusive: "I can't imagine anyone I'd rather have take the place. I've had an awful lot of people beating down the door—lots of U.N. people, particularly—but I'd much rather turn it over to you and Mary. You can have it for what I'm paying," he added generously. "Just send me a check every month and take over the lease when it's time to renew."

Mary and I sold our Encino house, shipped whatever we

thought we'd need to New York, and got on the plane with Richie to start our new life in the East. We had arranged for our two dogs, a small poodle and a German shepherd, to be in the cargo hold, each in its own cage. We were sitting on the port side of the first-class section as the jet engines began revving up. The roar had just reached full crescendo when Mary looked out the window and screamed. On the ground, right under the ear-splitting sound of the engines, were our caged dogs. Mary went ballistic. She ran up to the cockpit and just started yelling until the pilot turned everything off. We were sure the dogs would be dead or, at the very least, deaf, but Mary's quick action had saved the day, and we all made it safely to New York.

Kintner's place was gloomy and rundown. NBC lore had it that he and his dog, Lucky, watched television together every night while Bob drank. Anxious programmers worried whether Lucky would like their shows. Kintner's wife, Jean, seized every opportunity to be at their second home in Westport, and who could have blamed her? I spent my first night in the apartment alone; Mary had already left for out-of-town rehearsals. There was virtually no furniture there, and no window shades or curtains. As I was about to go to bed, I opened the window and looked down at Fifth Avenue. Across the street, next to the benches outside Central Park, was a derelict—not a common sight in the sixties. He was drunk or angry or crazy, or maybe all three, and he was shouting unintelligibly and shaking his fist at my building, seemingly at me. I stood there, transfixed by what I decided was the big city's way of welcoming me back.

Although we were only renting, we had Kintner's apartment completely redone, assuming we'd be there a long time. Several months later, it came time to renew the lease. The woman who owned the building lived in the penthouse, and I went to see her. To my outraged surprise, I learned that Kintner had been stiffing me for $250 every month. His rent had been $1,250 and he was charging me $1,500. To put it mildly, I was pissed. I called Bob at the White House. "Jesus, Bob, how could you do that?" "Grant," he rasped without a hint of embarrassment, "*everybody* does that."

With Mary away from New York, our dogs spent each day in the apartment with our not very competent housekeeper, whose scarred face looked as if it had been the loser in a few bar fights. Every morning, a young woman with six or eight dogs on leashes would come up in our elevator, add ours to her entourage, and head for Central Park. You'd think these animals, strangers to one another, would have been in a constant free-for-all, but somehow professional dog walkers don't let that happen. There was no fighting, the dogs did their thing in the park, and harmony prevailed.

Unfortunately, that was only in the morning. Mary and I had decided we would handle the job ourselves at night. "We" meant me, because Mary was out of town with the play. Every night around eleven, the dogs and I would walk down 63rd Street, turn right on Madison Avenue, and west on 62nd back to Fifth. While still in California, we had anticipated the no-backyard change in the dogs' lives and hired a guy to train them. He taught them to go to the bathroom on the cue of "Get busy." When *he* said it to them, legs came up and things happened. When I said it to them, they didn't even look at me. I spent countless nights walking around that tony block on the Upper East Side, yelling "Get busy!" to two dogs who couldn't wait to get home and get busy on the carpet.

I hadn't been ensconced in my fourth-floor office at the RCA Building more than a few days when Ted Ashley called and asked for an appointment. Ted was a veteran agent, powerful and influential. He normally dealt only with the top network people and got things done with seemingly little effort. I promptly invited him over. Ted got right to the point: "How would you like to be head of the CBS Television Network?" I stared at him. "It's a job you can have if you want it. I've been asked to find out whether you'd be interested."

For once I was quick to point out that it would be an unseemly time for me to jump ship. The truth was, I didn't feel ready for such an important and demanding job. I was also genuinely surprised that CBS management even had a clear idea of who I was, let alone thought well of me.

Twenty-five years later, when Frank Stanton and I were serving together as trustees of the Museum of Television and Radio, I learned that it was he, then the president of CBS and a towering figure in broadcasting, who had sent Ted Ashley to see me. Today, I can muse that if a man of Stanton's impeccable judgment thought I was ready in 1966, maybe I should have thought so, too.

As it turned out, right before Ashley's visit, I had been in consideration for the identical job at NBC—and didn't know it. After Bob Kintner's involuntary departure, the head of the television network, Walter Scott, had been promoted to chairman, and Julian Goodman, Kintner's protégé in NBC News management, was named president. NBC needed a replacement for Scott, and the decision was made in consultation with Bob Sarnoff, who had recently moved upstairs to run RCA. Mort Werner, my boss at the time, was also considered for the role, but Don Durgin, then head of Sales, got the nod. When I learned later that I had been one of the candidates, I was told it would have been awkward to jump me over Mort, and there was a good chance Don would have left if he weren't chosen. And he, at least, felt ready to run a network.

Later in 1966, things started to come apart for Mary and for me in different ways at the same time. *Breakfast at Tiffany's* struggled through rewrites in Philadelphia and, even with all those talented people doing their utmost, the play just wasn't working. I went down to see it on a Saturday night, and it was clearly in serious trouble. The next morning, I called Abe Burrows, who was holed up in the Stratford Hotel, wrestling with the Olympian task of turning Capote's book into a Broadway musical. I asked if I could come up to see him. "Absolutely," he said. After a couple of minutes of small talk, I got to the point. "So, Abe, what are you going to do?" I asked, eager to learn what miracle he had up his sleeve. "I don't know, Grant," the great director sighed. "What *am* I going to do?"

He never did find the miracle. Boston followed Philadelphia, and Edward Albee, an odd choice, was brought in to do the final rewrite. Not surprisingly, he hardly cheered up the material. *Breakfast at Tiffany's* closed after four preview performances in New York. I attended the wake at Sardi's, where the whole company could have a good group cry. Mary, who had put her heart and soul into the work, was hugely disappointed. She was also suddenly at liberty. Meanwhile, back at the NBC ranch, I was becoming increasingly disenchanted with the bureaucracy in general and with one member of it in particular.

In my new programming job, I reported to Don Durgin, who was a great guy and thoroughly equal to his assignment, but for one glaring weakness. He constantly deferred to a subordinate, Robert L. Stone, whom Kintner had earlier recruited from ABC.

Stone's title was vice president and general manager of the NBC Television Network. Though he reported to Durgin, he often overwhelmed him. Able and self-confident as he was in other respects, Don couldn't seem to keep Stone out of his office or his decisions.

Unfortunately, Stone had little feel for the creative component of the broadcasting business. Kintner had initially brought him in to reduce the size of the engineering staff, a job he took to with relish. His power grew as Durgin failed to control him, and to those of us on the programming side, his influence seemed almost entirely negative. His primary responsibility was overseeing the hardware and business affairs aspects of the network, and he appeared to resent those of us involved in more glamorous pursuits, who actually enjoyed our jobs. Our unforgivable sin, in his eyes, was that we were in the business of spending a lot of NBC's money on programs. Most of us came to work every day challenged by the almost limitless possibilities of network television; Stone's horizon stopped at the bottom line.

Behind his back, we called him "Doctor No," and we had a slogan for him: "Nothing ventured, nothing lost." Meetings that included Stone, held in Durgin's office two or three times a week, were often unpleasant and unproductive. Discussion was frequently about program opportunities, each of which required a considerable expenditure of NBC dollars. Without fail, Stone would jump in with a negative comment designed to preempt further discussion, or at least piss on the project at hand.

"Why the hell would you want to do that?" and "That's about twice as expensive as it ought to be" were typical Stone reactions to any recommendation, mine included, to spend money. It wasn't personal. In fact, he liked me and thought we were pals; he just couldn't help himself. But over the months his negativism became intolerable to me. It kept us from doing a number of things I thought we should have done, things that might have helped NBC competitively. I left most of those meetings steaming, and I was increasingly frustrated.

One evening, very close to Christmas of 1966, Mary and I were sitting in the den of our Fifth Avenue Kintner legacy, having a drink and talking about what she was going to do next. Would she do another television series or would she look for a movie? A movie made more sense, it seemed, because otherwise Mary would have to live almost full-time in California, while I remained locked in my long-term arrangement with NBC in New York.

All of a sudden it hit me that there was no reason in the world why we had to stay in New York. I could quit my NBC job, where I was getting Stoned to death, go back to California, and seek a job in production. The whole idea was appealing to me: trading New York, which I disliked, for California, which I loved; bidding farewell to the bureaucratic nay-saying that was making my life miserable; and getting active in television production. Mary agreed it was a great idea, and I went to the office the next day hoping NBC would, too.

After brief, encouraging conversations with Mort Werner and Don Durgin, I wound up in the office of Walter Scott, the elegant, dark-haired man who had run the television network during Kintner's reign. Now, more or less through attrition, he had become NBC's chairman of the board. Walter was a golf-playing buddy of many of the CEOs whose companies advertised on NBC, and had an old-school, white-shoe approach to business and to life. He was a truly nice man, very principled, but not intensely motivated. One NBC staffer had spoken for many of his colleagues when he said: "The brass ring reached out and grabbed Walter."

I explained to Walter that I wanted to resign and go back to California. He was genuinely shocked. He stared at me, searching for the right words to express his disbelief. "Grant," he finally managed, "that's simply unethical. It's immoral. You must honor your commitment." He went on to tell me how offended he was that I would even think of running out on a five-year contract. Didn't I realize how much the company had done for me, what a great future I had? Why would I want to leave? I told him why and watched his offended surprise turn to anger. He made himself clear: If not quite dishonest, it was surely outrageous of me even to entertain the idea of leaving. "But Grant, you signed it willingly," Walter said. To him, a contract was a contract, even if it meant involuntary servitude. It took me three meetings to convince him that if I didn't want to be there, NBC shouldn't want me there. He finally bought that, and we agreed to rip up the last four years of my contract.

I left the RCA Building that evening and turned up Fifth Avenue toward the apartment. Just past 53rd Street, I ran into Jennings Lang, the head of television for Universal, NBC's biggest program supplier. "What's new?" Jennings asked perfunctorily. "What's new," I told him, "is that I've quit my job and I'm going back to California." He didn't miss a beat: "Why don't you come with us?"

I had been out of work for four blocks.

By the early sixties, the networks had become masters of their own schedules and there had been important advances in technology—but that didn't mean the programs were better. Creatively, a certain homogeneity was setting in, not surprising when you consider that virtually all the programs were selected by three buyers instead of many. There were a few more program genres than would survive into later decades—westerns and variety shows had not yet bitten the dust—but network programmers were becoming less and less adventurous as the stakes got higher.

There were still some programming distinctions among the networks. CBS took dead aim at the most popular shows, always had the best ratings, and made the most money. Perennial runner-up NBC, under Kintner, aimed slightly higher, had the leading news organization, and was comfortably profitable. ABC, always disadvantaged by the weakest affiliate lineup, scrambled resourcefully, occasionally producing some interesting innovations—*Batman,* the first all-family show to play on two levels, satire for Dad and adventure for Junior; *Peyton Place,* the first prime-time soap opera; and *The Flintstones,* the first prime-time animated series.

CBS specialized in three kinds of shows: comedy (*Andy Griffith, Lucy, Beverly Hillbillies, Dick Van Dyke, Father Knows Best, Green Acres, Hogan's Heroes*), variety (*Garry Moore, Ed Sullivan, Jackie Gleason, Red Skelton, Carol Burnett, The Smothers Brothers, Judy Garland, Danny Kaye*), and game/people shows (*What's My Line?, To Tell the Truth, I've Got a Secret, Password, Candid Camera*). CBS also, less frequently, had good dramatic programs like *The Defenders* and *Route 66,* and a couple of fine westerns: *Gunsmoke* and *Have Gun, Will Travel.*

NBC's schedules in the sixties had much less comedy (*Get Smart, Car 54, Where Are You?, Hazel, I Dream of Jeannie*), far more drama and westerns (*Dr. Kildare, Mr. Novak, Star Trek, Alfred Hitchcock, Bonanza, The Man from U.N.C.L.E., Peter Gunn, The Virginian, Daniel Boone, Run for Your Life, I Spy, Ironside*), and were never without a few variety shows (*Perry Como, Andy Williams, Dean Martin, Mitch Miller*). There were also harder-to-characterize programs like *Walt Disney's Wonderful World of Color, Laugh-In*, and *You Bet Your Life*.

ABC had to do more with less, and got maximum mileage from an array of inventively selected series. There was an important ABC–Warner Brothers connection, reportedly the result of Leonard Goldenson convincing a foot-dragging Jack Warner that there was money to be made in television film production. The resulting schedules were heavy on action-adventure (*The Untouchables, Naked City, 77 Sunset Strip, The Fugitive, It Takes a Thief*), other drama and westerns (*Ben Casey, Maverick, The Rifleman, Wyatt Earp, Cheyenne*), some comedy (*Ozzie and Harriet, Bewitched, Donna Reed, My Three Sons, McHale's Navy, The Addams Family, The Flying Nun*), and a little variety (*Lawrence Welk, The Hollywood Palace, Shindig*).

With the networks now in total charge of what went on the air in prime time, programming had veered away from the live drama of the fifties to the kind of filmed programming Hollywood does best. That, of course, meant a much larger role for the television arms of the big motion picture studios, so Jennings Lang's invitation to come work for Universal arrived at an opportune time. Mary, Richie, and I returned to California, renting for a while before buying a comfortable old house on Beverly Drive. Mary made a few features and did some television guest shots, while I put in a couple of years at Universal and almost as long at Fox. Once again my timing was good. Just as I'd been in advertising when the big agencies were at the center of activity in network television programming, I was working at the movie studios when they had taken over that position.

Mary and I discovered Malibu, where we rented a small place on the beach. On Saturday mornings I'd usually play tennis at Jennings Lang's house, and then we'd go down to Malibu for the rest of the weekend. Tough life. Yet somehow the late sixties are the least memorable of all our years together, which may be a comment about more than our work situations.

Universal had rescued me, and I wanted to do well there. Jennings assigned me to get something going with ABC, where he hadn't been doing any business, and we did launch two very successful series with them. The first was *It Takes a Thief,* with Robert Wagner, a stylish drama that even attracted the guest talents of Fred Astaire, who played R.J.'s father in the 1969–70 season. Elton Rule, who had managed Channel 7, the ABC-owned station in Los Angeles, had been brought to New York by Leonard Goldenson to run the whole network. I had only a nodding acquaintance with Elton, but I bypassed the program department, pitched the show directly to him, and made the sale.

The other important ABC show was *Marcus Welby, M.D.* It was created by David Victor, who had written *Dr. Kildare* when I was at NBC Burbank. Universal and ABC were excited about the prospects of this new medical series, and Ralph Bellamy had been chosen as the lead.

I came into my office one morning, and sitting there was Robert Young, whom I knew only by sight. Someone had given him the script, and his opening words to me were, "I want to be Marcus Welby." Young was at that point semiretired and living in Rancho Santa Fe, outside San Diego. I explained to him that we were pretty far down the Ralph Bellamy track, and he said, "Let me test." That turned out to be unnecessary after Young or his agent went to see Marty Starger, ABC's head of programming.

Suddenly ABC decided Robert Young was a better choice than Ralph Bellamy, and it fell to me to call Ralph in Palm Springs to tell him "a funny thing happened on the way to the show" and excuse him from the project. It was an embarrassing moment for me, but Ralph, gentleman that he was, made the conversation much easier. *Marcus Welby,* with Robert Young, went on to seven successful seasons on ABC.

The network's insistence on Bob Young certainly didn't hurt the show's chances, and most would agree that he made a splendid Dr. Welby. Bellamy might have been equally good, but we'll never know, and today it's an unimportant matter. ABC's intervention stands as a good example of a network exercising its prerogative to call the creative shots. In this case the result was a wash at worst, salutary at best. Would that network "interference" were always so benign.

The couple of years I spent at Universal represented the first time I had been on the supply side of the television fence in any big-league fashion. The government had told MCA to choose one of its two businesses, and in 1962 the company elected to give up its number-one talent agency in favor of becoming a full-time production company. MCA bought Universal (including its four-hundred-plus-acre lot) for a bargain $11 million, and the company's characteristic zeal and initiative went into the new endeavor.

When I was there, and for years before and after, Lew Wasserman was the guiding, energizing genius behind the constantly growing enterprise. His predecessor, MCA founder Jules Stein, had turned the reins over to Lew at a very early point in the life of the company. Lew, in turn, spotted Sidney Sheinberg almost immediately after he joined MCA as a young lawyer in 1959. Looking back, I think Lew was even then grooming Sid to become president of MCA, and put him to work paying his dues in the television department, then headed by the dynamic Jennings Lang. The business affairs end of the work came easily to Sid, but he obviously loved the creative area as well. I have vivid memories of him, still in his office long after dark, in spirited script sessions and project discussions with Frank Price, Jack Webb, Roy Huggins, or another of Universal's cadre of producers.

One day in 1969, in ABC's tacky Vine Street offices, Sid and I made a major sale of forty ninety-minute movies to the network. To this day, ABC and Leonard Goldenson insist they invented movies for television, but actually NBC had done it a couple of years earlier, while I was still there. What ABC did originate was *The Movie of the Week*, and Barry Diller was the prime mover at the network. With Universal, NBC had earlier initiated *Project 120*, two-hour movies that really were the first made specifically for television. But the man who should get most of the inventor's credit is Jennings Lang, who was constantly searching for ways to make and sell more Universal product to the networks. In 1963, Lew Wasserman and Jennings visited NBC in New York to make a deal, which Bob Kintner approved, for three two-hour movies to be produced by Universal for prime-time use. Mort Werner and I spearheaded the effort in the Programming department, but the deal was really hammered out by the head of Business Affairs for NBC, Herb Schlosser, and Sid

Sheinberg, both of whom would later become presidents of their companies.

The first movie finished and delivered was *The Killers,* an adaptation of the Hemingway story, directed by Don Siegal and starring Lee Marvin, Angie Dickinson, and Ronald Reagan. It was rather violent by the television standards of the day, and we were a bit nervous about it being NBC's first foot forward in the form. Bob Kintner decided that we couldn't play it, and it was eventually released theatrically.

But the second and third films, both dramatic pieces, were approved for broadcast, and on October 7, 1964, a bit of television history was made. NBC presented the very first made-for-television movie, *See How They Run,* starring John Forsythe and Senta Berger, followed on November 18 by *The Hanged Man.* Their reception was encouraging enough for us to make a multi-picture, multiyear deal with Universal for more of these television originals, which came to be known as "made-fors."

Some of the scripts were adaptations of books; most were new material, turned in by writers eager to participate. These long-form shows would become an NBC staple, soon to be emulated by both other networks, and were usually scheduled in one of the time periods set aside for theatrical films. Five years later, ABC became the first network to schedule a weekly series of made-fors.

As colleagues in the television department at Universal, Sid Sheinberg and I were more than a little excited about our forty-movie sale to ABC that day. We raced back to the office in Universal City, where we were astounded to learn that Lew Wasserman wouldn't allow us to accept the order. We had been getting $800,000 for each NBC *Project 120,* and ABC wanted to pay only $500,000 for each of their ninety-minute movies. Lew felt the price differential wasn't equitable. In vintage Wasser-manese, he said, "Fellas, it doesn't make any sense," or maybe he said, "Forget it, fellas"—he owns both phrases. Later, the money got worked out and ABC began its *Movie of the Week* series.

One might have expected that the introduction of made-for-TV movies would tend to democratize the creative community. No chance. The moviemakers continued to look down their noses at the television practitioners, in spite of the fact that all were turning out product that looked very much alike. The only differences were that theatrical movies had much bigger budgets, acknowledged "stars," and, in terms of success, lower batting averages. Of course, that's the opinion of a guy whose whole experience has been television, and I might be considered a biased source.

Everything was going well at Universal, so naturally I left. I had joined the Los Angeles Tennis Club and there I got to know Bill Self, then in charge of television at Fox. Somehow, over post-tennis Cokes, he convinced me that I'd have more fun at Fox. Don't ask me why I bought that, but I did.

Almost from day one, I regretted leaving Universal. Fox wasn't in the same league—their network activity was on a much smaller scale—and I had no real opportunity to make a major contribution. I did sell CBS a pilot I put together, starring Herschel Bernardi, called *Arnie*. Bernardi played a blue-collar guy and the series was sort of a live-action *Simpsons* (though hardly of the same quality). It had been created by David Swift, a very good writer who scripted the pilot and then kited off to Europe. The series fell into lesser hands, and we really didn't deliver the show we sold.

But I do remember making the sale in the first place. The head of programs for CBS was Mike Dann, who was always distracted and difficult to pin down. After several futile attempts on my part to arrange a meeting, he phoned one day and said, "I'm at the Beverly Hills Hotel. Why don't you come over at seven o'clock tonight. I might have a couple of minutes." I drove to the hotel and went up to his room. Dann, obviously just out of the shower, was sitting with his feet up in the chair, picking at his toes, and talking nonstop. Before he could forget why I was there, I pitched him *Arnie,* he bought it, and it ran for two seasons on CBS.

Dann, whatever his attire, was never at a loss for words. Before his long CBS stint, he had worked in Programming for NBC when Pat Weaver ran the network. After Pat's departure, Bob Sarnoff, eager to instill some cultural changes, called in a group of NBC's senior executives for a pep talk. "We all want the same thing," he said, "and that's to make NBC the leader in all aspects of broadcasting. The fastest way to get there is for everyone to put an end to factionalism and start working together. From now on, let there be no more Weaver men or Sarnoff men. From now on," he concluded, "we're all NBC men."

Mike Dann raised his hand. Sarnoff called on him, pleased that the irreverent programmer wanted to participate. "I just wanted to say," Mike chirped, "that the regular five o'clock meeting of the Dann men is canceled."

During my time at Fox, Dave Gerber, then segueing from sales to producing, turned out his first network show. *The Ghost and Mrs. Muir,* a stylish comedy based on the 1947 movie, starred Edward Mulhare and Hope Lange in the parts created by Rex Harrison and Gene Tierney. It ran for one season on NBC, was canceled, and was then picked up for another year by ABC. Stanley Rubin produced *Bracken's World,* a drama about three starlets at a Hollywood movie studio. The series was forgettable, lasting little more than one season, but it wasn't a total loss: One of the actresses later became Mrs. Gerber and another married Dick Zanuck. The first is still Laraine Gerber.

I arrived at Fox during the first season of *Room 222,* which Jim Brooks had created and was producing with Gene Reynolds. Set in a big-city high school, *Room 222* starred Lloyd Haynes as an idealistic black teacher confronting problems like drugs and racial prejudice, problems that in 1969 were not often treated in prime-time entertainment television. It may not have been the first television show to mix comedy with substantial issues, but I can't remember any prior program that accomplished that difficult trick as well. *Room 222* was awarded the 1970 Emmy for Outstanding New Series, consistently won praise from educational and civil rights organizations, and went on to more than four successful seasons on ABC.

Jim brought in Allan Burns to write some episodes, and when Gene Reynolds had to leave the show for about six episodes to direct a pilot, Allan was asked to fill in as producer. For a few weeks I watched Jim and Allan in action on the same job, and that gave me a great idea that helped launch the next and best period of my working life.

For more than two decades, I had been attending the university of broadcasting, majoring in programming. I had never been uncomfortable working for others, being part of someone else's existing machine. But like most people, I was curious to find out whether I could start and run a company from scratch, and I was certainly aware of the considerable rewards success in the program business could generate.

Mary's career had been rather hit-or-miss since the *Van Dyke* show ended in 1966. When a CBS special, *Dick Van Dyke and the Other Woman,* offered a chance to reunite with her former partner, she was delighted. In his characteristically generous fashion, Dick more or less threw the show to Mary, and it proved to be a marvelous showcase for talents she hadn't had occasion to display for several years. The most significant result was that CBS got reexcited about Mary and offered her a show of her own. Mary was interested in simply doing the show, but I saw it as an entrepreneurial opportunity not to be missed. We sent Arthur Price, Mary's manager, to negotiate nothing less than a series commitment, although the network would have preferred to make just a pilot. That meant thirteen episodes and a virtual guarantee of getting on the air. In addition, it would improve our odds of having a success, and would allow us to go for broke and try to start a production company, which was my ultimate goal.

Obviously, there was financial risk in going it alone, but in those days it was still possible to produce programs for about what networks would pay for them. Even if we failed at the end of thirteen weeks, we would only be out the organizational start-up costs—not chopped liver, but manageable. And if we succeeded, Mary and I would have control of our mutual fate in an industry where bad management by a few could mean failure for many.

Most prime-time programs are made by companies that handle all the production details and then, in effect, rent the finished product to the network for two plays—an original and one repeat —in exchange for a license fee. As it turned out, the license fee paid by CBS covered our production costs for the first two years of Mary's show. Only a few years later, the changed economics of network television would make this kind of independent production start-up much riskier, if not prohibitive.

As the syndication market developed, producers had the potential to make large profits by selling their programs to individual stations, following the network run. The trick was to keep your program on the network at least four years, thus amassing enough episodes, perhaps ninety or more, necessary for a successful syndication sale. Most series never made it that far, but many that did brought back huge postnetwork profits. The network-producer marketplace reacted by changing the concept of the license fee. By the third year of Mary's show, license fees no longer covered the full cost of production. The producer was expected to take a loss on his weekly episode outlay in exchange for the possibility of getting rich on the back end. The deficit became part of the cost of doing business in the production community.

Once the CBS deal was made, I managed my first recruiting miracle by prevailing upon Jim Brooks and Allan Burns to cocreate and produce Mary's show. (Gene Reynolds, who produced *Room 222* with Jim, would join MTM some years later as executive producer of *Lou Grant*.) I've been dining out ever since on the invaluable notion of asking them to become a team.

I had separate preliminary conversations with Jim and Allan. The two had never worked head to head before; on *Room 222,* they'd work out a story together, and then Burns would go write it. Allan had done a couple of three-camera shows, including the highly regarded *He and She,* with Dick Benjamin and Paula Prentiss, but he found the format difficult, demanding "constant rewriting and a lot of late-night stuff."

"If I'm going to do more television," he told me, "I really really like this one-camera thing. But I'm thinking about movies." Allan wasn't entirely sure what I had in mind, and I was being circumspect because I was still at Fox. I did tell him that as the producer of the kind of show I was proposing, he would have more control. "If you're the guy in charge," I said, "you can call the shots."

Jim and Allan finally got the picture: Mary and I were starting a company to do *Mary Tyler Moore,* and we wanted them to do it as a team. A few years earlier, Allan recalls, he had tried without success to get Carl Reiner to put him on the staff of *The Dick Van Dyke Show,* "every comedy writer's favorite," and he found the prospect of doing Mary's show "enormously appealing."

But he and Jim had plenty of other projects on their respective plates. Jim had written and produced a pilot with Alan Alda and Louise Lasser, and Allan was thinking about a movie career. Both wanted to keep their options open, and weren't eager to commit to staying with just one show. They decided to come in and ask for the moon: to commit for a year, but only a year, because they didn't want to be tied up for more than that. Needless to say, I agreed, and they wound up doing the show for seven years.

Allan was surprised, he said years later, that I put my wife and our money in the hands of two guys who were, as far as I knew, "tyros at this whole thing." I knew Jim Brooks and Allan Burns were both exceedingly talented, and as simplistic as it sounds, it seemed to me that two talented people were better than one. At that point, the newly formed team had never met Mary, so we invited them to our house for a visit one evening. We had a staircase that descended into the middle of the living room. Mary came down the steps, did a drunken stumble, and sort of weaved into the room. Before they realized this was just her little joke, Allan remembers thinking, "Oh, my God. What did we get into? It's the best-kept secret in the world. All these years, Mary Tyler Moore has been a drunk, and we didn't know it!"

The first idea they pitched had to do with her being divorced, because "every writer we knew of had a divorce script somewhere in his trunk," Allan recalls. "I think we had her working as a leg woman for a Los Angeles gossip columnist. She would be a somewhat naive person coming out of a broken marriage, who goes to work for this harridan of a woman, working out of a building that housed a lot of writers. Except for the divorce part, it was pretty much a terrible idea, but Mary supported it." So did I, and Allan and Jim went in with Arthur Price to pitch it to Perry Lafferty, who ran West Coast programming for CBS. Since I was still technically at Fox, I had to operate by proxy.

"There's a dining room at Television City," Burns remembers, "that was the home of many horrible lunches over the years. Perry had a big grin on his face at the beginning, and the grin began fading, fading, fading as we went along. Finally, he said: 'No, you can't do this. You cannot have Mary Tyler Moore divorced. People hate divorce and there's no way that anybody is going to accept her.' We said she's the perfect person to do it with, because people will forgive her anything. We had already thought about how to deal with the problem, by making two characters on the show her former in-laws, who love her and can't stand their son. They blame him for the whole thing.

"You could see the little beads of sweat forming along Perry's hairline. 'But people will think she's divorced from Dick Van Dyke.' We had anticipated that one, too. No, no, we assured him, they'll see the ex-husband from time to time. Perry and his lieutenant, Paul King, begged us to rethink it, but we said no, this is what we want to do and it's what Mary wants to do." Before they went over to CBS, I had told Jim and Allan that the network could strongly advise, but couldn't tell them what to do.

At the end of the meeting, Perry said, "Well, I don't really think this is the right way to go, but I'll support you on it when we go to New York." So Jim and Allan and Arthur got on an airplane. "There's a very womblike room at CBS in New York," Allan recalls, "that had black felt or something like it on the walls. You go in and you feel like you're in the abyss. You sit in this room and there are special ceiling lights shining down. It was like being in a Kafkaesque kind of play."

They sat in a circle, surrounded by the CBS people, who included Perry, his boss Mike Dann, and Bob Wood, the new head of the network. "They wrung their hands," Allan recalls, "and said, You cannot do this, you cannot do divorce. And we said, Yeah, we can. Statistically, almost everybody in America is touched by divorce one way or another. We had this pitch all ready, and we were going over like a lead balloon. Finally, this heavy man from Research spoke up. When I say heavy, I'm being kind. Very ponderously, he said there were three or four things that Americans simply would not tolerate in their viewing habits. One was divorced people. The others were people from New York, people who were Jewish, and people who had mustaches. I looked around the room and what you had was mostly divorced Jewish guys from New York. Not too many mustaches."

Allan and Jim were excused from the meeting. It was clear to them that if they went ahead with their idea and CBS had to accept it, the network would give the show no support whatsoever. The door had hardly closed before Mike Dann was grilling Arthur: "Who are these guys? What are their credits? Hire somebody else, somebody we can deal with."

Brooks and Burns didn't know all that until much later, but they did know they had bombed. They flew back without Arthur, and told me that the idea was dead, that CBS hated it, and that they thought they should quit. "Remember that Jim and I had just come off *Room 222,* which was a reality-based comedy," Allan says. "We didn't want to go and do typical sitcom sort of stuff. CBS kept telling us Lucy was never divorced, Doris Day was never divorced, and we're saying, we can't do that kind of show. There's nothing wrong with it, but it's not what we do. We need some reality here, and the divorce gave us that. Gave us stories. Doris Day was the perpetual virgin and we just didn't want that persona for Mary."

What they wanted was to do something contemporary, that felt real to them, that would enable them to touch on current events. They decided to take a week off to think it over, and that's when they came up with the idea of the newsroom. "Jim had worked in a newsroom at CBS in New York and knew that arena very well," Burns remembers. "When he began to talk about it, we warmed to the idea very quickly and came up with the concept that later became the show. And which also included having Mary coming off a long-term affair." They repitched the idea to me and to Mary, and we loved it even more than the first one. The notion that Mary had been living with somebody sent shivers up CBS's spine, but they bought it. As Allan says, "Divorce to them was worse than living in sin."

While I stayed on at Fox, planning a timely but not unseemly withdrawal—my boss, Bill Self, was too good a guy to just run out on—Jim and Allan set up shop at an antiquated little lot, General Services Studios on Las Palmas Street in Hollywood.

Over the years, I've occasionally read that I played a significant role in the creation of Mary's show, but in truth I provided only support and enthusiasm. I do get credit for the choice of Jay Sandrich to direct, and he proved to be an inspired choice. He would become an integral, hugely contributive member of the show family. Burns, Brooks, and Sandrich winnowed out what eventually became the nonpareil ensemble cast that peopled Mary's show, a process in which Ethel Winant, vice president of casting for CBS, was enormously helpful.

After more than three months of looking, however, they still hadn't found anyone they liked to play Lou Grant. I suggested they read Ed Asner for the part, a fact I've never let Ed forget. He had played a chief of police in a really awful *Movie of the Week* for us at Fox. The material was so embarrassing that Ed played it kind of tongue-in-cheek, which suggested to me that he could do comedy.

"Ed was physically perfect for the part, but when we read him for it, he was terrible," Allan Burns remembers. "After he left, we said to each other: 'What are we going to do? We don't have anybody.' About ten minutes later, our secretary came in and said, 'Ed Asner's back. He wants to see you again.'

"Ed came in and said, 'What are you guys? You just sat there on your asses and let me bomb like that? I was awful. I knew it and you knew it. Why did you let me do it? Tell me something. Tell me what you want from this character.' So we started to talk to Ed and began to work with him a little bit. And good things began to happen. It was a great lesson for us not to sit on our hands and let somebody bomb. If you tell an actor what you want, he'll usually give it to you."

Even after Ed was cast, we continued to have problems with CBS. They needed something to show prospective advertisers before the show went into production, so we shot a sales piece— the now-famous "You've got spunk" scene with Ed and Mary. "It was done with one camera instead of three in a studio over on La Brea somewhere," Allan Burns recalls, "and it came off not that well. I remember Perry Lafferty saying to me afterwards, 'Ed Asner is a wonderful dramatic actor. Hear me, *dra-ma-tic* actor.'" The message from CBS was clear: Maybe we should think about somebody else.

"After that disaster," Allan says, "we did a test run in front of an audience and we really weren't ready. It was one of the worst nights I've ever spent. We knew we were bombing from the very first action to the last. Nothing worked. There was a postmortem in the huge office Jim and I had at the old General Services Studios. There must have been thirty people there, people we had never seen before. Arthur Price brought in people from his management firm. I remember seeing Andy Williams's brother and wondering what the hell he was doing there." It was true. Nothing worked; the material just lay there. Nobody laughed. I think disaster would be a fair word.

The real show was going to be filmed the following night, so I took Mary home, knowing the guys were going to stay and worry and agonize, and maybe rewrite a little. Around midnight, Mary, who has always been very professional—she comes prepared and lets other people do their jobs—finally lost it. She knew this show was her big chance and, crying, said to me, "You've got to fix it." More to appease her than anything else, I called the studio and got Jim and Allan together on the phone. I said, "Guys, I have a lady going to pieces here, and I'm calling you because I don't know what else to do. So I'm giving you one instruction: Fix it!"

I put down the phone, and Mary and I went to bed. The next day, there was a little more rehearsal, and they did the show that night. No serious rewriting had occurred, but there were some changes, including a number contributed by script supervisor Marge Mullen, who had worked with Mary on the *Van Dyke* show. Moreover, the actors and Jay had learned a lot from the previous night's fiasco. The transformation was fantastic—suddenly everything came together.

"It was the most euphoric thing," Allan Burns remembers, "going from the nadir, the absolute staring into the jaws of death, to the ecstatic reaction of the audience that night. Especially the 'You've got spunk' scene. That really kicked it off and set the tone for what the show was going to be. And we never lost it, from there on in."

CBS tested all its shows, and our pilot tested poorly. Mary was perceived as being a loser, because she was over thirty and unmarried. It was suggested that we get rid of Phyllis—Cloris Leachman—because she was seen as annoying, which was exactly what she was supposed to be. And we were advised to tone down Rhoda—Valerie Harper—or get rid of her, because she came off as too New Yorky and brassy (read: Jewish). Each of these ideas would have crippled the show, and it was easy for me to tell Jim and Allan to continue doing it their way.

But the battles with the network continued. Jim and Allan wrote a script called "Support Your Local Mother." It was about Rhoda's mother—Nancy Walker hadn't yet been cast—coming to visit Rhoda, who doesn't want to see her because she knows they'll fight. "So Mom ends up staying with Mary, who's trying to be the go-between," Allan recounts, "to effect some kind of truce between mother and daughter. In one of the scenes we had Mary antiquing a table in her room, beating it with chains and things to give it an antique look, when Rhoda's mother arrives. She doesn't understand why a woman is beating up a table with a chain, thinks Mary is sort of weird, 'but whatever makes you happy, dear.' Mary gets into a giggling fit, realizing how silly she looks in front of this woman, and it was absolutely a hilarious scene."

When CBS got the script, Allan says, "We got a phone call from the guy who was the network liaison to the show. We called him Dr. Death. He was very concerned with how he looked, how he was dressed, and he had this lugubrious voice. 'You can't do this show,' he began. 'You've got sadism in here with this hitting with a chain.' We couldn't believe what we were hearing. 'It's not funny,' he told us. 'It goes against all principles of family. Here's a grown-up who won't even see her mother. I forbid you to do this. You cannot shoot this show.' "

Jim and Allan called me and asked if I'd read the script. I had, and thought it was very funny. "We think so, too," they said, "but Dr. Death says we can't shoot it." "The hell with him," I advised. "Go ahead and do it." For all I know, it may have been the first time a network ever gave an order not to shoot a show and then had it shot. The "Support Your Local Mother" episode really *was* funny, and Jim and Allan won an Emmy for it that year.

Eight months before the series went on the air, and after some early ideas had been considered and discarded, Brooks and Burns had prepared for CBS a written presentation of the concept they had approved. They wrote it half in prose and half in dialogue. Incredibly, hardly one word of the dialogue changed from that first version to the show eventually filmed months later. Richard Slaughter became Murray Slaughter, and Marna Lindstrom became Phyllis Lindstrom, but the rest remained as originally written. The whole presentation runs twenty-one pages and ends:

> *This series will, as we hope you have noted, be comedically populated. But it is clearly about* one *person living in and coping with the world of the 1970's . . . tough enough in itself . . . even tougher when you're thirty, single and female . . . when despite the fact that you're the antithesis of the career woman, you find yourself the only female in an all-male newsroom.*

For seven years and 168 brilliantly executed episodes, Brooks and Burns never deviated from that simply stated concept.

Ever since my early radio days at NBC, I've always admired, sometimes to the point of awe, the performers, directors, and writers who make show business a different kind of business. I don't think of myself as a creative person, which is probably why I've been so star-struck about people who can do what I can't. In particular, I've always had enormous respect for good writers (a respect that's grown since I undertook this book). From my earliest days around and about television, it's been clear to me that good shows can be made only by good writers. That's why I asked two fine writers to create and produce a show for Mary, and history has already recorded how well Brooks and Burns executed that assignment.

What I didn't realize at the time was that I had found the ingredients that were to make MTM a *writers'* company. Before Mary's show had run its seven-year course, Jim and Allan, through their work, would attract dozens of first-rate writing contributors, a number of whom would stay with MTM to produce other wonderful programs.

Gary David Goldberg was one of the young writers who joined us in the early years. "There was such a generosity of spirit," he recalls, "by all the people you'd meet at MTM. I'd bump into someone like Jim Brooks and think, My God, I read about him in *TV Guide*. After you got out of your car in the morning and walked to the building, you'd see spaces marked 'Allan Burns' or 'Jim Brooks' right by the door. So you knew someday, maybe, you would move up. It was like playing for the Yankees."

Gary remembers the MTM version of peer pressure: "There was always this understated idea that your best was what was expected. You were there to bring to the table what was uniquely yours. Until I left MTM, I did not know there were writers who worked on shows they weren't in love with. The idea that writing was just a job was completely foreign to me. You were in awe that you could actually walk down and peek into Allan Burns's office and ask him a question. I mean, the Emmys glittering off the afternoon sun would blind you. The respect that was there made it Camelot for writers."

Why this happened should be a show business axiom: The best creative people love to work with other best creative people. That simple principle put in motion a magnet effect that made recruiting talented writers-going-on-producers surprisingly easy. Some of them, in those days before the agent/lawyer became king, even called us!

Another attraction was one for which I will shamelessly take most of the credit. MTM quickly became known as a production company that allowed its creative people almost limitless independence and authority. I respect such people, and feel privileged simply to watch them perform their magic. I don't try to do it for them, which I assuredly could not, and I've never understood the gall of executives who think they can. Not only did MTM give good creative people the freedom to do their work, but I became justly famous for throwing my body between our producers and network bureaucrats who sought to oversupervise or meddle in their efforts.

Steven Bochco, who later came to us from Universal, remembers his contacts with the network during the first year he produced *Hill Street Blues:* "You'd hear from Broadcast Standards or from your program executives, calling up after they'd read a script, 'Gee, we're nervous about this, we're nervous about that.' You'd get into a fight, you'd argue, then you'd say, 'Fuck you, we're going to do it our way.' "

Steven calls the knowledge that he had our total support on all creative matters "a really profound difference between MTM and a place like Universal." That kind of support made it possible for our producers to stand up to pressure from the networks. "You knew it and so did they," Bochco says. "It made the entire relationship different. At Universal, if the network ever had a problem, they never called me. They called some guy in a suit, who conveyed the message. And there was never a question: Just do it."

NBC was worried about *Hill Street,* and their own test results made them worry even more. A two-page internal NBC memo, dated May 14, 1980, was filled with bad news:

> *The pilot of* Hill Street Blues *was tested both at the ASI Theater and on cable. Results of both tests were generally negative. . . .*
>
> *. . . the most prevalent audience reaction indicated that the program was depressing, violent and confusing. . . . The pace of the program (too quick) undoubtedly added to the pilot's problems. Too much was crammed into this story and the many sub-plots contributed more to viewer disorientation than to interest. . . .*
>
> *The main characters were perceived as being not capable and having flawed personalities. Professionally, they were never completely successful in doing their jobs and personally their lives were in a mess. . . . Further, viewers found little warmth in any of the relationships. This would suggest that the cast be successful in dealing with most of their cases both inside and outside the station house, and that personal problems be introduced gradually and over a period of time and perhaps not to all members of the cast. . . . Audiences found the ending unsatisfying. There are too many loose ends. . . .*
>
> *. . . Frank Furilla* [sic] *was seen as not being capable or in control as chief of the station house. . . . Together with his personal problems, his profile was that of a cold, tough and not likeable person. . . . Joyce's profile was very similar to that of Frank Furilla—cold, tough and unlikeable, and not a good lawyer.*
>
> Hill Street *did not come off as a real police station. . . . There was also some feeling that there was too much chaos in the station house, again reflecting that the police were incapable of maintaining control even on their home ground.*

In other words, the network saw every one of the elements that were to make *Hill Street Blues* an enduring and memorable show as a problem to be overcome. The subtext of the NBC memo: Make it look like all those other programs.

In the early days of *Hill Street,* I would accompany Steven to Burbank for meetings with NBC. He did the talking; I was there as a symbol of MTM's support of his right to make the creative decisions. "Boy oh boy," he says, "it was like having a gun on your hip."

If you build a reputation as a place where creative people are encouraged to create, they will come. They did and they stayed. Charlotte Brown came to us as a writer on Mary's show and then produced *Rhoda.* Jim and Allan left *Rhoda* in 1977 to create *Lou Grant,* and got Gene Reynolds, with whom they'd worked on *Room 222,* to leave *M*A*S*H* and join them as co-creator. It surely wasn't because they made more money than they could have elsewhere. Partly it was the climate of the company, where writer/producers were free to do the shows they wanted, and partly it was my enthusiasm for what they turned out.

Comedy represented the entire MTM output in our earliest years, and the creative bloodlines of every successful series could be traced back to *Mary Tyler Moore.* In 1972, Dave Davis and Lorenzo Music, fresh from Mary's show, sat down to create the first *Newhart* show, tailored to Bob's unique persona. Aided by Burns and Brooks, and with Jay Sandrich's confident pilot direction, they turned out MTM's second series for CBS, one that would run for seven successful seasons. Tom Patchett and Jay Tarses would serve as early producers of the show, before peeling off to do other good work for MTM, and Pat Williams (also from Mary's show) did the music.

With the exception of one Friday night when I couldn't make it back from a New York trip in time, I was present for all 168 of the *Mary* filmings—not just as company boss or husband, but because I enjoyed watching the process. It was psychic income for me almost as much as it was for the actual participants. When *Newhart* was also shooting on Fridays, I often commuted between his stage and Mary's—and I witnessed a lot of awfully good television being made.

About the same time *Newhart* went on the air, Ed. Weinberger (since Ed. is unique, it's appropriate that he insists on the period) wrote and produced one of the best pilots our company ever made. Titled *Bachelor at Law,* it was a comedy about an idealistic innocent, fresh out of law school, who goes to work for a corner-cutting shyster. It was also directed by the peerless Sandrich, and starred veteran Harold Gould and a relative newcomer named John Ritter. In those days, most series sales were finalized in New York, and I had the pleasure of showing, and selling, the pilot to CBS. Then—network president Bob Wood, who already loved MTM for Mary's show as well as the promising *Newhart,* bought me lunch at "21" to help celebrate the sale.

I could have flown back to California without a plane; three shows on the air would put MTM in another league as a production company. The next morning I was sitting, fat and happy, in my office in Studio City, when Wood called from New York. As always, he was a no-bullshit, just-say-it kind of guy. "This is a crappy call to make," he told me, "but I've got to renege on the *Bachelor at Law* deal. Last night, after you left, we saw our one remaining pilot—from Fox. Grant, it is just fucking fall-down funny, and it's done by Larry Gelbart and Gene Reynolds"—two veteran talents whose *M*A*S*H* smash, after a staggering start, would become a landmark CBS show. "This is the situation," he continued. "We've got only one possible time period and we have to make a choice. Your show is a guaranteed thirty-five share, but theirs is an absolute breakout show. It's about a black military unit in Italy, and we just cannot not schedule it. I'll owe you one, pal."

Only a few years later, any network would have killed for a guaranteed 35 share, but then it wasn't enough to keep the Fox show, called *Roll Out,* from knocking John Ritter's first starring vehicle out of the box. *Roll Out* lasted exactly thirteen weeks on CBS. I've always believed *Bachelor at Law* would have been a long-running MTM hit. So has Weinberger. But the experience wasn't a total loss; Ed. would stay to produce Mary's show until it retired from the field in 1977. In doing so, he joined Jim and Allan, freeing them up to take on additional projects.

Consistent with my magnet thesis, Stan Daniels would become Ed.'s writing and producing partner in 1974. Heavyweight contributors David Lloyd and Bob Ellison came and remained aboard through the last episode of Mary's show. Together, they made as strong a creative team as any situation comedy has ever been blessed to have, and there were a number of other irregular-regulars who did their share, people like Treva Silverman and Earl Pomerantz. Some did other things as we went along, but they all continued to contribute to *Mary.* That was unusual then, and unheard of now, when writer/producers with one good year on one show routinely leave for more money to do something else. Characteristically, Jim and Allan saw to it that a number of women served in their corps of credited writers. Forty of the 168 episodes of *Mary* were written by women; Treva was the leading distaff contributor, with a record sixteen scripts.

Glen and Les Charles, who later left MTM to create *Cheers* with another MTM alumnus, Jim Burrows, were writers on the *Newhart* show. Jimmy was perhaps the only salutary result of Mary's ill-fated *Breakfast at Tiffany's* adventure. At the time, she had known him only as Abe Burrows's young son. A few years later, in 1974, Jim wrote from Florida, where he was directing little theater. He wanted to make the transition to television, and I told him I'd pay him $200 a week to watch other people direct our audience shows. When he turned up, I sent him to the *Newhart* stage to monitor the production. At dinner recently, Jimmy reminded me of what had transpired.

He watched the rehearsals and shooting of the show for four weeks. The first week, wanting to be unobtrusive, he positioned himself in the highest row of the empty bleacher seats where the audience would sit during the filming. He worked his way down a few rows at a time, until by the fourth week of rehearsals he was sitting right above the set where the actors were working. It was at that point that Bob Newhart told the show's producers, "Get that guy out of here. He makes me nervous."

That caused me to do what I should have done in the first place. I turned Burrows over to Jay Sandrich, who directed most of the *Mary* episodes. Jay and Jim hit it off immediately, and Mary's stage became Jimmy's home for a number of weeks, during which Jay became the mentor he has been to others before and since. Burrows was a quick study—a born director—and Jay brought him along as fast as Jim could absorb the process. Soon he was ready to fly alone and he became a fully participating member of the MTM family. Not only are Jay and Jim still close friends, but to this day they are the most sought-after comedy directors in television.

Every episode of every television show carries a "written by" credit, indicating the writer or writers to whom the original story was assigned. Because of the collegial, evolutionary nature of multiple-camera comedy, the participation of all the writers and writer/producers often leads to substantial changes and improvements in the script. In addition, some directors are so involved with the material that they could almost take writing credit. That was especially true of Jay Sandrich, who directed two out of every three *Mary*s and never hesitated to weigh in with his unfailingly creative suggestions. The consistently high quality of *Mary Tyler Moore* was a direct result of the stability of the creative team.

As one who revered such work and the people who did it, my respect for the many unusually talented individuals at MTM was palpable. That not only made me acceptable to them, it made my multiple jobs easy and enjoyable: encouraging them, supporting them, selling the results of their labors to the networks, and then protecting them from the network officials who were inclined to tell them how to produce their shows.

That last function was essential, because the kind of creative people who gravitated to MTM were not the kind to brook much network interference. They brought real meaning to the term *independent production*.

In the 1970–71 and '71–72 seasons, CBS Network president Bob Wood completely changed the character of his prime-time schedule. CBS was the leading network, but Wood knew that many of its high-rated programs were attracting an aging, rural audience. He bravely canceled a large group of still-popular series—*The Beverly Hillbillies, Green Acres, Hee-Haw, Petticoat Junction*—and replaced them with new, untried programs that promised a radical demographic change. The goal was to attract the younger, urban viewers that national advertisers were increasingly eager to reach. Breaking up CBS's successful schedule was particularly gutsy because Wood had no way of knowing if his replacement programs would do the job. They did. CBS maintained its leadership in homes reached, and bettered its audience profile in every important demographic category.

Many think Bob Wood was the best network president ever. He was a triple-threat executive: knowledgeable in the sales area, comfortable with the creative community, and popular and persuasive with the affiliates. *Mary Tyler Moore* was probably the beginning of the Wood "revolution," but in January 1971, the middle of *Mary*'s first season, the real engine of change arrived. That's when Norman Lear and Bud Yorkin introduced Archie Bunker to the world, and *All in the Family* exploded into our living rooms. It would be the top-rated program for the next five years, and it's fair to recall it as groundbreaking. Over the next few television seasons, MTM and Tandem (Yorkin and Lear's company) would become CBS's principal suppliers of literate comedy. Ours were frequently referred to as character comedies, theirs as issue comedies.

The CBS metamorphosis also extended to the dramatic form.

Wood kept several of the good holdover variety hours on his schedule, but more contemporary shows *(Mission Impossible, Mannix, Medical Center, Streets of San Francisco)* replaced the westerns. For one season, 1973–74, CBS had a memorable Saturday night lineup that for many was the most entertaining any network ever scheduled: *All in the Family, M*A*S*H, Mary Tyler Moore, Bob Newhart,* and *Carol Burnett.* (NBC's Thursday group of the eighties—*Cosby, Family Ties, Cheers, Night Court,* and *L.A. Law*—would be the only real competitor.) The following season *M*A*S*H* was moved to a Tuesday time period, one of six it would occupy before settling into its Monday night home for the last five of an eleven-season run.

Inevitably, though, even successful shows tire and go off the air, so production companies must periodically add new programs to their stables. One way to do it is the "spin-off," in which one or more established characters from a successful series become the leads of a new program. Our first use of the spin-off worked well. In a specially designed episode of *Mary Tyler Moore,* the Rhoda Morgenstern character was promoted to a show of her own. *Rhoda,* starring Valerie Harper, debuted on CBS in the fall of 1974 and was immediately popular. During its first two seasons, it was in Nielsen's top ten, finishing ahead of *Mary* both years.

In the eighth episode of the first season, we married Rhoda in an hour-long program, a stunt suggested by Fred Silverman, then program chief at CBS. That single episode drew a mammoth audience, but in the long term the marriage was a mistake, as even Fred has since admitted. People preferred the single, anxious Rhoda to the happily married one. Ultimately, in an effort to revive the flagging show, we put her through a divorce, but the audience didn't like that either. Shortly into the fifth season, *Rhoda* was canceled. Burns and Brooks were its executive producers for most of the run, succeeded by Charlotte Brown in 1977.

It was also in the fall of 1974, as *Rhoda* began, that we produced MTM's first show for another network. Created by Dale McCraven, *Texas Wheelers* was done for ABC, and bought by the network's vice president in charge of comedy: a young man named Michael Eisner, now the chairman of Disney.

Texas Wheelers starred Jack Elam, Gary Busey, and Mark

Hamill. It opened to enthusiastic reviews but lasted only a season. We had made a creative mistake for which I get most of the blame. The program was half an hour in length but should have been an hour. A half-hour show, through established programming habit and audience expectation, says to viewers: I'm a comedy. I'm supposed to make you laugh a lot. *Texas Wheelers* was not, in the industry vernacular, "hard-funny," though it certainly had comedic elements. In a word I think I invented at the time, the show was a "warmedy," really a scruffy *Waltons* that should have played as an hour at 8 o'clock. (In my judgment, CBS and Gary David Goldberg made the same mistake in 1992 with a very fine show, *Brooklyn Bridge,* based on Gary's growing-up years. It would be too glib to dub that one a Jewish *Waltons,* but the point is the same.) Most things in life are better shorter, but occasionally the reverse holds true with superior television material.

The fall of 1974 saw MTM introduce a comedy for CBS, clumsily titled *Paul Sand in Friends and Lovers,* in which Penny Marshall appeared in her first important role. Again, Burns and Brooks were the executive producers. The show, with Paul playing a musician in the Boston Symphony, never quite jelled and didn't make it through its first season. Jim and Allan took a bit of criticism for spreading themselves too thin. As the guy running the company, I was equally at fault.

In 1975, with *Mary, Newhart,* and *Rhoda* all thriving, we undertook three new programs. Weinberger and Daniels created a show that located Phyllis Lindstrom, Cloris Leachman's character on *Mary,* in San Francisco, widowed and out in the workforce. *Phyllis* was a funny show and a good try, but it survived only two years. The character had worked well as a counterpoint to the sense and sensibilities of Mary Richards, and not as well on her own.

Doc, another Weinberger and Daniels–created half hour, also premiered on CBS in 1975, this one starting as a late summer replacement. Barnard Hughes was wonderfully likable as a doctor practicing in New York in more of a clinic than an office, but the show struggled through a little more than a year before we and CBS gave up on it.

Our third entry that year, MTM's first hour effort, was created by Jerry McNeely and scheduled by CBS at 7 o'clock Sunday evening. The premise was a show that "traveled"—a professional photographer father (Alex Rocco) and his two sons (Leif Garrett and Vinnie Van Patten) having adventures wherever assignments took them. In such an early time period, *Three for the Road* lacked affiliate station clearances in too many important markets to ever have a real chance, and the road dead-ended after only ten shows. No one will ever know what would have happened if a young actor named Tom Selleck, who read for the part, had been cast in the Alex Rocco role. With exquisite judgment we turned him down. Who knew?

The good news for CBS was that they replaced *Three for the Road* with a newsmagazine called *60 Minutes,* and they've never had to make another change at 7 o'clock on Sunday.

The 1976–77 season found us making two more good tries, one of which should have been a long-running success. The first was a five-a-week daytime comedy/variety/talk hour starring the talented husband and wife team, Lorenzo and Henrietta Music. Five hours a week on virtually no budget is a difficult trick to master, and after a little over a month we admitted defeat. The one memorable aspect of the show is that we produced it for syndication, through Metromedia, directly to stations. But we were too little, too early for the now-common world of first-run syndication.

The Tony Randall Show was another matter. Created and produced by Tom Patchett and Jay Tarses, the show came very close to sticking to the wall, although it would survive only two seasons—the first on ABC and the second on CBS. It was well above average in the three-camera category. Tony was born to work in front of a live audience, and the writing was largely first rate. Ultimately, however, three strong egos could not live together. Since Tony was obviously essential, Tom and Jay retreated to their office and oversaw from a distance, giving two of MTM's younger writers, Hugh Wilson and Gary David Goldberg (just plain Gary Goldberg then) their first chance to produce.

Hugh had been in advertising in Atlanta, but wanted to make a change, and had come to work at MTM for $250 a week. It seemed he just observed for a few days, and suddenly he could do it. Gary, a college dropout who had run a day-care center in Berkeley, had been watching some television and saying to himself: "Jeez, I can do better than that." From the day he arrived, it was obvious that he was a writer.

"I used to sit in the window at home," Gary remembers, "and write. I must have had a hundred scripts I was trying to sell, so I was very carefully studying shows." He was turning out a script every few days, but had yet to land a paying job. "Then I got this call from *Newhart,* asking me to come in and pitch. There was no way I was going to leave their office without a job. I had twenty-six ideas worked out; I don't mean vague notions, I mean twenty-six real ideas."

Gary went in to meet with Gordon and Lynne Farr at MTM on a rainy day in February, and immediately sold three ideas. "This was exactly what I had thought work would be like—not like work at all," Gary says. "It was the most outrageous way to make a living that I had ever seen in my life. Here were these guys in T-shirts getting into their Ferraris and Jaguars. It was exactly what my fantasy was: You get the money but you don't change at all, and you don't have to wear a tie or anything. You're all of a sudden rich and powerful, but basically you're the same guy."

Hugh and Gary were naturals. They and Tony Randall were fond of each other and of challenging each other to do good work.

It *was* good work, and it deserved a better fate. Fred Silverman and I each get an assist for its early demise. As program head of ABC, Fred was pissed that Tom and Jay would not brook suggestions from the network's assigned program executive, wouldn't even let her in their office. Both immensely talented, they firmly declared independence and did it their way. (A few years later they would declare independence from each other and go on to solo successes.)

In excluding Silverman's delegate, Tom and Jay were really defying Fred. When the show completed the first season, having performed acceptably, he took his revenge by offering only a thirteen-week order for the second season, though our standard contract called for a full-season order if the show was picked up. He made it clear it was not negotiable; take it or leave it.

Now it was my turn to be pissed, and I decided to leave it. Silverman's limited order freed me to offer the Randall show to another network. I paid a visit to Bob Daly, then Fred's counterpart at CBS, told him about the situation at ABC, and offered him the program for a full second-season order. Somewhat to my surprise, Bob said he'd buy it. Thinking to stick it to Fred while also benefiting the show, I turned down the ABC half order and moved it to CBS. Mistake.

Everyone at MTM was pleased, but it turned out I had shot us in the foot. The program had been building an audience at ABC, but that audience was not yet devoted enough to follow it to CBS. At the end of the second season, we were canceled, which I don't think would have happened if I had just taken Fred's short order and stayed put.

Goldberg and Wilson were each ready to fly alone. In 1978, Hugh created *WKRP in Cincinnati,* a radio station cousin of Mary's show. It ran on CBS for four solid seasons and has since had even more success in syndication, easily the biggest dollar-producing show MTM ever made. CBS would have enjoyed several additional, profitable years of *WKRP* if they hadn't moved it around their schedule seven—count 'em, *seven*—times. A high-ranking program functionary named Harvey Shepard preferred a Universal comedy, *House Calls,* which he stubbornly kept in the 9:30 Monday slot that would have been ideal for our show.

Eventually and inevitably, the audience gave up trying to find the peripatetic *WKRP,* while *House Calls* simply died of its own mediocrity. Harvey Shepard later went on to head Warner Brothers' television division, where I presume his program judgment improved. His intransigence about finding a permanent home for *WKRP* caused me to badger him constantly, and it drove Hugh Wilson up the wall. On one occasion, Hugh vented his frustration on me and, indirectly, his good friend Gary Goldberg. It's not only a fine illustration of how passionately people can feel about their programs, their "children," but also demonstrates that MTM was not just about kissing and hugging.

The Last Resort was an ill-fated comedy try Gary made for MTM and CBS in the 1979–80 season. It seemed that audiences were not interested in looking back on Gary's personal experiences as a waiter at a bucolic summer resort. During its brief existence, CBS decided to try it once in a coveted Monday night time slot. As a result, Hugh Wilson felt that an important special hour effort of his show was being sacrificed and that I was at least part-architect of this perfidy. He fired off a note:

> *Grant,*
>
> *It was a very big deal for all of us to have a special one-hour presentation of our show. It gave us a sense of finally arriv-*

ing, and we worked ourselves to the point of exhaustion to do what I think is the very best show we have ever done. To learn now (from CBS, not MTM) that the one-hour slot is being denied us mainly through the efforts of MTM—leaves me stunned, embarrassed and pissed.

Our success is being jeopardized and used as leverage to save another show.

KRP was pre-empted repeatedly last year during sweeps and nobody seemed to mind that. We were pre-empted two weeks in a row at a critical time so that Last Resort *could have a shot behind* M*A*S*H. *We have been sent to the Russian front of Monday night to try and lead in* Last Resort. *When's it going to stop?*

Week after week we've watched Resort *writers get into their cars at 9 p.m. on nights we re-wrote until 2 in the morning. We don't give a shit what happens to them. We only care about ourselves and it's a damn good thing, too.*

Nobody even thought to ask this, but since I was told we did have an hour, I wrote it that way. The show is badly damaged by splitting it up, for whatever that's worth.

Hugh

My reaction to Hugh's note was uncharacteristically strong. Although CBS had made the scheduling decision, he was accusing me of favoring one MTM show over another. I also felt he was taking a gratuitous shot at Goldberg. I wasn't so naive as to think there was never competition among creative people within the company, but I did fancy the notion that the competitors were friends. I fired back my own memo:

Dear Hugh:

I hadn't realized how much our friendship meant to you until I got your note.

I don't know what's troubling you—hopefully it's nothing in your personal life, maybe something as transitory as a concept that won't quite turn into a script—but I want to tell you as quickly as I can dictate this that you just qualified for the Absolute Shit Award for 1980.

I wish I'd known how far apart you and Gary have grown

since you worked on Randall *together. If you're an example of Gary's friends, he surely doesn't need any enemies.*

*I'm so fucking angry with you that I don't want to belabor the many points your note excites. I'm sorry about the Russian front of Monday night, I'm sorry about the re-writes that go on until 2 a.m., and I'm sorry that you lost your post-*M*A*S*H *time period once to* The Last Resort.

Most of all I'm sorry you don't realize that I would do all of the same things for you if the situation were reversed. Perhaps I would then get the same note from Gary; somehow I doubt it.

G

I don't remember whether Hugh responded in kind, but I'm sure we talked out the matter in some fashion. He's a good guy and still a friend. Equally talented at writing and directing, Hugh has since been active in features as well as other television. In 1987, after his years at MTM, he produced one season of a CBS half-hour, *Frank's Place,* that many critics felt was "too good" for television in tackling serious issues in the comedy form. CBS erred again by moving *Frank's Place* four times in that single year, and again the audience never found the show.

Following *The Last Resort,* Gary David (now) Goldberg made a more interesting try for MTM in 1980; in fact, he made two versions of what became my favorite Goldberg project to date, counting even his more successful efforts. Born probably a decade too early, the show was called *Bureau,* and its hero was a journalist in Vietnam. CBS wasn't too crazy about the locale from the outset, but out of respect for Gary and for the MTM auspices they ordered a pilot. It also didn't hurt that we suggested the show would have overtones of *M*A*S*H.* When selling to a network, it's effective to describe your project in terms of something or someone that's already a hit: "Picture an ensemble cast like the people around the bar in *Cheers*" or "Think of a Mary Tyler Moore type."

Whatever his original intentions, the pilot Gary wrote became more dramatic than comedic. I lobbied for it to be made into an hour, Gary agreed, and CBS added its reluctant approval. The show that resulted found no particular favor at the network, and it tested badly. I think the CBS executives considered it moralizing and self-righteous, and too left-leaning in its antiwar attitude. Moreover, it was deemed slow and too heavy. Other than that, they loved it.

It was a measure of Gary's and my determination to do *Bureau* that we were able to persuade CBS to let us try again, this time in a lighter half-hour form. Gary supervised two other writers to put together the second effort. But the comedy version didn't bowl anybody over either, and we finally admitted defeat. Not long thereafter, Gary's representatives came up with a deal at Paramount that he couldn't turn down and I wouldn't match.

A sea-change was occurring in the business of television production. "By 1980," Gary remembers, "the studios had started the system where they guarantee you millions of dollars against your earnings. It was the beginning of free agency and the end of independence. I had been approached, and my lawyer, Skip Brittenham, had typed out an eleven-page deal, saying, 'We can make this deal at any studio in town.' A lot of it was based on guarantees; Skip had basically taken the definition of profits out of the reach of studio accounting: As soon as you hit the sixty-seventh show, you got a $3 million bonus, and then you got a $25,000 bonus for each episode as you went along. In effect, you were getting your profit participation in advance of the studio, and it had no relationship to whether the studio ever made a dime or not."

As much as Gary wanted to stay at MTM, there was no way we could compete with that. So, Gary recalls, "Skip took the deal, as written, to five studios. Each one not only agreed to it 100 percent, they started to add stuff, like making movies. Instead of having something like 5 percent of the net of *The Last Resort,* if it had succeeded, I would now have 35 percent of the gross of whatever shows I did."

I told Gary that if he could make that kind of deal, he should do it and not feel bad about it. We had a parting lunch at La Serre, Gary went to Paramount, and, he recalls, "did my best to create a mini-MTM within the studio walls. I tried to do for other people what had been done for me: to encourage their best work, not to hold on to them when it was time to go, and to think of ourselves as part of a community bigger than our bottom line." I've always been sorry that *Bureau,* our last venture together, was such an exercise in futility, but I've been happy to have Gary's friendship ever since. And if Gary is in your life, so is his very special wife, Diana Meehan, making me doubly blessed.

As business events turned out, Paramount more than earned back its investment. Gary created and produced *Family Ties* for the studio, and all parties were hugely rewarded.

Once every season during the seventies and eighties, a network "suit" would come out from New York to give a luncheon speech to the Hollywood television community, deploring the ever-escalating cost of programming. Frequently the speaker du jour would refer to the goose and her golden eggs, and suggest that the same gloomy end was in store for a business that didn't control its costs. After each of these speeches, we producers would go back to our offices and do in the afternoon whatever we'd been doing all morning. That heedlessness was to contribute directly to the debilitation of our goose.

In September 1970, the same month *Mary Tyler Moore* was having its premiere, a show called *The New Doctors,* produced by Universal, was about to start its second network season. Eight one-hour episodes, starring E. G. Marshall, David Hartman, and John Saxon, were to be broadcast at 10 P.M. Sundays as elements of *The Bold Ones,* an NBC tripartite series that eventually had a four-year run.

Stu Erwin, who was then the Universal executive in charge, remembers: "We shot the show in five ten-hour days on the set, plus one twelve-hour day on location. Each script had to be turned in to the production department at least two weeks prior to shooting, and shooting was to be completed no later than eight weeks before the scheduled airdate." Of the eight episodes later broadcast during the 1970–71 season, seven were completed by mid-September—safely in the can before the season even started.

The budget for each episode was $229,849—little more than one-sixth of the production cost of a similar show twenty years later. The "above-the-line" portion, covering all the creative elements—cast, script, director, etc.—was exactly $69,853. In those glorious days of yesteryear, budget and final cost were expected to be the same. When the first seven episodes went over budget by a total of $26,873—a minuscule 1.5 percent—Stu wrote a memo to the producer, Cy Chermak, asking that he "do everything possible" to make up the difference in the last show.

All that changed during the seventies. The Consumer Price Index (CPI) doubled during the decade, but television seemed immune to the perils of inflation. As fast as the CPI was rising, network revenues were rising twice as fast, doubling every five years. Ninety-eight percent of American homes had acquired a TV set, more than had indoor plumbing, and they kept it on seven hours a day. With no competition other than relatively weak independent stations, the three networks maintained better than a 90 percent share of this vast national audience, and advertisers were falling all over themselves to buy network time. The goose was thriving, and the cost of programming continued ever upward.

In the late seventies, after Farrah Fawcett did *Charlie's Angels* and became a household name, her agent, Sue Mengers, called me. "Farrah might be interested in doing a comedy," she said. "Why don't we meet with her tomorrow?"

I drove to Farrah's house on Mulholland Drive with Stu Erwin, whom I had lured away from Universal in 1974, and we had a long and encouraging meeting, exchanging substantive creative ideas. Sue Mengers called back the next day. "Farrah thought you guys were terrific and she's very interested. I thought I'd give you some idea of what she costs."

"How much per episode?" I asked. "One hundred and twenty-five thousand dollars," Mengers replied. Knowing I could get Mary for that—three times—I closed the subject: "You could have saved me the trip."

That was an easy call, but most of them weren't. Salaries and fees were ballooning. The desire by a series lead for another few thousand an episode would result in a visit by his agent to the production company that held the talent contract. Then someone from the production company would go to network Business Affairs to plead the actor's case. "Obviously, we can't do the series without him," was the usual opening line, and in those years it was often enough to get the job done. The raise would be approved, resulting in more money for the star and a higher net-work license fee for the producers. The network would cover its additional costs out of constantly increasing ad rates. Each jump in cost-per-thousand homes caused groans and hand-wringing on Madison Avenue, but no national advertiser could afford not to be in network television.

While this was happening, the various unions representing stagehands, wardrobe, electricians, cameramen, makeup, and all the other trades and disciplines necessary to produce a television program were negotiating substantial raises for their people. New contracts containing work rules that drove costs higher were approved by studios and networks eager to get on with the business of making money in a rising market. It was a self-inflicted Ponzi scheme, and we were all willing participants.

Toward the end of the seventies, just about the time some of our comedy heavyweights—Jim Brooks, Ed. Weinberger, Stan Daniels, Gary Goldberg—were being wooed away by Paramount's unlimited checking account and substantial backing from ABC, MTM began producing hour-long dramatic shows. That transition was simply a function of the kind of creative people we were able to attract; as our comedy specialists were halfway out the door, their dramatic counterparts were coming in.

We didn't surrender our comedy trademark without a fight. We continued to do occasional comedy pilots, but only *WKRP* made a real noise. Even *The Betty White Show,* produced by Weinberger and Daniels and several other *Mary* graduates just as Mary's show drew to a graceful close, lasted only half a season. I attribute its failure to the difficulty of presenting Betty in a new character while Sue Ann Nivens was still fresh in viewers' minds, and to CBS giving up on the show too quickly, as nervous networks so often do.

Occasionally we made movies for television, under the supervision of Stu Erwin. I had brought Stu on board to be an important member of senior management and to supervise our dramatic shows. That proved to be a master stroke. For some companies, long-form production is a business in itself; for MTM it was usually prompted by the desire of some of our creative people to treat a specific subject or piece of material.

In 1977, Jerry McNeely wrote and produced *Something for*

Joey. Directed by Lou Antonio, the picture attracted the largest TV movie audience of the year. It was the true story of Heisman Trophy winner John Cappelletti and his much younger brother, Joey, who died of leukemia. The last scene, in which John received the trophy and dedicated the award to his brother, was a moving re-creation of the moving real-life event.

In 1978, Phil Barry produced and George Schaefer directed *First You Cry*. Mary starred in this adaptation (by Carmen Culver) of Betty Rollin's book about losing a breast to cancer. Dick Crenna played her husband, and Tony Perkins was the third point of a triangle—a man to whom Mary (Betty) turned during a very traumatic period.

The shooting of *First You Cry* was marked by one of several personal tragedies in Mary's own life. It occurred while I was in New York for a day or two of location filming. Early one evening I got back to our suite at the Regency Hotel ahead of Mary, and the phone was ringing as I walked in. It was Mary's aunt Berte Hackett, who gave me the news that Mary's teenage sister, Elizabeth, had died in a senseless accident. Shocked and saddened, I stared out at the lights of Park Avenue, waiting for Mary to return. Despite the considerable difference in their ages, there was real love between the two, and Mary had been proud of the way Liz, a happy, well-adjusted girl, comported herself. For her part, Elizabeth, equally proud of Mary, had handled her sister's celebrity well. When Mary arrived, there was nothing to do but just tell her. She's a woman of great fortitude, and she needed all of it that night. It wouldn't be the last time I had to bring her bad news.

Thornwell, produced in 1981, was another MTM television movie worth making. It was a true story about a black soldier in the U.S. Army who was accused of theft and given LSD without his knowledge in an effort to extract a confession. *Thornwell* was the kind of docudrama that tries its best to tell a story just as it happened. It was brought to us by Harry Moses, who had originally dealt with it for *60 Minutes,* where he was a segment producer. A condition of our deal was that he would get to direct the film, his first such assignment. Coincidentally, Harry was the son of John Moses, with whom I had worked in the early fifties. Appropriately, Mark Tinker was the producer.

There were six MTM shows on the CBS schedule at the beginning of the 1977–78 season—five comedies and one new dramatic hour. The drama, *Lou Grant,* was the work of several of our best and brightest, plus one distinguished draftee. It was an unusual spin-off.

Unlike Betty White, Ed Asner was spun off Mary's show in his well-established and much-loved character. What was unusual was the double departure from the accepted spin-off approach, in which great pains are taken to make transition to the new show as natural as possible. In this case, not only did the venue and workplace change—from a joke of a television station newsroom in Minneapolis to a respected daily newspaper in Los Angeles—but the persona of the lead character metamorphosed from a hard-drinking small-time news director to a highly professional big-city editor.

The people who managed this neat trick were Allan Burns and Jim Brooks and, very importantly, Gene Reynolds, fresh from his triumph as the co-developer and executive producer of *M*A*S*H.* Those creative auspices plus the popularity of the Lou Grant character got us a series commitment, instead of the usual single pilot order, from CBS. That meant that we would get on the air, unless we absolutely stunk up the joint with the prototype episode.

During the five years the show ran (113 episodes), other important contributors, especially as writers, were Michele Gallery, Seth Freeman, and Gary David Goldberg. Jim Brooks was off to Paramount after the first season, and Gary followed about midway through the third. Gene Reynolds, a man of considerable strength, whose determination occasionally borders on stubbornness—almost always for the right reasons—was executive producer from the first episode to the last.

Halfway through the first season of *Lou Grant,* the show had not yet found its audience (or vice versa). The CBS program executives did what network functionaries all too frequently do: They decided they knew best. Gene, Jim, and Allan resisted their suggestions, so CBS summoned us to a meeting in Television City. We sat with relative patience while the networkers politely but firmly told us what they perceived the creative problems to be, and made some strong suggestions about changes. My colleagues took a few minutes to articulate some token responses, but I knew them too well to let that go on for long.

"Guys," I said as courteously as I could, "let's cut through all the shit and save everyone some time. You're sitting here with three of the best producers in television. They are making the show you bought and the one they want to make. If you're that unhappy with it, then cancel it now and let them get on with other projects. Otherwise, just have a little faith, as we do, that success will come."

MTM had spoken. A guy in my production company role, facing down the network on behalf of such peerless creative partners, could always get off on a scene like that. Officialdom wisely folded its useless cards, and we returned to the studio, where for the next four years those peerless creative partners made a successful and critically acclaimed program called *Lou Grant.* Using the multiple concurrent storytelling technique frequently employed in today's ensemble shows, the Reynolds-Brooks-Burns team always saw to it that at least one of the story lines in each episode was *about* something. They explored issues on which people—their audience—had strong opinions: rape, corruption in business and government, aging, automation and job loss, blacklisting, health care abuses, abortion, the death penalty, drugs, the environment, homelessness, and many others.

Most television (and movie) writers are somewhat left-leaning, and it's probably fair to say that the *Lou Grant* group leaned a bit more than others. The result was that CBS and certain advertisers were always a little anxious about the show's politics and stances on the more controversial subjects treated. And through those on-air years, Ed Asner became increasingly vocal and visible about his own liberal views, frequently going public with not entirely popular opinions on a variety of topical matters.

As Ed spoke out, conservative reaction grew, and so did the pressure on CBS. After receiving numerous letters denouncing the actor, who was often perceived to be speaking in character, more than one of *Lou Grant*'s sponsors defected. During a strike by the Screen Actors Guild in 1980, when for a time we in the company (management) were rather estranged from Ed (labor), I voiced my own complaint: "Ed Asner is talking with Lou Grant's credibility but thinking with Ed Asner's judgment."

That disagreement with Ed was entirely a business matter; personally, I have cherished his friendship since he first became Lou Grant on Mary's show in 1970. I respect and admire him as well. He's a stand-up guy who never sells out, even when he is almost certain to pay a price professionally. His public support of several liberal causes unquestionably killed off his Lou Grant character before its time. And, of course, the show went with him.

The establishment may have been vexed with Ed, wishing he would cut down on the rhetoric, but not everyone was put off. In November 1981, a couple of months after the show began its fifth season, Asner was elected president of Screen Actors Guild. That sort of validation probably encouraged Ed, and he continued to make his views known. When CBS announced the prime-time schedule for the fall of '82, *Lou Grant* was not on it.

By that time I was more than six months into my new NBC gig, so I am certainly no expert on why the show died. While it's fair to say that in terms of ratings it was tiring somewhat, most objective observers would agree there was still a lot of life in *Lou Grant*. But the executives at CBS were no longer objective. They had been on the catching end of all the flak, and probably no one in the decision-making process wanted to go to bat for the program. Moreover, there was one man in that process whose opinion mattered more than all the others. My guess is that a fly on the wall during the network scheduling meetings would have overheard something like this:

> WILLIAM PALEY (CBS chairman): *What are you going to do at ten on Monday night?*
> SENIOR PROGRAM EXECUTIVE (carefully): *We haven't absolutely decided that one, Mr. Paley.* Lou Grant *is still pretty strong and has good demographics.*
> PALEY: *I'm still getting those damned letters. Have any more sponsors dropped out?*
> S.P.E: *Not lately, sir, but a number of them are kind of antsy.*
> PALEY: *Why don't we just dump it and get rid of the problems for good?*
> S.P.E: *Fine idea, sir. We've got a new drama called* Cagney and Lacey *that should play well in the time period.*
> PALEY: *Good. Now let's talk about Tuesday.*

That exchange would have happened after I left MTM. While I was still there, I had the fun of watching *Lou Grant*'s first four years of solid, provocative hour-long dramas. There were occasional lapses, but more often than not the show said something. From its premiere, it exemplified the best of MTM. That calendar year the company was on a major roll. It was 1977, we had been in business seven years, and seven of our series—*Mary Tyler Moore, The Bob Newhart Show, Rhoda, The Tony Randall Show, The Betty White Show, Lou Grant,* and *We've Got Each Other*—made the network schedules. Each of them contributed to MTM's growing reputation as a place where quality counted, and several were (or were on their way to becoming) long-running audience favorites. We were simultaneously beloved by Nielsen and by the critics—a balancing act that had become the company's signature.

Mary not only contributed her own exquisite performance each week, but she also set a work ethic standard the entire company emulated. (Most of the actors on *Mary Tyler Moore* were masters of the quick study, but the all-time champ was Mary herself.) My job was to recruit the creative people we wanted—many of them simply walked through the door and volunteered—encourage them to do their creating, and take them by the hand to network offices to sell their creations.

Deal-making was Arthur Price's department. Once I had identified the talent we wanted, frequently with the advice and encouragement of those already at MTM, Arthur would arm wrestle lawyers and agents to conclude the necessary deals. Then, after we had sold one of our series to a network, Arthur negotiated with their Business Affairs people to get the best terms for MTM.

He handled the business side of MTM from the outset, particularly during the company's first few months when I was managing a graceful exit from Fox. We both did our jobs well, and we made an effective team. Trained as a talent agent in New York, Arthur had been Mary's personal manager for some years when MTM was launched in 1970. She valued his advice and trusted him. I trusted him, too, and never had reason to regret it while I was running the company. The regrets came later.

One sunny day in 1977, I said to Mary, "I want to give Arthur a piece of the company."

"Okay," she said. "How much of a piece?"

"Thirty percent."

That produced the predictable reaction, even from someone

who paid practically no attention to any MTM activity beyond her own show. "That would give Artie almost as much as we would each have left. Why does it have to be 30 percent?"

"Because I think it should be a meaningful interest," I said, "and he deserves it. You and I together will still easily retain control." To her credit, Mary didn't argue, although later I would wish she had. When I told Arthur the good news, he expressed, in his characteristic low-key style, surprise and gratitude.

From that day forward, there was a change in the way Arthur comported himself, a change that the entire company noticed. He had been validated. Now he was an owner. That meant that all the people who worked for MTM worked for him, and he radiated newfound confidence.

As I think back to those days and the change in Arthur's manner, it's easy to understand how he felt. To that point in his life, he had always been an agent, never a principal. He considered; he never *decided*. He advised; he never *did*. Ultimately it would prove to be a role change he couldn't manage. He might own something, but he couldn't run it. Norton Brown often called Arthur "the best number-two guy in the business." Later we were to discover just what an accurate assessment that was.

Norton Brown was the co-founder and president of Brown, Kraft & Co., an accounting and business management firm. Mary and I had been clients since 1962. As Mary's manager and on other matters, Arthur had also worked with Norton. MTM became one of Brown, Kraft's best accounts, and in return we got some very good outside advice as our company grew.

During my time at MTM, the first eleven years of the company's life, we purposely kept the management team very small. That meant everybody was busy and an important part of the whole, and it allowed me to stay close to all our creative activities, current and in development. In addition to Arthur, Stu Erwin, and Norton Brown, there were only a couple of other key players.

Years earlier, Norton had introduced Mary and me to Harold Hertzberg, a partner in a Beverly Hills law firm. Like Norton, Harold is rock-solid and low-profile. In the early days of MTM's evolution and growth, his wise counsel was invaluable. Eventually, the legal work we required became more time-consuming and routine, and Harold turned the bulk of it over to a younger member of the firm, Mel Blumenthal. Mel turned out to be eager, capable, and industrious. His billable hours increased to a point that led me to suggest to Arthur one day, "Why don't we just bring Mel into the company?"

I have never had a worse idea. Mel Blumenthal's role was entirely restricted to business affairs, and he was supervised by Arthur. There was an evasive quality about Mel that I soon found more than slightly off-putting, but Arthur seemed satisfied with his work and I mostly ignored my reservations. MTM was humming along, and I had plenty of more pleasant matters to occupy my time. That, I was to learn much later, was a major oversight. At the time, it never occurred to me that I would leave the company I founded, and I didn't realize that my management team was not just lean but dangerously thin. How thin, I would observe from a distance when it was far too late.

But more ominous clouds were forming. For a couple of years, Mary and I had been working so hard at our jobs that we didn't notice we weren't working as hard at our marriage. But the neglect slowly took its toll, until the damage was irreversible. Onlookers may well have thought that sharing a business gave us a double bond. Ironically, that part of our relationship was what survived; gradually, the company became the principal thing we had in common.

We had what might be characterized as a quiet disengagement. No one hit anyone or threw anything, but we were finally giving up on great expectations born eighteen years earlier, and that kind of failure inevitably engenders clenched teeth. Still, there remained a lot of *liking,* and we didn't fold the tent easily. In fact, several tents—houses, rather—played a part in our efforts to hold the marriage together.

Our first try was the beachfront property we bought in the Malibu Colony, where we built a great house. It's as though we thought the sea air would provide a salutary, remedial effect. We commuted separately, because I left earlier in the morning and came home later at night. Unfortunately, the Malibu cure didn't take; we still had more problems than solutions. I moved out and into a rented guest house behind the much larger main house of some sort of half-assed diplomat. Its principal appeal to me was its remote location, high above Benedict Canyon. The day I looked at the place, there were some laundered shirts hanging in a bedroom closet; they turned out to belong to Jerry Perenchio, Norman Lear's business partner, who apparently had used the same way station just ahead of me. There was a second guest house across the pool from mine. It was inhabited by Candice Bergen, whom I never once saw during my three or four months in residence. I swear.

My separation from Mary was an odd one. We worked on the same lot, where I paid a great deal of attention to her stage and her show. *Mary Tyler Moore* was the company's proudest product. My presence at run-throughs and filmings was a bit awkward, but understood to be in the line of duty. Most afternoons, as she drove off the lot, Mary would wave to me sitting in my fourth-floor office—an act that seemed both civilized and poignant. The truth was, neither of us wanted to give up on the marriage, and after several months and a number of heart-to-hearts, we agreed to try yet again. We decided that the longer, separate commute was part of the problem. That led to selling the Malibu house and buying another in Bel Air, on Chalon Road, from a retired CBS executive and his wife, who were heading for Palm Springs.

But marital matters did not improve at the Chalon house, although we were working at it. One Saturday afternoon I was leafing through a coffee-table book in Martindale's, a Beverly Hills bookstore that no longer exists, when I spotted a piece of property directly above and behind the Bel Air Hotel. A little investigation disclosed that the whole thing was just over five acres, much of it hilly. I inquired further. It turned out that the owner of the land had just given up on getting both the house he wanted and a tennis court on the part that was level. To Mary and me, the privacy the location offered was important, and we bought the property. Over the next couple of years, we designed and built exactly the kind of home we both liked, somewhat in a Spanish motif, but mostly just comfortable. And as it turned out, we were also able to build a tennis court into the side of the hill, with a large ballet/rehearsal studio for Mary underneath half of it. David and Laraine Gerber would later buy the Chalon house for more than we had paid for it, a singular event in my lifetime of real estate adventures. My timing has always been buy high and sell low. With me, it's a law.

The new house was approached by a long, curving driveway that began at the end of Lausanne, a short dead-end road. There were only two other houses on Lausanne, and the one directly below us belonged to the president of Technicolor, Arthur Ryan, and his wife, Ingrid. We made a point of introducing ourselves as the building process got underway, because we knew the Ryans would be a bit inconvenienced by the mess our construction would create.

"A bit inconvenienced" doesn't begin to suggest what transpired. For at least eighteen months, huge construction vehicles and earth-moving equipment lumbered noisily up and down the road past the Ryan house, sometimes blocking it entirely. Each day, every day, pickup trucks owned by the workers were parked the entire length of Lausanne, all of which made the Ryans's comings and goings a nightmare. Not once did they call to complain. Mary and I, still living comfortably in our Chalon home a couple of miles away, grew increasingly embarrassed.

At last the house was finished, the road was clear, and we moved in. We had one immediate and pressing duty, the first part of which entailed the purchase of a large silver bowl; around the edge we had inscribed a heartfelt message of gratitude, addressed to Ingrid and Art. I've forgotten the exact text, but the sense of it was that theirs had to be a special marriage for them to have endured so long and so patiently the torture we had inflicted on them. On a Sunday afternoon we called on the Ryans and in a short, rather stilted visit, delivered our gift of insufficient atonement. They expressed their appreciation in polite fashion, and Mary and I departed, thinking our new neighbors really had been more upset with us than they had ever let on.

Three weeks later we discovered a better explanation when the Ryans separated and subsequently divorced. We never knew whether we had unwittingly provided the last straw or, for that matter, who wound up with our sterling peace offering.

When it came to failed unions, unfortunately, Mary and I weren't far behind the Ryans. We delayed the actual split somewhat while Mary was away on location near Chicago, making her considerable contribution to *Ordinary People*. I visited the location only once, over a weekend, and there was very little connection between us. Not long after Mary returned to Los Angeles we decided to call it a marriage. By that time an unhappy ending had been in the air for so long that we had become resigned to it, and we were able to deal with the actual event almost casually, or so it might have seemed to anyone looking on.

I guess it was my penchant for neatness that made me choose New Year's Eve, 1979, just as the decade was ending, to move out. I had a sense of history about it, and I knew it would be a date even my bad memory could always dredge up. I had already rented a house at the end of a cul-de-sac just off Coldwater Drive, and late in the afternoon I started throwing stuff in the back of my car, thinking at first to take only the bare essentials. Somehow the sad task became an assignment I had to finish that day, necessitating a number of trips from Bel Air to a couple of miles above Beverly Hills. And that was the easy part. A few weeks before, I had undergone surgery that left me with no cartilage in my right knee, and the recovery was not going well. While I struggled up and down the stairs with my belongings—as a Depression kid, I'm a packrat who never throws anything out—the pain became quite severe and my limp increased. As light turned to dark, I knew I was coming off like an overloaded Chester on *Gunsmoke*. All the while, Mary sat reading (or at least appearing to) in a chair in the bedroom, through which I had to pass with every agonizing load. Finally, in the sweet manner of Mary Richards—or perhaps Laura Petrie—she inquired, "Would you like some help?" Staggering under the burden of assorted suits and haberdashery, I lied, "No thanks, I can handle it myself." The whole thing was a scene out of a Myrna Loy–William Powell comedy, and we both started laughing. Still, that did nothing to lessen the sadness and sense of failure we were both experiencing. I finally completed my departure, and the marriage and the decade ended simultaneously.

I've said earlier that really good shows can be made only by the best creative people. In 1978, MTM captured two of the very best, largely through the good work of Stu Erwin. Early in the year, Bruce Paltrow arrived, after shopping a development deal with CBS around town. He was looking for a production home, and he and his agent, Lee Gabler, finally chose MTM over Columbia and MGM. Six weeks later he was followed by Steven Bochco, whom Stu had known and worked with at Universal before joining us in 1974. He and Stu had stayed in touch, and more than three years later, when Steve felt the need for a change of scenery, he caught up with Stu at MTM.

"I had made pilots at other places," Paltrow says, "and MTM was different. It was very small, very unpressured. At some point, it dawned on you that everyone else there was all-pro. And if you didn't measure up, you really didn't belong. So you tried to play up, because everybody was kind of watching to see how good you really were. You just knew good work was being done all around you by good people. And no one ever interfered with who you hired, on what basis you hired them, or what you did with them."

Whatever attracted Bruce and Steven, their subsequent efforts ensured that MTM would not go down in television history as just a comedy company. Though they came from different directions, the two were already friends, and their first MTM work was done together. They turned out an hour pilot for NBC, a comedy-drama called *Operating Room* about some young, bachelor doctors in a Los Angeles hospital. Although each would go on to individual success with dramatic shows that incorporated considerable comedy, this joint Paltrow/Bochco effort just didn't work. Perhaps it was because *Operating Room* was lopsided in favor of comedy; their subsequent landmark shows were built on more substantial dramatic foundations.

Bruce brought with him a pilot commitment from CBS, which resulted in *The White Shadow* and was followed by a five-episode order. In November the show, about a white basketball coach (Ken Howard) in an inner-city, mostly black high school, began a solid three-year run at 8 P.M., first on Monday night, later on Tuesday. There was plenty of story opportunity to address real issues, much of which was mined in the three years the program lasted. In my opinion, it would have lived longer had CBS not asked for more comedy and less "heavy" material in the third season. The lighter version blew away just about the time I left for NBC.

CBS owned the Studio Center lot where MTM lived, and while *The White Shadow* was still in production, held its annual shareholders' meeting one morning on another soundstage. Retired CBS president Frank Stanton, the man probably as responsible as Bill Paley for building the company, was there, relegated to the audience as just another shareholder. A few years earlier, Paley had insisted that Frank retire at sixty-five, although he waived that company rule in his own case. Stanton had many years of potential service left in him, and the entire industry thought Paley had treated Frank badly and ungratefully. For a number of years, they were virtually estranged, although Stanton never went public with what had to be very hurt feelings, and Bill behaved as if he had been the injured party. In the last decade of Paley's life there was, happily, a rapprochement, brought about largely by Stanton's valuable service to the Museum of Television and Radio, which Paley had founded and considerably funded.

After the shareholders' meeting ended, the CBS directors toured the Studio Center lot. Work stopped on *The White Shadow* stage as they walked onto the basketball court that was the show's major set. Ken Howard greeted them and, as always happens when business meets show business, there followed a brief, stilted conversation. As it limped to an awkward end, Ken, standing at about three-point distance, casually threw a basketball toward the basket. It fell cleanly through the hoop. Exclamations and applause followed, which Ken took with appropriate modesty. One of the CBS directors said to another, "Let's see you top that, Frank. You're the hotshot athlete."

Frank was Franklin Thomas, who runs the Ford Foundation and is still on the CBS board. He was standing exactly at mid-court in a suit and street shoes. Unable to ignore the challenge gracefully, Thomas caught the ball someone threw him, took one quick look at the basket, and fired. *Swish!* He, too, shrugged off the applause for a feat that would have won him $10,000 at halftime of an NBA game, but I'm sure that shot was a high point for him.

Bruce Paltrow was creator and executive producer of *The White Shadow,* and my oldest son, Mark, was credited as producer. For several years, Mark had been paying his dues in entry-level production jobs at other companies, Lorimar for the most part. He came to MTM first as associate producer on *Three for the Road,* and served in the same capacity on a number of pilots and TV movies, as well as the original *Bob Newhart* series.

Mark's association with Bruce Paltrow was easily his most valuable, both in terms of learning and career progress. He was given as much responsibility as he could handle, as fast as he could handle it. Bruce is justly renowned (as is Steve Bochco) for bringing young people along, helping them to realize their goals. Many of them have been talented minority aspirants, among them actor Denzel Washington and, on *The White Shadow* alone, actors-turned-directors Thomas Carter, Kevin Hooks, and Eric Laneuville.

Bochco's first solo flight for MTM was *Paris,* an hour-long police drama starring James Earl Jones, a natural segue from the highly praised work Steven had done at Universal on such series as *Columbo* and *Delvecchio.* We shot thirteen *Paris* episodes, of which CBS aired only eleven. Some observers suggested that the show failed because not enough audience would buy a black lead, but I think Bochco feels the work just wasn't good enough. Everyone in the television program business, from whatever vantage point, experiences more failure than success.

But you can't keep a good writer down, and Steven Bochco is far more than a good writer. Television lore has it that Fred Silverman, with the feature movie *Fort Apache, The Bronx* as his inspiration, originally suggested Steven's next project. Fred certainly deserves credit, but he has to share it with two of his NBC colleagues, Michael Zinberg and Brandon Tartikoff, and with one of mine at MTM, Stu Erwin, all of whom served as midwives in one way or another.

On January 2, 1980, Tartikoff and Zinberg had lunch at La Scala in Beverly Hills with Stu, Steven, and Michael Kozoll, another MTM draftee from Universal. It was then that Brandon first floated the television *Fort Apache* arena Silverman wanted to develop. At first Bochco and Kozoll were less than enthusiastic about doing yet another cop series, but their fellow lunchers were persistent. Within a couple of days they had invented the show that would become *Hill Street Blues*.

A week later, Stu and I went with Steven and Michael to Tartikoff's office in Burbank. Not only was the concept approved, but Bochco made it very clear that he and Kozoll would have to be guaranteed freedom from network interference to do the show they had in mind. That sort of agreement is one thing in a programmer's office; there would be plenty of wrestling later with the network's Standards and Practices people, who are paid to be considerably more tight-assed.

Remarkably, Steven and Michael turned out a pilot script by early February. Stu and I loved it and, more important, so did NBC. There was considerable input from several quarters, and in recent years many have claimed involvement, but *Hill Street Blues* was clearly the co-creation of Steven Bochco and Michael Kozoll. Period. And none of us yet foresaw that the project would take television drama to a new level.

By happenstance, I did make one substantial contribution to the pilot and the series. Bob Butler, a highly talented director I had known for years, came to see me to resubmit an idea for a show he had first brought to me at Fox in 1969. Later, he and Michael Gleason, a writer/producer recruited by Stu Erwin, would develop that program, *Remington Steele*, from Bob's original concept. For the moment, however, Butler's appearance in my office gave me the idea that he was a great candidate to direct the *Hill Street* pilot. I'm not sure Bochco and Kozoll were all that keen on the suggestion at first. But when Bob returned to Steven's office to tell them how he proposed to direct it, Steven stopped him after only a few pages. "We don't have to hear any more," he said. "That's great."

Bob's vision complemented and enhanced what Bochco and Kozoll had put on paper, the final ingredient in a stunning marriage of talent. Butler would go on to direct the next four episodes, all of them written by Steven and Michael. By the time the series was turned over to other directors, a style had been set that would characterize *Hill Street* throughout its network life. Watching the show, I always felt—and I think most viewers did, too—that I was *in* that cop-house, and *out* on those mean streets.

The exquisitely chosen cast of *Hill Street Blues* was perhaps the strongest ever assembled for a dramatic television series. The production team wouldn't settle for anything less. It wasn't easy. Bochco ran into what would have been a stone wall for a more fainthearted producer. NBC's head of casting, Joel Thurm, voiced an "over my dead body" objection to Daniel J. Travanti for the lead role of Captain Frank Furillo. Where others would have been intimidated enough to go on to the next candidate, Steven went to the mat. He simply wouldn't take no for an answer, and, with total support from the rest of us at MTM, he finally prevailed.

We also got a negative response from NBC about casting Veronica Hamel in the Joyce Davenport role. The network had a flashier sort of woman in mind and was ready to give us a turndown until Fred Silverman overruled his subordinates. (It was one occasion when Fred's penchant for doing everything himself was a godsend.) It's a daunting challenge even to imagine what other actress would have brought to the character so many qualities—believability, versatility, professionalism, sexiness, elegance, and integrity—in one package.

There was also disagreement over what to call the show. The original title was *Hill Street Station,* which I still like, but NBC pressed for something catchier. Stu Erwin gets credit for suggesting *Blues,* which satisfied everyone. For me, the series was so good it could have been called *My Mother, the Car* and still have enjoyed the same success.

There was one other casting dispute, which proved that not all the tormentors of a producer necessarily work for the network. Bochco had decided that actor Bruce Weitz was perfect to play the bizarre Mick Belker. I was not so sure, and said so in stronger terms than I normally employed in second-guessing a producer's casting choices. Since I was Steven's boss, he was a bit more patient than he had been with Joel Thurm. He called one afternoon to ask if he could see me. "Come on up," I told him, in keeping with my practice of making myself available to our creative people. In short order, Steve arrived with Michael Kozoll, associate producer Greg Hoblit, and Bob Butler.

Steven led off: "We're here to take another shot at convincing you that Bruce Weitz is Belker."

"Forget it," I said. "He just can't be that scary. Belker is menacing, almost crazy, and—"

I didn't get any further. With an unearthly roar, something not human flew into the room and leapt onto my desk. Terrified, I almost tipped over backward in an attempt to get away from what seemed to be a crazed animal. It crouched, growling, on my desk as I cowered in fear I didn't even attempt to hide. Suddenly it smiled, and laughter erupted from everyone else in the room and from the outer office, where other onlookers had been tipped off. Bruce Weitz jumped down from atop my desk, and Bochco went for the kill:

"So, what do you think?"

I mustered what little dignity I had left. "I think that's Belker," I croaked.

By the beginning of the eighties the combination of high profits, availability of new technologies, and the arrival of ABC to competitive parity with CBS and NBC was having a lethal effect on network programming costs. Money was plentiful, and while more money didn't necessarily result in better programs, no one in Hollywood wanted to test the opposite theory.

The announcement of each network's fall schedule—CBS traditionally made theirs on Washington's Birthday—had been pushed back to May. Each network now waited until the last possible moment to lock in its programming, hoping that something wonderful would pop out of the development box. That gave producers less time, two months less, to get their shows ready for the new season. In television, having less time always means spending more money. Long hours of overtime became routine, and shooting schedules for hour-long shows slid from six ten-hour days to seven twelve-hour days, and sometimes to eight.

Some inefficient practices had become institutionalized: Instead of scripts being delivered at least two weeks before the start of production, they often arrived the night before. Directors found themselves prepping with only a first draft or, worse, nothing but a bare outline. The old requirement that shooting be completed eight weeks before airdate was long gone.

Moreover, satellite technology had made it possible for producers to deliver their shows at the last minute. This allowed the networks, in their zealous pursuit of the strongest possible weekly episode, to make changes right up to the airdate, which they sometimes did. Listings in *TV Guide* would be wrong, confusing viewers and prompting that important publication (with its readership of 40 million) to threaten reprisals unless the offending network shaped up. But the potential for last-minute changes offered by the satellite went hand-in-hand with network indecision, and producers often frantically worked overtime to complete a show that was to be broadcast that same week.

All this resulted in skyrocketing costs. By the end of the inflationary seventies, when the price of everything else had doubled, program costs had nearly tripled. Hour shows were now routinely budgeted at $550,000 to $600,000 a week. This steady increase had been accepted with only minor flinching by the networks. Their craving for hit programs had become even more urgent since ABC, which had always been the Arnold Stang of networks, transformed itself into Arnold Schwarzenegger in 1976, taking the prime-time lead for the first time. As a result, its network operating income went from $29 million in 1975 to $165 million in 1977. Now there were three evenly matched networks fighting for every inch of prime-time turf, and if a series appeared to offer the potential of a 30 share, well, no one wanted to quibble over a few dollars. After all, the networks were all making money and the leading network sometimes made more than the other two combined. Until the eighties, the three networks had very little competition for viewers' attention. Cable was not yet established, independent stations were generally weak, and ABC, CBS, and NBC consistently monopolized more than 90 percent of the prime-time audience. Hit shows often had 40-plus shares, and programming success performed real magic on the bottom line.

Paul Klein, once NBC's audience measurement expert and later head of programs, developed a theory in the mid-seventies that the lowest share any network could possibly get in prime time was a 10. It didn't matter what the program was; even a test pattern would get at least a 10. His reasoning was simple: Remote controls were not yet in common use, and a substantial number of Americans were bedridden. Ergo, until someone else came into the room to turn the set to another channel, these viewers were, quite literally, a captive audience.

On January 9, 1980, NBC unintentionally tested the theory. The network presented a ninety-minute special, *Live from Studio 8H,* devoted entirely to classical music. It got a 9 share, the lowest of any prime-time program in NBC's history. But Klein had a ready explanation. "Viewers hated this program so much," he suggested, "that all across America, thousands of disabled people threw themselves out of bed and crawled to the set on their elbows, just to turn the dial."

When Klein was head of programming in the late seventies, NBC commissioned the production of *Holocaust*. There was some concern that a nine-and-a-half-hour miniseries based on life and death in the concentration camps of Nazi Germany might be more than the American television viewer was prepared to accept. But Klein was never among the doubters, particularly after he looked at the finished work. Others at NBC agreed that *Holocaust* was a superb production, but questioned whether viewers accustomed to television's steady diet of lighter fare would tune in.

They needn't have worried. At a time when NBC had major ratings problems throughout its schedule, *Holocaust* turned out to be a blockbuster. For that one week, NBC was back on top and Klein was a hero. A visitor to his office who knew that Klein's wife had a realistic perspective on life at the networks wondered about her reaction when the good ratings numbers had come in.

"It's awful that six million Jews had to die," Janet Klein had said to her husband, "for you to get a forty share."

A big, sidewalks-of-New York guy with a saturnine demeanor, Klein was never at a loss for a one-liner. While he was at NBC, he contributed a number of original words, phrases, and concepts to the television lexicon: event programming (specials that he hoped would make up for NBC's lack of successful series), jiggle (his disparaging term for the bouncing bodies on some of Fred Silverman's popular ABC shows of that era), and the L.O.P. (Least Objectionable Program) Theory. In his view, people were so committed to watching television every night that they'd sit down in front of the set, flip the dial, and watch the L.O.P.

Klein may have had his finest moment at a news conference in Los Angeles in June 1978. The occasion was Fred Silverman's first meeting with the television press since leaving ABC to become the president of NBC. More than a hundred reporters and editors, joined by a gaggle of NBC executives eager to get a look at their new boss in action, packed a large room in the Sheraton Universal Hotel. The session went routinely until one reporter stood up to ask if he might direct a question to Paul Klein. Silverman, happy for the chance to take a breather, called Klein to the microphone. "We'd sure be interested, Mr. Klein," said the interrogator, "to hear your reaction when you learned Fred Silverman was going to be your new boss. For the last few years, you've been widely quoted saying very disparaging things about Mr. Silverman himself and about the programs he scheduled on ABC. Since the announcement that he was coming to run NBC was made way back in January, I'm wondering what these last five months have been like for you."

Klein leaned into the microphone: "Other than a brief period of impotence . . ."

Each of the networks fishes in the same production pool for its programs. The Hollywood studios and independent companies that form this pool all function under the same labor agreements and talent requirements. Consequently, a new one-hour program made at Studio A for Network X will cost about the same as a new one-hour program being made across the street for another network. The big increases have come when series are renewed for additional seasons. Creative people seek new agreements reflecting their individual importance to a program's success, and production companies in turn demand a higher license fee consistent with the contribution their show is making to the network's schedule.

MTM's *Hill Street Blues* premiered on NBC in January 1981. The average cost of each show in the first season was $613,072, of which the above-the-line segment (actors, writers, producers, director, and associated creative costs) accounted for $241,072. While somewhat on the high side because of *Hill Street*'s complexity, production values, and large cast, that fell comfortably within the prevailing parameters of what new prime-time series were supposed to cost. The show was renewed for a second season and then swept nearly everything at the 1981 Emmy Awards. After a rocky start, *Hill Street* had clearly established itself as a fixture on NBC's Thursday night schedule. Its emerging success was accompanied by an above-the-line budget increase of 22.4 percent as the cast, producers, director, and writers all got increases.

By the following season, 1982–83, *Hill Street* was that rarest of network birds, a top-twenty program with superb demographics, equally cherished by audiences and advertisers. Steven Bochco had succeeded in bringing a new form to television, combining police drama with a multilayered plotline and a literate script. It was network television at its very best, and the standard by which other dramatic work came to be measured. The above-the-line costs increased that season by another 47.5 percent, helping to bring the total episode budget for *Hill Street* to well over $800,000. By then, this was a nonevent. The production cost of lesser series, even those in their first year, had risen to more than $700,000, network revenues were zooming, and the goose was still pumping out golden eggs.

Over the years I've enjoyed good relations with almost all the folks who write about television for the print media. I've taken my lumps on occasion, sometimes deservedly, for a show that disappointed a critic or for an executive decision someone felt compelled to second-guess. But throughout my management of MTM and NBC, I had generally approving and kind press, and when the Television Critics Association presented their first annual Outstanding Career Achievement Award, I was honored to be the recipient. Over the years that I've been reading the critics' columns and reviews, it seems to me the breed has improved substantially.

In the early days of network television, the job of covering the business often went to the last guy through the door, or to someone who hadn't made it on some other part of the paper. Unlike film and drama criticism, the TV beat carried no prestige and was frequently handed to someone with no particular interest in covering it. There were some early, literate observers—John Crosby of the *New York Herald Tribune* and Jack Gould of *The New York Times,* for example—but they were the exceptions. More often, television critics fell into the hack department, and much of their work was on a fan-magazine level. Gradually, as the new medium grew from infancy into an omnipresent giant no one could ignore, the territory was turned over to more-skilled, intelligent hands.

The critics I've read in recent years tend to come in one of three varieties: (1) good, (2) not so good, and (3) a few who could be in the first category but believe they are more talented than the people they cover. As a result, their typical show review is unduly negative, less a service to readers than an effort to prove that the critic can be more clever or amusing than the material being critiqued. Usually the effort fails.

Readers of *The Washington Post* have for years enjoyed the best one-two punch in television coverage in the entire country. Why that combination occurs in our nation's capital, and not in New York or Los Angeles—the centers of the business— is to the credit of the former executive editor of the *Post,* Ben Bradlee. Bradlee recognized, long before his counterparts did, that a medium that would occupy the average American home for seven hours a day was deserving of serious attention from his newspaper.

From the time he took over the *Post*'s TV beat in March 1977, Jack Carmody has written the most complete, most accurate, and most engaging column dealing with the daily business and trends of broadcasting—everything from schedule changes and executive comings and goings to network and station plans and activities. If it's happening, Carmody knows it, and he usually knows it first. And his column is written with such insight and wit that many people with no connection to the television business—most of the *Post*'s readership—find it worth their time.

Also represented in the Style section of the *Post* has been Tom Shales, hands-down the best reviewer ever to cast a critical eye on a television show. An observer nonpareil, he's also an imaginative, superior writer, informative, and vastly entertaining. (And has a Pulitzer Prize to prove it.) Shales clearly *likes* television. Though his reviews can be devastating, he never gives up on the possibility that just beyond the next station break there may be a landmark show. And he's a lightning quick study. Consider just part of his September 1982 assessment of *Cheers,* after seeing only one episode of a show that was to remain popular for eleven years:

> Cheers *is for cheering. It's the best new series of the season and the most substantial new comedy since* Taxi. . . . *It grows out of the traditions of ensemble character comedy perfected by these folks and many others at MTM Enterprises in the days of* Mary Tyler Moore—*comedy that starts with good writing and lives or dies on the basis of performance. By happy fortune or clever design, both elements combine in*

> Cheers *to create a new instant favorite, a comedy series with*
> *potential to enter the ranks of the all-time greats.*
> *What a swell place to hang your hat* Cheers *is.*

Tom Shales, the critic, is a national treasure. Would that he worked *in* the medium.

The Goliath of television coverage, because of its huge national circulation, is *TV Guide.* During my MTM service, I had a half-kidding running battle with the magazine over its often cynical aim at the lowest common denominator. It was fun to twit the editorial people about the infantile crossword puzzle ("_____ in the Family") found in each issue, which, I contended, betrayed their clear contempt for the intelligence level of their readership.

In early 1981, however, *TV Guide* ran a two-part article by Frank Swertlow that took our differences to a more serious level. The article purported to expose rampant cocaine use in the television industry, and contained some shocking allegations, including:

> *"Coke is all over the place," said a high-ranking network official, who requested that his name not be used. "It's directors, writers, producers, actors, everyone. It's horrendous."*
>
> *One studio head joked about his creative bookkeeping. "There are three kinds of costs: above-the-line, below-the-line, and cocaine-line," he said.*
>
> *Many observers believe that the widespread use of cocaine is the biggest problem facing the television industry.*
>
> *"If you don't have a bowl of coke on the table in Hollywood, you're a nobody."*
>
> *And now people in Hollywood are beginning to wonder: will it also destroy the television industry?*

I fired off a letter of outrage to Roger Youman, the magazine's editor, pointing out that the article was long on scandal and short on substantiation:

> *Names,* Roger, *where are the* names? *Where are the* facts? *Who are the using and abusing producers? Who are the network people who demand cocaine before (and as a condition of) buying a show?*

If there is cocaine in this community, and no doubt there is, it plays no part in the selling and buying of television shows. I've never seen it, I've never been asked for it, I've never been offered it, I've never heard from any of my colleagues or counterparts of any cocaine currency within our business. And as the present chairman of the Caucus for Producers, Writers and Directors (over 100 of network television's premier contributors who collectively account for the bulk of prime time), I get around a lot among my peers. . . .

You owe the creative community out here proof—names, dates, facts—or you owe us a public apology. Failing either, just sell the book to Rupert Murdoch or Generoso Pope, so we will know once and for all what TV Guide *stands for.*

For three weeks, there was no response. Then a full-page ad appeared in *Variety* on March 23:

To the Hollywood community:

Grant Tinker and others have suggested that TV Guide *owes the television production industry an apology for publishing a two-part series on cocaine use in Hollywood and the way it affects programs that reach the air. According to Ben Stein in the* Wall Street Journal, *the* TV Guide *pieces are viewed as an attempt to aid the Jerry Falwell attack on television. . . .*

Names could not be used because cocaine is an illegal drug and our sources did not want to be part of prosecuting their friends and colleagues. We will continue to protect those sources.

Grant Tinker and Ben Stein apparently passed over the paragraphs in the articles that said those who use the drug are a minority, that many of the top people in production are not even aware of the extent of cocaine use in the industry. But because there are some producers and network people who are either users or who employ the drug as currency, it does have an influence on some of the pilots that are assigned and even on some of the programs that have reached the air. And the few actors and writers who work stoned—despite Stein's denial about the writer—certainly affect the programs.

Much as we respect Grant Tinker in his more temperate moments, we see no reason to apologize for a factual, accurate article. . . .

One would hope that the industry, instead of perceiving our series as an insidious attempt to discredit television, would take action to correct the situation.

The ad was signed by Merrill Panitt, *TV Guide*'s editorial director, and both its tenor and its prominence marked it as a response to an outcry from others in "the Hollywood community." But the ad was more than self-righteous; it downplayed the sensationalistic tone and message of the original article. My already high dudgeon was raised to world-class levels, and I decided to retaliate with a *two*-page trade ad of my own. I joined forces with David Rintels, a past president of the West Coast Writers Guild, who had shared with me his own letter of protest to the magazine and allowed me to quote him liberally. Like me, Rintels took strong exception to the vagueness of the charges, and the refusal to cite sources:

You and I met last year at the TV Academy's conference on Standards of the Docu-Drama, and you must know that the standards of this article—the anonymity and sheer lack of balance of it—would not pass the standards that we all agreed television should be bound by.

Why didn't Frank quote me, or someone else in the industry, as saying it was all wrong? I told him that, twice, as strongly as I could. How can he or you expect to be taken credibly in the industry unless you cite sources? If you're not willing to cite sources and produce evidence, I think decency requires that you not fall back on blind charges. Are they real people? Fringe people? Many or few people? We have no way of judging the article when it is so deliberately vague. . . .

Speaking for myself, I feel we have been libeled, unfairly and irresponsibly, by an article that is wrong, published in a magazine that, this once, chose ratings over higher standards. And I think that, while impressing the impressionable outside the industry, you have undermined your credibility with the people inside it.

I got in the last word:

> *I think you'll agree, Merrill, that the above is telling, temper-ate and indicting. It cannot be dismissed with "we stand by our story" or "we must protect our sources" ritual responses. You've made some serious charges about an entire industry. You willfully published them, you energetically promoted them, and now you blithely defend them without offering one iota of supporting evidence.*
>
> *A lot of us would like to see you put the matter right.*
>
> *Grant A. Tinker*

Neither Merrill nor Roger ever mentioned the subject to me again, and we all moved on to more constructive pursuits. In cool hindsight, I also realize that I could rightfully protest only on behalf of the television industry. I've never been in the movie business, and simply hanging around town a few years ago left me with the impression that some noses were being used for more than smelling the roses. More recently, Rupert Murdoch has come to town (via Fox), and it's clearly simplistic and wrong to connect him with tabloid journalism alone. Although I was on the right track with another of my suggestions: In 1988, *TV Guide* was indeed sold to Murdoch.

For a guy who likes to be alone, I don't live alone well. That's one reason I've spent virtually all my adult years living with someone. A better reason is that over a span of forty-three years, I have loved three women in turn, each special and wonderful in her own way.

Ruth gave me twelve years and four children in a period when I probably needed more emotional support than I ever would again, though I would only come to realize that, and the extent of Ruth's selfless contribution, years later. Mary and I were compatible and complementary, to say nothing of being in love for most of our marriage. Though she is ten years younger (she says eleven), we were equal marital partners throughout our eighteen years together (she says seventeen). It turned out that we also became business partners, and that connection had more staying power than our personal relationship. But one thing that never really waned was our mutual sense of humor. To this day, we tend to laugh at the same things.

Divorces, and their causes, are painful experiences. But the emotional bruises heal, and eventually the good memories outweigh the bad. And life goes on. Both Ruth and Mary have remarried, happily as far as I can see. We seldom meet, but it's no sweat when we do. Phone conversations are comfortable and welcome, at least for me. What Ruth and I have in common are four great kids, now grown. And Mary and I share a lot of memories of the good years, when two people who belonged together were together.

And then there is Melanie, the final instance of my good fortune in finding the right person at the right time. She came into my life when she stepped into my MTM office in 1978. I needed

a new secretary (today properly labeled an assistant) and called
Blanche Runge, who had served me in that capacity in the early
sixties in Burbank. Blanche was still at NBC, now as an executive, and I thought she might be able to help, since she knew
the territory—me. "I know exactly the person," was her instant
response.

A day or two later I welcomed Melanie Burke to my office and,
after a short interview, hired her. I liked her right off the bat,
though there was certainly no hint of the relationship to come.
That would develop out of personal, reciprocal feelings, but in
the beginning my appreciation of Melanie came from the kind of
woman she is, from her character and her integrity. The fact
that she quickly became indispensable helped, too. She was the
kind of secretary who's always several steps ahead of the boss;
she knew what I should and would do before I did, or so it often
seemed. And she had spent a couple of years in the Entertainment division of NBC, so she knew how the business worked.
She was also a huge help when I bought and remodeled a house
up in Benedict Canyon, high above Beverly Hills.

When I first entered that house with a real estate agent, a
bathrobed figure was sitting in a darkened den staring at a television set. It turned out to be O. J. Simpson, house-sitting for a
friend and trying to cure a bad cold before a broadcast assignment that weekend. He was long gone before escrow closed.

It was in that same house late in 1980 that I got a phone call
around two o'clock one morning—the kind that's like a punch in
the stomach. It was from my son Mark, whom the police had
contacted when they couldn't get a number for me. The news was
tragic: Mary's son, Richie, was dead. He had been visiting two
girls just off the USC campus. While showing off with a sawed-off shotgun, twirling it, Richie had shot himself in the head,
dying instantly. Why he was carrying the gun we'll never know,
but through his own father's interest in the outdoors, he was not
unfamiliar with firearms. That alone should have made him
more careful. The tragedy was heightened by the fact that Richie
had only recently "found himself" after a number of troubled
teenage years. He hadn't been living at home for some time, but
we had seen enough of him to know he had made it through his
personal rough patch and come out safely on the other side. I
think he was closer to Mary at the time of his death than he had

ever been. Her only child, Richie was always a sweet kid, perhaps too naive to deal with the more sophisticated, sometimes cynical world into which he was born. Mary had patiently struggled for years to help him deal with an unforgiving society, as had I to a lesser and less successful extent. Finally, it had all come together for him, mostly through his own doing, and now he was gone.

I had two difficult tasks to do, only one of which I could handle. The first, the call to Mary, could wait until morning, I decided; there was no point in waking her in the middle of the night with such cruel tidings. I had also been asked to identify Richie, but I wasn't up to that. My son Michael, a member of the Los Angeles Police Department—the family proudly calls him "Michael the Cop"—drove with me to the morgue. I waited outside while he went in and carried out the necessary identification. It's the kind of task a big-city police officer has to do too often. I finally phoned Mary in the morning, and she was devastated. Yet again she needed all her considerable strength.

A couple of days later, after appropriate funeral services, there was a well-attended memorial reception at the Lausanne house. It seemed to me that the presence of so many people said a great deal about their love for Richie and about their abiding respect for Mary.

Then there was a more personal good-bye. In a chartered Lear jet, we flew Richie's cremated remains to a quiet, pastoral area in northern California. Richie's father guided us to a spot along a small river where they had sometimes fished together. In that peaceful place, we surrendered Richie's ashes to the swiftly running stream.

Throughout this period, Melanie was becoming important in every aspect of my life, and perhaps it was inevitable that my dependency on her would develop into something much stronger. Somehow the considerable difference in our ages didn't seem to matter. When the house in Benedict Canyon was finished, we moved into it for the beginning of some very happy years together.

The day of my second lunch with Thornton Bradshaw, June 9, 1981, was a day of unrelated extremes. I had barely arrived back at my MTM office that afternoon, having committed the next five years to NBC and wondering what the hell I was doing, when suddenly the answer seemed not very important. Betty White, Allen Ludden's wife, was on the phone:

"Allen died a few minutes ago," she told me. "He went very peacefully."

For months, Allen Ludden had fought the good fight he would eventually lose to cancer. Until recently, he and Betty had been in Carmel, where they were building their dream vacation house, and he had gone into the hospital there. When his condition temporarily improved enough for him to be moved, we had flown him down to Good Samaritan in Los Angeles. He died just a few weeks later, with Betty holding his hand. She's as strong a woman as I've ever known, but that afternoon her voice betrayed her, as she asked, "Do you think you could take on the job of getting a few of his good friends together to be part of the services?"

Of course I could. The hard part was limiting the number of participants—Allen had innumerable friends. Two days later, Burt Reynolds, Mark Goodson, Dick Martin, Tom Kennedy, Gene Rayburn, and I had the honor of saying a few loving words about Allen, not all of them sad. Many of the memories we shared of Allen were funny, happy ones. He was that kind of guy and he would have been pleased by the tone of the gathering.

Weeks later, Betty, who has always brought unmatched meaning to the word *thoughtful,* discovered that her call to me had come on the day of my NBC decision, and she apologized for having "bothered" me. Since Allen's death, she has continued her one-armed paper-hanger pace, doing *Golden Girls* and other television projects while involving herself in a full schedule of do-good activities, particularly where animals are concerned. Don't let your dog stray too far; Betty will find it, think it's lost, and take it home. And if she does, the dog will be better off.

Before long, I was so caught up in my fixation about saving NBC that I failed to think clearly and responsibly about the post-Tinker stewardship of MTM. I simply decreed that Arthur Price would become president. As it turned out, the decreeing took a little doing.

With Arthur, Mel Blumenthal, and Norton Brown in tow, I flew to New York to fill in Mary. Even though I had always made the corporate decisions, common courtesy called for me to tell her face-to-face. History said she wouldn't question my judgment.

History said wrong.

Mary had set up temporary quarters in the Waldorf Towers, and all four of us trooped into her suite. She was characteristically gracious, though a bit formal. Her reserve toward me was but a harbinger of what lay ahead that evening. I quickly recounted the plans for my imminent departure for NBC and my designation of Arthur as my successor at MTM. Hindsight later told me I presented the case rather presumptively, an error that stemmed from eleven years of having made all the business decisions for the company.

Her reaction made it clear that that was then and this was now. "I'm not sure Artie should run the company," she said, right there in his presence. I was shocked and angered and embarrassed. "Why the hell not?" was my immediate response.

"I'm not sure it's something he'll do well. And if he did become president, I think there should be someone on the outside overseeing MTM."

That suggestion made me furious. "That's just ridiculous! Anyone from the outside wouldn't know enough about the company to be of real help and would just get in the way. Arthur's been with us from the beginning and he's thoroughly capable of running MTM."

Mary continued to resist, an attitude I attributed to our personal situation, never giving her credit for having prescient instincts in an area to which she had never paid any real attention. Arthur, Norton, and Mel looked on like the Three Stooges at a tennis match, which only served to make me apoplectic. Finally, I lost it entirely. "Goddamnit, Mary, you're just being stupid," I yelled. "You don't know shit about how the company runs, and you're pissing on a guy who's busted his ass for it. And he's sitting right here, for Christ's sake. What the hell is wrong with you?"

I ranted on for a while, concluding with a door-slamming exit, aware that throwing a complete fit might actually get the job done. Which it did. When I rendezvoused with my fellow travelers later that evening, I learned that Mary had indeed relented and had agreed to let Arthur take the reins of MTM unsupervised.

The passage of time would one day result in two unanticipated ironies. Irony No. 1: Mary would turn out to be absolutely right to question whether Arthur should run MTM. Under the stew-

ardship of Arthur Price and Mel Blumenthal, a vital organization came to a creative standstill.

"During the very first week of Arthur's presidency," Stu Erwin
remembers, "a workman came into every MTM executive's office
with orders to install an automatic door closer. The symbolism
was startling. Overnight, when our creative people dropped by
for a visit, they discovered that everything had changed, that,
literally, MTM's open-door policy had ended." The company
quickly shifted its focus to the bottom line, Stu says. "For a
while, Arthur set up a good-cop, bad-cop approach, with Mel as
the villain. Everyone was told that 'we're gonna start running
this place as a hard-nosed business.' Arthur was making an effort to establish a relationship with the production people, while
Mel was meeting by himself with Bochco, Paltrow, and the other
executive producers to lay down the law."

In the fall of 1982, three MTM shows—*Remington Steele, St.
Elsewhere,* and the second *Newhart* series—made the network
schedules. After that, Stu says, "Arthur ended his good-cop role
and started to beat people up on budgets and contract negotiations. The priorities had changed forever." The very qualities
that had made MTM special had been destroyed, and the company never had another good year. Then, in the summer of 1988,
Arthur and Mel engineered the sale of MTM to English buyers,
who paid $320 million, far more than the stalled company was
worth, erroneously anticipating a future that would match the
past. So the approval I had to browbeat Mary into granting
would ultimately work to her colossal financial benefit.

Irony No. 2: Leaving MTM to return to NBC would ultimately
cost me tens of millions of dollars when I was later required, by
anxious RCA lawyers, to dispose of my 35 percent interest in the
company I had built. And Arthur, the object of my passionate
recommendation, was to be both the biggest disappointment and
the principal beneficiary. Not that Blumenthal didn't give him a
run for his money in both departments. Never have two people
been so richly rewarded for such a lackluster performance. It
never occurred to them (or perhaps it did) to share some of their
ill-deserved spoils with a number of loyal, contributive staff people, as Norman Lear and his partners did when they sold their
company.

For me, a constant painful reminder of how far MTM has fallen has been the once-beloved pussycat logo. It was created as a spoof of the MGM lion, because I wanted something distinctive as our imprimatur. We had the gall to dispatch Dave Davis, an Emmy Award–winning producer who arrived with Jim Brooks and Allan Burns when Mary's show began, just to shoot pictures of kittens, one of which would appear at the end of every episode of every show the company produced. Always conscientious and deliberate, Dave spent a whole day on the project. The product of his work was to become more than mere corporate identification for MTM—it became a symbol of quality television.

I held our meowing cat in high esteem, not only for itself, but for the superior work it represented. I loved it when different shows had fun with the logo, no matter how silly the alteration. At the end of *White Shadow* episodes, the cat was dribbling a basketball, *St. Elsewhere* had him (maybe her) wearing a surgical mask, and on more than one occasion the final show of a canceled series saw the kitten roll over on its side and die. Sometimes producers felt the meow was a bit frivolous, and when program material was too serious, or ended on a down note, the cat fell silent.

The talented writer/producers who made MTM the cat's meow have long since departed; now the logo signs off product the original company would not have watched, much less made. These days, I don't watch many MTM repeats, but when I do see one of our shows, I tend to switch channels before the logo appears. It's somehow too painful a reminder of those proud and productive days in the seventies that are now just a memory.

In late June 1981, Melanie and I headed for my favorite vacation retreat, the Hotel de la Voile d'Or on St. Jean Cap Ferrat in the south of France. Having said yes to Bradshaw, my idea was to manage one last escape before jumping with both feet into the formidable challenge awaiting me at NBC. The escape lasted about one day. The entire world seemed to discover my news at once, and everyone I knew (and some I didn't) wanted to discuss it with me. Bradshaw called, seeking my concurrence, which I gave him, that NBC should hang on to Tom Brokaw, whose new deal with the company now needed my approval. Many of the other calls were from the press.

Back in Los Angeles, I turned official attention to my assignment. I took off for New York, pausing only to pay a necessary visit to the Rodeo Drive clothing store of my longtime friend Dick Carroll. I ordered a whole bunch of new suits to take the place of the more casual attire I wore at MTM, where sweaters and jeans were considered dressy. During the next five years, I kept complete wardrobes on both coasts. My sartorial needs alone ensured that the Carroll family would continue to live in the style to which they had long been accustomed.

As I undertook the NBC assignment, I wanted a place where Melanie could have full-time live-in help, particularly because I would be in New York so much. Mary had wound up with the house on Lausanne Road in the divorce, but she had moved to New York herself. I bought it back, lock, stock, housekeepers, and dogs. With some redecoration and some staff changes, the house served nicely throughout the NBC stint and longer.

In 1990, I was to buy yet another house in Bel Air and put Lausanne on the market, expecting to make a killing. Following my lifelong practice, I would acquire the new house at the height of the real estate market, and be unable to give the old one away, until movie producer and now mogul Peter Guber virtually stole it from me—though he might not characterize the transaction quite that way.

Melanie would feel more comfortable in the new house than she had in the one Mary and I had built. Over the next few years, she would return to UCLA for a Master's degree from the School of Social Welfare, leading to a more-than-full-time role as a therapist at the Rape Treatment Center in Santa Monica.

But for the first half of the eighties, besides having her own life to lead and a big house to run, she had a relentless role to play on my behalf. Without complaint, she managed my weekly absences, the frequent gatherings of the affiliates, and all the other business-related functions. Her selfless dedication and her character kept me on an even keel during more than five years of demanding duty at NBC.

Most of the early days and weeks of my new NBC adventure were necessarily spent in New York, headquartered in the RCA Building. I moved into the sixth-floor office Fred Silverman had recently vacated, inheriting tastefully decorated digs I wouldn't change for the run of my stay. At the time, I had enough to do just learning to act like a chairman. The fact that those quarters were the very ones to which I had delivered mail and messages thirty years earlier gave me a satisfying sense of completion.

The company was indeed in terrible shape; if anything, it looked worse from the inside. When Bob Butler, our chief financial officer, briefed me on the network's year-to-date performance against business plan, the figure at the bottom of every column was in parentheses—each representing seven- and eight-figure misses. Had it not been for the shooting-fish-in-a-barrel certainty of returns from the television stations NBC owned in New York, Washington, Cleveland, Chicago, and Los Angeles, the company would have reported a loss in 1981.

Profits were one-sixth of those at ABC and CBS, there had been several affiliate defections, and morale was at an all-time low. For the 1980–81 broadcast season, which had just ended as I arrived, NBC had no regular series in the top ten (and only *Real People* and *Diff'rent Strokes* in the top twenty). The company had lost its credibility with every important constituency—affiliates, advertisers, the press, the general public, and its own employees.

Our program schedule was so weak that Sally Bedell Smith, then the able television reporter for *The New York Times,* wondered out loud whether NBC would ever be able to regain the "critical mass" of audience that could make it competitive again. NBC's affiliates and the advertising community wondered, too; the only welcome aspect was that their expectations were so low that any shred of good news was going to be well-received.

In truth, you didn't have be a rocket scientist to run NBC, but strong leadership was essential. Oddly, it was a quality I hadn't really thought about at MTM. We had started the company from scratch and I knew just about everybody on the lot. We'd simply made up the rules as we went along. At NBC, with its fifty-five years of history and thousands of employees, I was to discover I was a pretty good leader.

I was keenly aware that morale at NBC was so low that many in the company wondered whether it even had a future. In an effort to suggest stability and continuity, I quickly appointed Bob Mulholland as president and chief operating officer and Irwin Segelstein as vice chairman. I really didn't know Bob at all, but he had been with NBC for virtually all his executive life and had served in top management in News and then as president of the television network. I figured that he knew everybody in the company and vice versa, and that his prior roles represented excellent credentials.

I had worked with Irwin at Benton & Bowles twenty years earlier, and remembered him as bright and analytical, with virtually a Talmudic approach to broadcasting lore. He had been president of Columbia Records and had held senior programming posts at both CBS and NBC. In the relatively undefined role of vice chairman, I saw him as a roving centerfielder who could roam the organization as I asked him to, and who would provide me with intelligence about matters with which I was not yet familiar.

Bob's appointment turned out to be a serious error on my part, one that would not be resolved for more than two years. Part of the problem derived from differences in our management styles. Meetings with affiliates and others would often find us at opposite ends of the table, and the contrast in our styles got in the way of effective communication. Bob's approach was very direct, sometimes confrontational, while I move more slowly, often waiting for a troubled situation to find its own resolution. There are pros and cons to both approaches, but Bob was not the boss. I was.

There was yet a worse problem. We were really doing the same job, and we were constantly running into each other. I had inadvertently created a superfluous layer of management. In effect, most of the company reported to Bob, he reported to me, and I had no intention of leaving. That left him as the odd man out, a situation of my own making.

Having to fire the president of NBC was a prospect I dreaded, but by early 1984, it was clear that I could temporize no longer. I went to see Bradshaw, and whatever his more humane feelings may have been, he didn't join me for a minute in the temporizing department. As soon as I had outlined the problem and my guilt over having been its author, he inquired, "So, what's the trouble?"

"The trouble is that the only course is to fire Mulholland."

"Sounds that way to me."

I returned to my office and buzzed Bob on the intercom. When he arrived, I was seated on one of the couches, not at my usual place behind the desk. "There's something we have to talk about," I began.

"You want me to leave, right?"

"Yeah, that's it."

I made an effort to explain, but Mulholland didn't need or want that. As I had agreed with Bradshaw, I sent him up to RCA's head of personnel to work out his exit arrangement. Throughout the difficult process, Bob's professionalism made his departure less painful for all those who had worked with him. Some months later, I made a pass at reestablishing contact with him, but he didn't call back, and it was clear he had drawn a line through my name.

My interaction with others in the company was far happier. I had inherited from Fred Silverman a group of first-class, experienced top executives, some of whom I rearranged as I began to understand our collective job. I also asked Bud Rukeyser to return from a fifteen-month stint at *Newsweek,* to which he had defected after twenty-two years at NBC. His replacement as head of corporate communications had lasted only a few months with Fred, and that job was open when I became CEO. With the exception of Bud, whom I remembered from our days of mutual service in the sixties, I recruited no new senior executives as I arrived.

The reorganization following Bob Mulholland's departure put most of the operating divisions of the company under Ray Timothy and Bob Walsh, respected broadcasters with decades of service at NBC. Both had come up through the ranks and had successful track records managing NBC-owned television stations.

Ray had the network to run, and his areas of responsibility included Sales, Affiliate Relations, and Programming. He was totally comfortable with the first two, which dovetailed with his own experience, and less comfortable with the last, in which Brandon Tartikoff, president of the Entertainment division, reported to him. Given my own program background, Ray was happy to have me stay close to Brandon, which was made easier by my being in Burbank on Fridays.

Walsh, like Ray, had run stations himself, so he was thoroughly prepared to supervise all of the NBC-owned television stations. Also reporting to him were NBC's eight radio stations and three radio networks. For good measure, we added Sports to his portfolio. A couple of other operating departments went to Bob Butler, whose principal contribution was as chief financial officer. That area was my weakest suit and, during my tenure, Bob would prove to be a patient instructor, frequently saving me from embarrassing myself when the numbers were under discussion.

My weekly commute gave me plenty of time to consume and assimilate the relentless accumulation of reading matter a company like NBC generates. But it also meant that for ten or twelve hours a week, I felt cut off from my job, effectively unavailable. In order to stay informed and involved, and to ensure that senior management was on top of everything that was happening, I invented something we called the Chairman's Council. There were nine of us, including me. The others were Timothy, Walsh, Butler, Segelstein, Rukeyser, Gene McGuire, who headed up Personnel and Labor Relations, Cory Dunham, our general counsel, and, when he later joined NBC as president of News, Larry Grossman.

The group met on Wednesday afternoons for sessions of an hour or two. Problems, plans, programs, procedures, and policies —to be alliterative about it—made up the agenda. The final responsibility for company decisions was mine, but it was immensely useful to have several experienced broadcasting minds brought to bear on whatever problem was on the table. I think the most valuable dividend lay in the esprit de corps that developed among nine executives with disparate responsibilities. That spirit radiated out and down into the company, and I am convinced that the collegial approach that was the essence of the MTM style played a real part in resuscitating NBC.

Morale throughout the company was at a dangerously low point in mid-1981—dangerous because in such a climate people don't do their best work and the best people begin to look outside the company for other opportunities. It's a self-perpetuating spiral of failure. I've always believed that if you don't have a job you go to happily each day, you should get another job. NBC employees were clearly not racing to work every morning.

Bud Rukeyser and Gene McGuire arranged a number of employee meetings to begin to address the problem. The first was held in historic Studio 8H, the old Toscanini radio venue and now the home of *Saturday Night Live*. Everyone was invited, and NBCers of all levels crowded into the studio. Most of them looked uneasy. That wasn't surprising; NBC had sunk to last place by all the measurements of television success, scores of people had been hired and fired, and, from reading the papers, you'd think that the company had acquired a new name, "beleaguered NBC."

The closed-circuit setup permitted two-way communication with all network locations, as well as our owned television and radio stations. Bob Mulholland and Irwin Segelstein joined me on stage, and I identified the members of the Chairman's Council positioned in the first row, along with Arthur Watson, president of Sports; Al Jerome, president of the Television Stations; Pier Mapes, president of the Television Network; Mike Sherlock, president of Operations and Technical Services; Bob Blackmore, head of Sales; and Bill Rubens, in charge of Research. Then we switched to all the other locations, introduced the senior person at each one, and showed wide shots of everyone in attendance.

I made some opening remarks, mostly about why I returned to NBC and what I expected—at that time it was nothing more than a hope—that we would accomplish together. I promised everyone that this meeting, and others to follow, were not going to be speeches, they were going to be dialogues. I wanted questions, suggestions, complaints—anything any employee in that studio or elsewhere wanted to discuss.

The Q&A began a bit slowly, but soon people began to speak up. I addressed most of the questions myself, but Bob and Irwin and the other executives pitched in. A couple of hours into the session hands were still being raised, but it was time to quit, which we did with my assurance that we would come together again on future occasions. I also promised we would make a swing through the other NBC locations for local versions of this sort of get-together.

Looking back, I think the revival of NBC began then and there. Probably there were a few cynics who thought these meetings were a Boy Scout exercise, but their candor paid exponential dividends in morale. Over the next five years, we held many more such meetings. Those in New York and Burbank were closed-circuited to everyone, and I know they fostered a sense of family that only became stronger as NBC began to experience success. After Bob Mulholland's departure, I began to do a single at the gatherings, calling on executive experts as needed for special information. Not only did I develop a comfort level about being able to answer the questions, but I began to get off on the give-and-take itself.

The interaction and exchanges with my co-workers were the closest I ever got to realizing the core reason I had answered Thornton Bradshaw's original call for help. These were the people, or at least they represented the people, with whom I had worked twice before at NBC. The irresistible challenge was to restore, together, the company of which we used to be so proud.

There was another constituency whose support would be essential to the turnaround we hoped to achieve. It was made up of just over two hundred affiliated stations that comprised the NBC Television Network. Without them, there *was* no network. Without their support, particularly in terms of clearing, or carrying, NBC programs, we simply couldn't succeed. And without the visible and vocal team-playing of the largest market affiliates and station groups, we would ultimately die.

When I came on board, the affiliates had had it with the network's broken promises. A few had defected to ABC, and some that remained often replaced network programs with syndicated fare that produced more income. These preemptions weakened an already weak network. In the long run, only a complete turnaround of NBC would restore affiliate faith and real partner participation.

But of course the relationship between a network and its affiliates is complex and mutually dependent. On bad days, it's been compared to two scorpions in a bottle, who must either learn to share their resources and live together in peace, or die. More often it's called a partnership, although the word is defined variously and loosely, depending on the relative positions and clout of each party. In some cases there were critical rifts that urgently needed repair. Strong stations in important markets, many of them part of the NBC family since radio days, were still being wooed by ABC and CBS. Several were sorely tempted to jump ship—to defect to another network that offered a more profitable association. Ray Timothy and his Affiliate Relations operatives worked hard to hold a number of reluctant feet to the fire while NBC was performing so inadequately.

I was pressed into service in a number of ways. On occasion, Ray would set up a one-on-one meeting with a particular station owner in need of some TLC. There were also opportunities a couple of times a year to present our case to NBC's affiliate board, a dozen or so intensely interested owners and general managers elected by their affiliate peers to represent all of them with the network. These get-togethers usually took place over a couple of days in some salubrious locale, where morning work sessions could be followed by afternoon tennis or golf. Such congenial conditions gave us our best shot at buying some time to get our network act together. It was a holding action at a time when, for the most part, we were selling spit. But since the majority of our partners didn't have immediate better options, they gave us additional slack, sometimes grudgingly. They would return home to disseminate to their fellow affiliates assurance that the network had been taken to the woodshed and would redouble its efforts. It was at these affiliate board meetings that I was particularly on display. I knew there was plenty of skepticism in the room, but my principal assignment was to radiate confidence and competence.

In truth, most of the board members were easy for me to relate to. They gave me points for my successful production background, which made them believe I knew a good television show when I saw one. For my part, I've always cottoned to broadcasters, so it was easy for me to have genuine interest in matters important to them. I can't really say what they thought of me at that early stage of our relationship, but I enjoyed those meetings even when we had nothing to be joyous about.

One other strategy for improving interaction occurred to me almost immediately. I sought out several NBC affiliate elders, men who had spent their lives in broadcasting and were highly regarded by their peers. I asked them to play a special role, ex officio, as a committee of expert advisers. They were a small group: Ancil Payne of King Broadcasting, who was stationed in Seattle; Jack Harris of H&C Broadcasting, in Houston; Al Flanagan, who ran the Gannett stations from Atlanta; and Fred Paxton, then chairman of the affiliate board, who owned and managed the NBC affiliate in Paducah, Kentucky. Most of them had one foot out the retirement door—Al Flanagan, in fact, was gone before he could really contribute—but that gave them objectivity. Fred Paxton wasn't the graybeard the others were, but he was wise and sensible beyond his years. We never held formal meetings, but they knew they were particularly prized counselors and were available, mostly by phone, whenever I needed advice from the affiliate point of view. And they brought more: They were longtime NBC "partners" and had a sincere appreciation and concern for the network/affiliate relationship and how it worked best.

I didn't keep secret the fact that I looked to them for special advice, knowing that I would get good marks from the rest of the affiliate representatives for seeking them out. I'm sure Ancil, Jack, and Fred were aware of that public relations aspect, but their sensible counsel was so clearly in the best interest of both sides of the partnership that no one minded.

I seldom got into matters involving the hardware of broadcasting, but occasionally it couldn't be ducked. One afternoon, I took a call in my 30 Rock office from Jay Sandrich, who was toiling at NBC's antiquated Brooklyn studios, directing the entire first season of *The Cosby Show*. He would go on to direct all the episodes in the second year, as well as many in subsequent seasons; it's impossible to overstate the importance of Jay's contribution to that landmark program. As always, he got to the point quickly: The RCA cameras he was expected to use were frequently breaking down, causing unacceptable delays, or there would be color mismatches, necessitating retakes. Could he rent another brand of camera to replace them?

Sandrich is a hard man to say no to, but I persuaded him to give the RCA cameras another chance. This was a knotty corporate matter with which I was already familiar. Other NBC shows had found the parent company's equipment wanting, but all were given the same reasonable rationale: How could RCA sell its cameras to outside customers if it became known that NBC's own shows wouldn't use them? New RCA cameras were dispatched to Brooklyn, and of course they quickly came up as short as their predecessors. My next call from Jay was an announcement, not a request: "We can't turn out this show every week with second-rate equipment. I'm going to rent some Ikegamis."

I knew better than to argue. Far easier to incur the wrath of a few RCA executives (and the raised eyebrows of my boss, Thornton Bradshaw) than refuse a determined Sandrich, who knows better than anyone what it takes to turn out superior television.

One matter that had to be decided was how NBC was going to distribute its programs. The years of delivery by coaxial cable were gone, superseded by satellites. NBC's Operations and Technical Services staff, run by Mike Sherlock, recommended we reject the C-band system chosen by ABC and CBS in favor of the more expensive Ku-band. I could pretend now, as I did then, that I fully understood the virtues and shortcomings of both, but I do remember that Ku-band was costlier, reportedly not guaranteed to be weatherproof (I remember hearing the phrase "rain attenuation"), and ran counter to the conclusions of our competition and our RCA parent. Despite that, with the considered advice of the Chairman's Council, the poorest network sprang for the highest cost. That would prove to be the right decision, and NBC programs and program traffic have been moving around reliably ever since—a fine example of a dumb CEO being smart enough to accept good counsel when it's available.

Toward the end of my stint as NBC chairman, it became known that the RCA Building's landlord, Rockefeller Center, Inc. (RCI), was not only planning to raise NBC's rent when the current lease was up, but they were also turning down our urgent request to upgrade our woefully outdated studio space. The studios had been originally designed with radio, not television, in mind.

In the belief that two can play hardball, we floated the not entirely false report that NBC would be looking for a new home. Instantly, we had major real estate movers and shakers coming in the windows, and a couple were beckoning ardently from New Jersey. Mayor Ed Koch heard about the latter activity and promptly invited me to bring a few friends over for breakfast on the back porch of Gracie Mansion. He couldn't imagine NBC moving out of the city, much less to another state. We explained that prudent business conduct called for us to examine all our alternatives.

Donald Trump jumped on the bandwagon, with a vision of NBC as the "Television City" centerpiece of the monster development he planned for his valuable riverside property between 59th and 72nd streets on Manhattan's West Side. He may also have viewed such an arrangement as the key to getting city help on the project, in grateful return for having kept NBC in New York.

Bob Butler was our point man on all this activity, and for months he played the various interested parties like instruments. Clearly, RCI could hear the music, which they eventually faced. So in the end, NBC stayed put. I was gone by then, but Butler's masterful tactics won for new owner GE not only better lease conditions from RCI, but tax benefits from the city of New York.

Butler was also the man in the middle of NBC's brief romance with Ted Turner. We were the more aggressive party, while I think Ted saw a visible potential marriage to NBC as useful in accomplishing other goals he had in mind. Turner was in a cash bind at the time, and in a meeting in the RCA suite at the Dorset Hotel, Bob presented a $225 million offer for half of CNN. The negotiations didn't go much further, though, because Ted rejected out of hand our firm condition that NBC have editorial control.

For years, ABC was the network that successfully bid for and carried the Olympics. In 1985, beginning to feel our NBC oats, we decided to make a determined run at the 1988 Games. First up for competitive bidding were the Winter Games, to take place

My father, Arthur, with Joan, me, and Phyllis.

Ruth and I—the big day.

With Jodie, Michael, Mark, and John.

Portrait of the author as a new
NBC vice president, 1961. (NBC)

Robert E. Kintner, NBC's president from
1958 to 1966. (*Broadcasting* magazine)

Mary's Richie.

MTM's founding couple.

All these people to make one show—the cast and crew of *Mary Tyler Moore*.

Jay Sandrich directing the star.

Ted Baxter with his idol, Walter Cronkite. (CBS)

Betty White, Mary, Georgia Engel, Gavin MacLeod, Ed Asner, and Ted Knight; Cloris Leachman and Valerie Harper had already spun off into their own series. (CBS)

Allen Ludden,
Betty White
Ludden, CBS's
Bob Wood,
Mary, and me.

Writer/producer Allan
Burns contemplates
directing.

Steven Bochco.

Lew Wasserman,
Thornton Bradshaw,
and me. Normally, I
would be listening.

*Hill Street*ers Michael Conrad,
Veronica Hamel, and Daniel J.
Travanti. (NBC)

St. Elsewhere originals. (NBC)

Cheers stalwarts
John Ratzenberger
and George Wendt.
(NBC)

At sea with
Thornton Brad-
shaw, Mike
Wallace, David
Wolper, and
Art Buchwald.

With Gary Gold-
berg and Brandon
Tartikoff on a panel
at Harvard.

The Chairman and
the King. (NBC)

Bud and Phyllis Rukeyser with Bruce Paltrow.

With Melanie.

A more private moment.

in Calgary. That kicked off some detailed, coordinated homework done by Art Watson, president of Sports, and his boss, Bob Walsh, with input from Bob Blackmore, head of Sales, and some of Butler's financial guys. We sat around for a couple of days and nights conjuring with dollar numbers—our estimates of what the other networks, particularly ABC, might bid for the rights, and how much Blackmore might collect from advertisers. We decided that $300 million was the highest bid we could reasonably justify, and even that had a small built-in premium— rationalized as the value of the message NBC would be sending by picking off ABC's traditional prize.

At the last minute, we nudged our bid up to $305 million, on the theory that ABC would come in just above $300 million. Privately, I felt we had reached just a little too far, that we would not "get out" at that level, no matter how much of his customary magic Blackmore performed. I'm sure my immediate colleagues shared the feeling that we had let our hearts get in front of our heads. When we got word that ABC had gone to $309 million and been awarded the rights, we were disappointed but relieved that we'd been bailed out.

When bidding came due on the Summer Games to be held in Seoul, our luck improved. This time we did all the same homework and wound up with a number that made sense, that sales expectations could support. Accordingly, Walsh and Watson headed off to Lausanne, Switzerland, headquarters of the International Olympic Committee, authorized to bid $300 million. Once there, they called back to recommend that we go to $325 million, which I authorized without any real optimism that ABC wouldn't again outbid us. But ABC had been unable to get Madison Avenue to come up with enough advertiser money to justify their Winter bid. That caused them to be uncharacteristically cautious in Lausanne. They passed, and NBC was the highest bidder.

The host Koreans, however, had been badly misled about how much Olympic Games staged halfway around the world would be worth in this country. They had anticipated rights offers as high as a billion dollars. They were insulted by our bid—the only one—and there were bad feelings all around. Walsh and Watson took the NBC bid off the table and came home.

But with no other interest, the Koreans had a problem, which we "solved" for them. We lowered our bid to the original $300 million and attached, as a face-saving gesture, a revenue-sharing plan that would kick in at a level everyone knew would never be reached. Nor was it, and the upshot was that our fortunate failure to win the rights to Calgary became a success in Seoul.

A fair amount of my day's work simply arrived in my office uninvited, by mail, memo, phone, or in person. As time passed, and I learned more about the company, dealing with those matters became almost automatic. The knottier problems came up in meetings; that's what meetings are for.

When I arrived in mid-1981, Bill Small was president of NBC News. He had been hired during Fred Silverman's administration by Dick Salant, the retired president of CBS News, whom Fred had brought to NBC as vice chairman. Small had served with distinction in CBS News management for almost two decades, but he resigned from NBC in late February 1982 after a rocky couple of years. He had reported to Bob Mulholland, and it was never a happy relationship. Mulholland persuaded me that Reuven Frank, a former president of the News division, should return to that job. Reuven agreed to step into the breech with what seemed to me a distinct lack of enthusiasm. I think he preferred the role of producer, and felt he had already paid his management dues. But he answered the call, and one immediate dividend was that he was known and liked by his News division colleagues.

Late in 1983, I was watching a round-table discussion on C-SPAN. One of the participants was Larry Grossman, whom I remembered favorably from my second NBC tour in the sixties, when he was head of Advertising. Larry had been president of PBS since 1976, and I had pretty much lost touch with him. His impressive performance on C-SPAN gave me the idea of asking him to return to NBC. Shortly thereafter, while we were in Hawaii for the November meeting of the affiliate board, I told Reuven he was off the hook, that I had found a replacement who would make it possible for him to return to the producer function he clearly enjoyed. Never a demonstrative sort, he took the news with no particular comment or visible reaction. Much later, I would learn from a book he wrote that he felt my action had been peremptory. That gave rise to my own thought that he might have protested too much about not wanting the job.

Grossman came to work as head of News early in 1984. After Mulholland left, he reported directly to me. Evidently, the news purists in the department thought of that as the blind leading the blind, although given NBC's eventual success, they would probably give me a good executive grade. But as bright and thoughtful as Larry is, and despite his years of experience in broadcast management, he never quite achieved acceptance from many of his departmental colleagues.

Two of the best News presidents who ever worked in television, Dick Salant at CBS and Roone Arledge at ABC, came to their jobs with no previous experience in news. But for some bullshit reason that is more conceit than sense, there is still a myth among news types that unless you began your working life in the womb of that business, you cannot ever really belong to the fraternity. Larry was the victim of that ridiculous shibboleth, no matter how well he performed or how fiercely he fought the good fight for his assigned charges. Tom Brokaw, whom I respect and consider a friend, was the heaviest of the heavyweights who never really got on the Grossman bandwagon.

No one had to tell me to stay out of the affairs of Larry's department, particularly in terms of its output. When it comes to coverage and content, and everything in between, News must operate free of corporate pressures. Still, I paid close and interested attention. Along with many others who have spent their lives in the fiction arena, I find the reality end of broadcasting fascinating, and I made myself accessible whenever the News division asked for advice or help. I've always felt the output of the people who work in News is the primary responsibility of broadcasting. The rest of us largely exist to serve and fund that output, and I wanted everyone in the division to know how keenly I cared about what they did. When Tom Brokaw's *NBC Nightly News* led its competition, or when *Today* blew by ABC's *Good Morning, America,* I think I was more pleased than when our prime-time schedule became dominant.

For many years, NBC had tried with no success to keep a news magazine—its counterpart to *60 Minutes* or *20/20*—on its weekly prime-time schedule. Many formats had been tried by many different news managements; all had failed. Now Larry wanted Roger Mudd and Connie Chung to co-anchor a new program, titled *1986,* to start in June. But Roger was having none of it, and events in his recent past helped explain why. He had left CBS News in 1981, disappointed when Dan Rather had been given the job as Walter Cronkite's successor. He joined NBC News, assured by the incumbent management that he would be the successor to John Chancellor as anchor of *NBC Nightly News*. Then, in 1982, Roger was importuned to share the *Nightly News* anchor duties with Tom Brokaw, only to have Tom replace him as sole anchor a year later. He also knew that newsmagazines, even the successful ones, take a long time to build an audience, and he was dubious about NBC's commitment to *1986*. Would Brandon Tartikoff be willing to tolerate the inevitable low ratings and keep the program on the air? Would I? Roger Mudd wanted some assurance.

With Larry playing the role of moderator, Brandon and I met with Roger early in the year, when NBC was making plans for its fall schedule. Roger sat facing us, as skeptical as a desk sergeant questioning two accused felons. Brandon had come prepared. "We're going to be number one again next season," he told Roger, "and the last thing in the world I'd want people to say is, 'Sure, NBC's in first place, but there's an asterisk in the record book.'"

Roger bit. "Asterisk?"

"We'd be the only network without a newsmagazine in prime time," Brandon said. "I want to win the right way."

Mudd was almost sold. "But what happens if the ratings are low?" he asked, staring at me. "How long do you stick with it?" "Forever," I replied. And I meant it.

Unfortunately for Roger (and possibly for the cause of good journalism), I would leave NBC before *1986* could turn into *1987*. The early ratings were indeed low, NBC's new management had other priorities, and "forever" became December 30, 1986.

Late one foggy afternoon, I was going on a quick trip to Washington for some long and easily forgotten obligatory function. Because of the weather, the West Side Heliport was socked in, and my NBC driver, the (mostly) reliable Chester Reed, was taking me to the New Jersey location where RCA kept its air force. The phone buzzed. It was Tom Wyman, then president and CEO of CBS, with whom I had a friendly relationship but normally no reason to conspire. After the pleasantries, he inquired, "How do you feel about that long-distance camera position, the one from which we all get pictures of the Reagans horseback-riding at the ranch?"

"I think it's a stupid invasion of their privacy. I guess it's there in case the president falls off his horse."

"Assuming we've never talked, how would you feel about losing it?"

"I'd feel just fine."

That was the only time I ever "managed" NBC News. It turned out that Larry Grossman also felt it was an expendable vantage point, and I don't think we spied on Mr. Reagan's rides ever again. Presumably, CBS didn't either. Whether Wyman made a similar call to someone at ABC, I don't know. I think it was an appropriate action, and I was kind of pleased about it. Screw the news purists.

Every month there was an RCA management meeting, at which the six or seven people who collectively ran the various RCA businesses—NBC, Hertz, the record company, consumer electronics, and the rest—came together to tell each other, and Chairman Bradshaw, how we were doing. I also attended the monthly RCA board meetings, and on those same days I chaired NBC's board meeting. I found all these sessions a bit onerous at first. At MTM most "meetings" were just me, in jeans, muttering to myself in my office, or talking briefly with three associates. Or it might be an even more informal schmooze with some of our creative people, where I was more listener than speaker.

Now I was attending meetings as the CEO of a company in real trouble, about which, in those early months, I knew too little to contribute much. In addition, at every one of these sessions, I was sitting there representing the most rotten business in the RCA family. The abysmal NBC "financials" had to be presented, along with those of the other divisions. Ours were always by far the worst, an obvious albatross around the neck of RCA. When the numbers went up on the screen, I'd find myself sliding lower and lower in my chair. NBC's horrendous condition was not of my doing, but in that room I was its embodiment, and as the group listened to our bad results, I sensed a number of "Who farted?" looks.

At my second RCA board meeting, Ed Griffiths, who had been replaced as chairman by Bradshaw but was still on the board, made an earnest case for the immediate sale of NBC. Its plight was hopeless, he said, and RCA should get rid of it at once. He didn't seem the least bit troubled that I, the guy who had just been recruited to save the company, was sitting right next to him. And I'm not at all sure he didn't have support from some of the other directors. After a few minutes of discussion, Brad took the suggestion off the table as being premature—as opposed to unthinkable.

The NBC board meetings went more smoothly, despite my distinct lack of experience at chairing such things. They immediately followed the more substantial RCA sessions and were attended by many of the same cast. Most of the NBC directors were cordial, and some—General David Jones, Tom Paine, Pete Peterson, Bob Cizek, Andy Sigler, John Petty, and John Brademas, in particular—came with a clear and friendly rooting interest. As, of course, did Brad. William French Smith, who joined the board shortly after he resigned as U.S. Attorney General, was memorable for a different reason. His first question about any action the board was considering, no matter how innocuous, was invariably, "Do the directors have any personal exposure or liability here?"

My least frequent trips to the fifty-third floor were to see Brad. It turned out that when he said, "You run it," he meant it. Which is not to say he wasn't available. If I felt the need for some sound advice from an older, wiser head, all I had to do was call him. The response was invariably an immediate "Come on up," as though he had nothing else to do, which was hardly the case. I think he made himself particularly available to me because I was his invention; it had been entirely his idea to bring me to NBC as the "savior." If I didn't get the job done, it would be on his head.

In retrospect, most of the discussions we had were inconsequential, but particularly during the early, difficult months, when the problems were overwhelming and morale was so low, the occasional lift from Brad was very welcome. I also sought his counsel on various protocol matters with which I'd had no experience, often related to a board activity or an upcoming RCA event.

As chairman of NBC, one of my annual chores was to attend the RCA shareholders' meeting. Once there, I was fair game for any question about the company's broadcasting activities. My first such meeting was May 4, 1982, and I wasn't looking forward to it. First of all, there was no good news about NBC. We had stabilized the program schedule to some degree, but all our new shows were struggling to find an audience and we were still very much the third-place network. But worse than that, for me, was the prospect of shareholder questions about technical and engineering minutiae. If a shareholder needed an explanation of the relative merits of C-band and Ku-band satellite transmission, for example, I knew the answer couldn't be, "How should I know? I was an English major."

The solution was to be found in the four hardcover loose-leaf books prepared by the RCA and NBC law departments. These fat volumes were crammed with facts, figures, policies, and procedures on every aspect of NBC's operations, and were designed to answer every conceivable shareholder question. On several of my transcontinental round-trips, I took the books along and virtually memorized their considerable contents. By the day of the meeting, I was ready for anything.

I accompanied Bradshaw and the other company officials to Studio 8H in the RCA Building, where Brad started the meeting with a few state-of-the-company remarks. After some random questions—some quite testy—for others on the RCA team, I sensed that my turn at bat was imminent. Despite the tension, I was reasonably confident that there was nothing in those four black books that wasn't, at least temporarily, in my head.

My moment of truth arrived. A woman stood up, captured one of the roving microphones from an NBC page, and said, "I have a question for Mr. Tinker. Judy Woodruff, one of your news correspondents, is pregnant, hardly a condition to be hidden in this day and age. But every time she's reporting on television, you show her only from the waist up. Why is that?"

I could have kissed her. I waited until the roomful of people quieted down, and responded, "At NBC it's our custom, when photographing one of our reporters, to shoot only half of that reporter. Almost invariably, it's the upper half."

The place erupted with laughter. For the remainder of the meeting, I didn't get another question. In three days I would forget every fact I'd crammed from those four books, though in subsequent years I'd prepare just as carefully for each shareholders' meeting. But I never again sweated them.

There was one small compensation for having to wear a suit and attend all those meetings: a chauffeured limo. My driver,

Chester, had served in the same role for NBC's two previous CEOs, Herb Schlosser and Fred Silverman, both of whom lived in New York City and kept him busy. Experience had taught Chester that bosses may come and go, but the front seat of a Cadillac can be forever. With me, his main responsibility was meeting my plane from Los Angeles on Mondays and returning me to JFK on Thursdays. Late one evening, after a flight that was delayed several hours, Bud Rukeyser and I arrived in New York. Chester, as always, was a tall and visible presence at the airport gate.

It was immediately apparent that he was less than fully alert. Executive action was called for. "Give me the keys," I said, and moved into the driver's seat of the stretch limousine. A chastened Chester got in next to me, Bud climbed in the back, and I proceeded to chauffeur our group into Manhattan. Chester attempted a mumbled story about a trip to the dentist that afternoon, but it was clear he had made at least one other stop. When we arrived at the Dorset Hotel, I got out of the car and removed my briefcase from the trunk. Chester, still not himself, had remained in the passenger's seat. I handed him the keys, and his instructions: "Now you can drive Mr. Rukeyser home."

With the rare exception of a *Cosby* show that takes off immediately, new series need time to find an audience. And the more they vary from the tried and true, the more time they need. The art of programming is in making the correct judgment about what, if anything, can and should be done to help them succeed. Too often, network programmers, with their jobs on the line, look at dismal early ratings, decide they were wrong about a show's potential, and yank it off the air.

But if you believe that the show the producers are delivering is as good as you hoped it would be, you must have some confidence that the audience will eventually think so, too. Leave it alone, suffer the low ratings, and know that you're in it for the duration. If your program judgment is good (and if it isn't, you should be doing something else all day), the show will slowly build its audience, and you won't have to worry about that time period for years.

Hill Street Blues, St. Elsewhere, Cheers, and *Family Ties*—four series that came to represent NBC's (and television's) best while I was there—were all slow starters. Each was a best-of-breed, brilliantly written and produced, but the early ratings made strong men weep. Throughout its first season, *Cheers* ranked near the bottom of Nielsen's prime-time list, some weeks finishing dead last. That didn't mean *Cheers* was a bad show; it just meant hardly anyone was watching. Staying with *Cheers* until the audience found out how wonderful it was solved NBC's problems at 9 o'clock Thursday for eleven years.

Family Ties, which also premiered in 1982, had a similar track record. Gary Goldberg's show, always of high quality, had abysmal ratings its first season, entirely a function of having to face entrenched competition from the other two networks. By year two, *Family Ties* was attracting a loyal audience; once it began to follow *The Cosby Show* in 1984, it became a genuine hit. And *Hill Street* finally succeeded only when it was locked into one time period, 10 P.M. Thursday, after the nomadic scheduling of its first season.

St. Elsewhere was also slow out of the gate, and when it came time to bite the bullet on that one, I was looking at an MTM show from the network side of the fence. The genesis of the series went back to very early 1981, when Josh Brand and John Falsey were working for Bruce Paltrow as story editors on *The White Shadow*, then in its final season. They wanted to create their own next assignment, and they talked to Stu Erwin about a new series based on the experiences of a friend of Brand's at the Cleveland Clinic. I had still been at MTM when we authorized a research trip they made to Cleveland, and I remember talking *St. Elsewhere* to Brandon Tartikoff as "*Hill Street* in a hospital." For me, that was just the usual selling jargon, but neither Paltrow nor Bochco was fond of the analogy.

By early spring, five *White Shadow* alumni were developing what would become *St. Elsewhere*—Brand and Falsey, my son Mark, John Masius, and team leader Paltrow. Brand and Falsey stayed with *St. Elsewhere* through the first season and, though they moved on in 1983, received a "created by" credit for all its seven years. Among their celebrated work since then have been *I'll Fly Away* and *Northern Exposure*.

By the time the project began to come together, and approvals and go-aheads were finally forthcoming from the network, I was already at NBC, trying to look and act like a chairman. The birth of a television series is almost always tortuous, but *St. Elsewhere*'s was a little more so than most. In the end, what were probably too many cooks turned out a provocative pilot, but not before Bruce decided that the first few days of shooting on the pilot were unacceptable. All that footage was scrubbed ("eaten," in Hollywood-speak), and production was halted for some late recasting (Ed Flanders as Dr. Westphall) and a new director, Thomas Carter. (Thomas had started with us as an actor on *The White Shadow,* and was yet another beneficiary of the Paltrow practice of helping talented young people.) Once Bruce had it going the way he wanted, there was no doubt in my mind *St. Elsewhere* was going to be a keeper. It was both quirky and solid.

On April 27, 1982, NBC announced its fall prime-time schedule. In 10 o'clock time periods on Tuesday, Thursday, and Friday were three MTM hours: *St. Elsewhere, Hill Street Blues* (returning), and *Remington Steele*. The last was the result of Stu Erwin's notion to put Bob Butler and Michael Gleason together to fashion a show from the idea Bob had first proposed to me at Fox thirteen years earlier. The three series, each of which had a stutter-start, became exactly the kind of double-value successes network sales departments covet: respectable-to-good ratings and demographics that led the league. The audience for these shows was largely the 18 to 49, better-educated, higher-income viewers so beloved by most advertisers. All three series would serve the network until after I retired in late 1986, and all three played important, contributing roles in NBC's recovery. Ironically, they would eventually cause me grief, in one case in an important and expensive way.

Industry observers would occasionally remark on NBC doing so much program business with my old production company, and that caught the attention of the habitually nervous RCA Law department. For several reasons, not the least of which were the priceless FCC-granted licenses of the stations NBC owned, any seeming conflict of interest that might give rise to even a hint of potential impropriety caused the legal eagles high anxiety.

Suddenly, the blind trust Bradshaw had assured me would be a workable way to conserve my 35 percent interest in MTM wouldn't fly. My choice, though no one quite said it out loud, was either to return to MTM or dispose of my interest in the company I had founded and built for eleven years. The first option was out of the question; I was going to get the NBC job done or die trying.

I would have to sell out, which I did. In retrospect, I should have gone hunting for an outsider to buy my share of the company, but at the time the thought seemed heretical, particularly as it would affect Mary. She certainly deserved to recapture at least a third of my interest. As it turned out, she wound up with no part of what I sold back, which went instead to Arthur Price and Mel Blumenthal, both of whose original interests had been gifts. To put it mildly, it has galled me ever since that those two, who managed MTM to a creative standstill, together owned almost two-thirds of the company when it was sold.

But no one, not even Thornton Bradshaw, had held a gun to my head, and my failure to pin down his assurance about the blind trust was no one's fault but my own. I had left MTM of my own free will, and I divested with my eyes wide open—for a fraction of what my 35 percent was going to be worth. The price was a function of what constituted those assets at the time I sold. Television programs are in a network schedule at the pleasure of the network; they can be canceled unilaterally at any time. Episodes not yet produced, delivered, and paid for are not yet assets. For example, I was credited with my estimated interest in only the first thirteen episodes of *Hill Street,* and no interest whatsoever in all of the eventual episodes of *St. Elsewhere* and *Remington Steele.* Just those three cases together represented a total of 376 hours of quality television on which I realized no return.

The first season of *St. Elsewhere* was brilliant creatively, but almost no one watched. It was seldom ranked among the first fifty shows in the Nielsens, and twice finished dead last among all the shows in prime time. When discussions started about whether or not to renew it for 1983–84, most of our NBC decision-makers wanted to dump it. In a rare overrule, the chairman (guess who) called the shot. "It's a good show," I said. "Let's pick it up."

With characteristic irreverence, Bruce Paltrow says the only creative suggestion he ever got from me came from what he thinks is my aversion to "the whole idea of people being sick." He claims that when the show got renewed, I said to him, "Who wants to go to a hospital? It's depressing. *St. Elsewhere* should be brighter." In the first episode of the second year, the opening shot showed the doctors walking about the hospital, where workers were painting the walls a lighter color. One of the doctors turned to another and said, "The chairman of the board told us if it's brighter and lighter here, maybe we'll live longer." That was Bruce, having the last word.

I also voted to retain *Remington Steele,* which was not quite as endangered. The pickups saw both shows begin to prosper in their second seasons, ensuring solid success and many more episodes. Working strictly for the benefit of NBC, I thus made a huge contribution toward boosting the price for which MTM would ultimately be sold.

It was bad enough that my decision to take the NBC job wound up costing me tens of millions of dollars. But when it became generally known that I had played a strong role in the second-year renewal of *St. Elsewhere,* a few stories in the trade and consumer press suggested that part of my motivation might have been the desire to keep my son Mark, one of the show's producer/directors, from being out of a job. I didn't bother to think about what those reporters would have said had they known that Paltrow would add my youngest son, John, to his writing staff in that second season. I've always been proud as hell that both Mark and John are considered superior creative talents by people more knowledgeable and objective than I.

Bruce, Mark, John, Tom Fontana, and John Masius were the team that took the show to its considerable heights. And *St. Elsewhere*'s literate style attracted an audience so demographically desirable to advertisers that Bob Blackmore, the talented head of NBC Sales for many years, told me it was the fourth-best selling program on the network.

But for all these successes, skyrocketing production costs were catching up with NBC and the other networks. By the mid-eighties, they had risen so sharply that some half-hour comedies were budgeted at about what an hour of *Hill Street* had cost in 1981. At the start of the eighties, $550,000 to $600,000 had been the average budget for a one-hour drama; in the nineties that might buy only thirty minutes of a multiple-camera comedy. The production costs of *Hill Street* itself, after all the increases that accompanied its first five successful seasons, had risen by a million dollars an episode over the 1981 budget. And more typical one-hour dramas, with similar production values to what *The New Doctors* was delivering in 1970 for $230,000, could now easily cost more than $1.2 million.

That's exactly when advertising sales, the fuel that feeds the system, hit the wall. After a ten-year period of more than 300 percent growth, the total revenues of ABC, CBS, and NBC declined in 1985 and remained flat for the rest of the decade. Their combined prime-time rating—the percentage of all sets tuned to the three networks—had reliably totaled in the high 50s for more than twenty years. Now it fell to the 30s, a victim of toe-to-toe competition from cable, Fox, videocassettes, and other new players.

The new proprietors of the network companies—Capital Cities, Larry Tisch (Loew's), and General Electric—immediately instituted cost-cutting measures. But their problem was that the major expense of running a network, accounting for some 70 percent of the total, was the aggregate cost of programs—entertainment, news, and sports. Most of these costs, in the short run, were fixed, and annual increases were built into every contract.

The ever-higher price of entertainment programs, as we have seen, had become institutionalized over two decades. Talent with household names were asking, and sometimes getting, more than $100,000 an episode, and a substantial number of writer/producers were being paid like baseball stars, with multimillion-dollar deals and escalation clauses. Every existing show had contracts in force, and no fiat from the top was going to bring those dollars down. So the networks got tough with license fees.

It had been more than fifteen years since the fee they paid the producer covered the actual weekly production cost. That made sense while the domestic syndication aftermarket stayed healthy, and while producers could look to an immediate sale in foreign countries as soon as the network contract was signed. That income from overseas, while not substantial in comparison to the potential dollars available from U.S. syndication, was paid up front and helped reduce the weekly deficit to a manageable amount. It allowed producers to keep their shows on the air, hoping for the repeated network renewals that would give them the ability to enter the domestic syndication big-money game.

Until the economy and the advertiser marketplace stalled, deficits didn't cause producers any sleepless nights. License fees and production costs rose more or less on parallel tracks. The average license fee paid by a network for a new one-hour program had risen in the early eighties to about $800,000, which was within $100,000 or so of what most shows cost. But in the second half of the eighties, the networks' desperate need to save money, and their limited options for cost-cutting, led them to freeze license fees. For producers of all but the megahits, deficits climbed perilously high. While license fees stopped at $900,000, or even less, for new one-hour series, Hollywood-produced hour dramas on film, a thirty-year staple of prime-time television, could cost upwards of $1.2 million. Half-hours budgeted at $625,000 to $700,000 or more were licensed for only $400,000 to $450,000.

And just as deficits were getting totally out of hand, the bottom fell out of the off-network syndication market.

Starting in the seventies, for producers of network shows, syndication had become the potential pot of gold, the huge payoff that could erase years of weekly deficits. The FCC's Prime-Time Access Rule (PTAR) went into effect in the fall of 1971, prohibiting network affiliate stations from scheduling syndicated shows, after their network runs, in the lucrative early-evening time periods.

At first, some affiliates tried these shows in the late afternoon, but met with little success. It soon became clear that strong off-network programs worked best when scheduled in early-fringe time, 6 to 8 P.M., when local audience levels were higher, advertising dollars greater, and the competition was news. Since network affiliates were foreclosed by PTAR and their own news programming from use of those early-fringe time periods, independent stations were given their first chance to play with the big boys. The number of independents exploded from about eighty in 1971 to well over three hundred, all of them eager to buy programs with established network track records. Successful shows with four years or more on a network, enabling them to accumulate enough episodes for syndication, were snapped up at increasingly higher prices.

The full effects of PTAR on the syndication marketplace were not felt immediately. The hit series that first went into syndication—*Mary Tyler Moore, Bewitched, I Dream of Jeannie, The Bob Newhart Show,* and others—were sold for a fraction of what they would have brought just a few years later. In 1977, when Mary's show was completing its seven-year run on CBS, we were delighted when the 168 episodes were sold for $37.8 million, or $225,000 per episode. By 1980, another round of syndication brought in an additional $150,000 for each negative, but we were still a few years early.

By that time, independent stations, always struggling for an audience, had figured out how to use PTAR to achieve a competitive breakthrough. They learned to schedule off-network hits against the network affiliates' news programming. The deals were for several years, during which time the station could usually broadcast each episode six times. *M*A*S*H* was the watershed that changed the marketplace. It was so successful in winning time periods in which independents had always languished that it created fierce competition to buy shows like *Happy Days, Laverne & Shirley, Barney Miller, Three's Company,* and numerous others to follow. Some of these comedies broke the million-dollar-an-episode barrier on their first foray into syndication, tripling or quadrupling what hit half-hours had brought just five years earlier. Total syndication revenues for a successful series often topped $100 million.

Even those boxcar numbers were demolished in 1987 when the first 125 episodes of *The Cosby Show* were put up for sale. NBC was still running original episodes on Thursday nights, and it was far and away the number-one program in television. Viacom, with counsel from syndication consultant Bob Jacobs, was handling the distribution, and their pitch to stations was simple: "What else has the potential to give you a 50 share every night and turn your station around? Are you going to let your competition get it?" There was such a frenzy to acquire *The Cosby Show* that written bids were required, hand-delivered to a public accounting firm.

No station could know what its competitors were offering, so preemptive strikes were the order of the day. Someone close to the sale remembers when MCA, which owned WWOR-TV in New York, sent in its bid: "Not only did they offer $350,000 for each episode—no New York station had ever paid more than $140,000 for *anything*—but they attached a check for $44 million. In Atlanta, where the previous high was $45,000, Gannett's WXIA bid $105,000—and turned out to be the only bidder."

Nationwide, the *Cosby* syndication brought in $4 million an episode, multiplied by the two hundred episodes eventually made. Then, in 1990–91, three years after the first sale, all two hundred were resold for broadcast when the initial five-year run was completed. This time the revenues were $1 million for each episode, bringing the overall total for *The Cosby Show* syndication to a nice, round $1 billion.

For a while, particularly in the early eighties, one-hour hits like *Magnum, P.I., The A-Team,* and *Fall Guy* were also attracting per-episode prices well over a million dollars. *Magnum* broke all records at more than $1.7 million, but its ratings fizzled well before its syndication run was completed. CBS's three prime-time soap operas, all of them long-running network hits, found syndication a whole new, and much tougher, ball game.

Dallas sold for more than $100 million but was a ratings disappointment and went off the air quickly. That expensive failure, together with the short syndication life of *Magnum,* changed everything. *Knots Landing* was sold at distress prices, and *Falcon Crest* never got sold. Even *Miami Vice,* NBC's upscale, high-demographic hit, found no takers at the asking price, and was eventually placed on the USA cable network. The difficulty of scheduling hour-long series in the highly profitable early-fringe time periods and the competition of hit comedies snuffed out the syndication marketplace for these longer shows.

Eventually, the flood of off-network situation comedies so saturated the sales arena that even those half-hour syndication staples fell victim to the law of supply and demand. Real hits like *Cheers, Roseanne,* and *Golden Girls* had no trouble attracting per-episode dollars as high as $2 million, but lesser shows had considerably less success. The marketplace had changed, probably forever, and producers were often faced with an unpleasant alternative: no sale, or sale to cable, where the dollars might barely cover the years of deficits.

The drying up of the syndication market, together with bad industry-wide economic conditions and the difficult new competitive environment, led to fundamental changes in programming. Piling up huge deficits each week without the real possibility of a big payoff on the back end had little appeal for producers. Hour-long shows suffered the double whammy of abysmal syndication prospects and weekly deficits that ran into the hundreds of thousands.

Universal, which had built its huge television production company with thirty years of successful one-hour series, now periodically grumbled, through MCA president Sid Sheinberg, that they no longer would produce them. Bob Daly, Warner Brothers' chairman, set a policy that his company no longer would produce programs that cost more to make than the network license fee plus immediate overseas sales revenues. Stephen Cannell, one of television's most successful independent producers, told *Variety* in 1992, "The networks' message to us has always been 'go ahead and lose money because you'll make it back on the other end.' They always want to give us a $900,000 license fee per hour and have us spend $1.2 million. But now we've got to tell them we can't survive doing business that way."

The short-term remedy was to cut production costs. Some producers of filmed dramatic shows found savings by moving away from the high union costs and large studio overhead of Los Angeles. Overall costs in places like Canada, Utah, Washington State, and Virginia could be as much as 25 to 30 percent lower, and shows could be shot in six days instead of seven.

Other savings have come from abandoning expensive carry-overs from the movie business. Not as many takes of each scene are being shot and instead of using 35mm film, the staple of the Hollywood studios, some shows are shooting in l6mm. Production staffs have shrunk as well. In the late eighties, a typical one-hour network show might have had:

> *3 executive producers at $17,500 each, per episode*
> *1 supervising producer at $15,000*
> *1 producer at $12,500*
> *1 executive story editor at $8,500*
> *2 story editors at $6,000 each*

Today, the staff might comprise:

> *1 executive producer at $25,000*
> *1 supervising producer at $17,500*
> *1 producer at $12,500*
> *1 story editor at $6,000*

That's four people instead of eight, and a salary savings of almost $40,000 an episode. Similar reductions have been effected throughout the production process. Fewer scripts are being commissioned, casts tend to be smaller, and gone are the days when every actor automatically makes more than he got in his last series. In addition, networks are less demanding about requiring big names for each role, so producers can use less-experienced actors who get paid less.

To viewers, the most noticeable change has been the proliferation of so-called reality programming. Long before economic conditions got to the crisis stage, the success of *60 Minutes* on CBS and then *20/20* on ABC led each network to start looking to its News division for prime-time help. At that stage, the attraction was not low cost but longevity, as well as schedule balance. Successful news programs seemed to stay on the air forever, unlike hit entertainment series, which invariably petered out after a few years and had to be replaced. But the hard part, as always, was to produce a program that would win the attention and loyalty of the prime-time audience.

When bad times hit in the late eighties, the networks had a more urgent reason for seeking reality programs. They cost less —much less. Often independently produced, the new reality shows feature everything from cops and emergency rescue teams to re-creations of actual events to home videos sent in by viewers.

Well after David Wolper's breakthrough in 1960, ABC, CBS, and NBC had maintained a no-outsider-need-apply rule for reality program production. Now, the pressures of the bottom line made that taboo a relic of the past. Networks were only too eager to turn over prime-time reality to producers of the tabloid fare they used to disparage, and to programs that looked suspiciously like that very fare. Bill Carter of *The New York Times* has called this category "the last refuge of desperate programmers," but the shows have spread across the schedules. They don't have high-priced stars and writers, they're done on tape instead of film, and the price is right. Some hours are made for as little as $400,000, less than half the cost of a studio-produced network drama. And they have the authoritative look of news programs.

The blurring of the line between reality and re-creation was noted in a December 1991 story by Carter, quoting Don Ohl-meyer, then the executive producer of ABC's *Heroes of Desert Storm:* "We're telling a real story. When we show a tank being blown up, what's the difference whether it was news footage or whether we blew it up ourselves?" Ohlmeyer—according to Ken Auletta's definitive book *Three Blind Mice*—had been offered the presidency of NBC News in 1989 but declined. Four years later, NBC put him in charge of its entire West Coast operation.

Networks began to whip their own News divisions to beef up their reality development. Ironically, these are the very divisions whose staff, bureaus, and budgets they had slashed during an earlier wave of serious cost reduction. Now, in the nineties, some news organizations are managed less as world-class journalistic institutions than as in-house sources of low-cost programming.

The glut of prime-time reality and news-related shows bought from various producers may have played a small part in acceler-ating the loss of network identity that began in the latter half of the eighties. In truth, that identity began to erode as the time-honored responsibilities that had always been part of the territory of network broadcasting gave way to the exigencies of business—or, to be more accurate, to how the new owners viewed those exigencies.

Viewers watch programs, not networks. So any network is known by its programs, and the programs that most identify a network are the ones it generates from within. Mostly, that means news. The flagship news programs have always represented the best work of the organizations, and justified the upkeep of bureaus and correspondents around the globe. Jennings, Brokaw, and Rather quickly suggest their respective employers, as do *Today, Meet the Press, 60 Minutes, 20/20,* and *Face the Nation.* Each of those programs serves almost as a logo for its network. Today, the proliferation of reality programming, with its dramatically altered journalistic standards, and the financial pressure on network news to use affiliate staffers domestically and stringers and foreign news agencies abroad, has homogenized the process. In the nineties, networks have become less likely to be known and identified by the news programs they produce, and the importance and quality of news have, sadly, diminished.

I have considerable impatience with the maximum profit fixation of the current network owners. Throughout the glory days of radio, and flowing naturally into television, certain obligations were understood to go hand in hand with being a broadcaster. Those fortunate enough to possess government-granted broadcasting licenses realized there was a quid pro quo. They owed their communities, from which they profited so handsomely, something in return—call it public service or just good citizenship. Their contribution could take the form of news, or informational, religious, and educational programming presented for the enlightenment of the audience. It might mean participation in a worthwhile community project. Invariably, the short-term financial result would be cost, not profit. Most network chieftains and station owners have always understood that, and paid their dues.

Networks are nothing more than a collection of some two hundred affiliated local stations, a handful of which they own themselves. While networks per se are not licensed, they used to be run by people who acknowledged the same unique franchise obligation on a national basis as each station did locally. Again, discharging that obligation usually represents cost, or at least foregoing profit opportunities. The whole history of network news, at least until the mid-eighties, is a case in point.

Unlike every newspaper in America, the fundamental business of a television network is not news. Television networks, whose only income is from advertisers who want to reach the largest possible number of viewers, are in the mass-appeal business. Entertainment programs with low ratings—meaning rejection by the public—don't survive. But for decades news not only survived, it thrived. Networks used to support their News divisions with annual budgets in the hundreds of millions, often with red ink on the bottom line at year's end. The people who ran the networks from the time there *were* networks—broadcasters all —"paid the two dollars" as a matter of course. No one thought of a News division as a separate company obligated to run at a profit; news was the jewel in the crown that was to be cherished and supported by a highly profitable entertainment schedule. It was what made a network great.

The most vivid example of how broadcasters feel about news came in the seventies, when ABC finally fought its way to competitive parity with the other networks. After finishing third in prime time for fifteen years, ABC won its first season ever in 1976–77. Now that it was finally making good money, Leonard Goldenson's network chose to spend a lot of it on news. They gave the vastly talented Roone Arledge, who had made ABC Sports the best in the business, the additional responsibility of running ABC News. As Goldenson said in his own book, "Our prime-time schedule was going like a house afire. We were starting to make progress in daytime and in morning; and now, I felt, we could at long last start pumping in the resources to make ABC News competitive with CBS and NBC." Goldenson believed, as we all did, that no network could lay claim to industry leadership without a world-class news organization. And he put his money where his mouth was.

The new owners come from a different world, and they do not share the traditional values of network broadcasters. Their focus is on the bottom line, and every part of the company is expected to pull its financial weight. That philosophy works fine in the manufacturing world; get rid of unprofitable divisions and you grow and prosper. In television, some of the activities that may not produce a profit, particularly news, are the very elements that give a network its special character—and distinguish it from all those other choices on the dial.

In the past, for reasons ranging from romantic to self-serving, network heads always felt there was more to life than just the Nielsens. That was the attraction of network broadcasting, the intangible that made it a different kind of business. Here was this great national franchise that gave three companies direct access to every home in the country. The possibilities seemed limitless. Pat Weaver invented the *Today* show not as a moneymaker—it was in the red for ten years—but because he saw it as a valuable service that only network television could provide. Bob Kintner built NBC News and encouraged and promoted Weaver's legacy of specials in order to be better than CBS—even when the competition made more money. But these kinds of decisions would have no counterpart in the nineties.

Laying off correspondents, closing bureaus, and deep-sixing documentaries certainly saves money in the short run. But to the degree that corporate financial pressures injure the credibility of a news organization and shift its programming focus from good journalism to ratings, they are disastrous. News producers who allow the rigging of a car crash to produce a spectacular fire do so because they believe attracting a big audience is what they've been hired to do. It's up to top management to get the priorities straight.

As the nineties arrived and the economic downturn began to exacerbate the already declining fortunes of the big three networks, still other dollar-saving measures were employed. Not entirely surprisingly, very few of the people in the Entertainment divisions walked the plank even in those days of company-wide austerity. That was because management knew that the big bucks were generated in the prime-time periods those folks were charged with programming. What management should also have known, though, was that those same divisions were vastly overstaffed, resulting in the creation of make-work jobs. Too many high-paid executives meddled with producers' creative work, which thus became less efficient and more costly to the buying networks.

There were many areas of NBC in which I had never worked during either of my two prior tours. When I returned as chairman and CEO in mid-1981, I knew I would need to go slowly while I got a little education. That delay wasn't going to be necessary in the Entertainment division. In one way or another, I had been in the program business since I first joined NBC in 1949, and I returned to NBC with some firm intentions in that area.

My most explicit resolve was to thin out the Entertainment division at least by half. This was not so much a cost-saving measure, though that would have been a desirable by-product, as a belief, based on my experience across the whole spectrum of the business, that leaner is better. I had seen too many promising programs spoiled by having too many cooks, usually in the network kitchens. And the best creative people, I knew, need help the least and resent and resist it the most.

MTM had grown and prospered by *not* trying to do the producers' jobs for them; some of the most celebrated television ever produced had been the result of noninterference. The only way to ensure that NBC would enjoy the same kind of results would be to behave, as a network, in a similar manner. Fewer people would mean less opportunity to smother creative work with too much "supervision."

But when I rejoined NBC, resolve notwithstanding, I hesitated to implement that plan. I rationalized that to take so harsh an action so quickly would send exactly the wrong signal to a company that already had a considerable morale problem. Moreover, Brandon Tartikoff clearly did not feel he had too many troops. He was a graduate of another school of thought. It may be useful to take a quick look at that school and its founder/headmaster.

Let me start with a disclaimer: I am a great admirer of Fred Silverman, both for what he accomplished as a programmer at CBS and ABC, and equally for his truly remarkable comeback in the production business after his rough sledding at NBC. But Fred, at least in his network days, was a walking contradiction. He wanted a zillion lieutenants and foot soldiers around him twenty-four hours a day, yet he was a complete hands-on executive who never thought a job would get done unless he did it himself. He was a one-man band who always had a whole lot of other musicians simply sitting around holding their instruments (so to speak).

In my opinion, Fred invented the Entertainment division bureaucracies as producers have come to know and deplore them. And because he worked successively at all three networks, like Typhoid Mary he infected them all as he went. Not only did he overpopulate each one as he arrived, but he left a lot of disciples behind when he moved on. To this day, they continue to multiply like rabbits, destroying whole gardens of potential programs as they trample over all but the most celebrated and stalwart producers. Today, Fred Silverman, the producer, must contend with legions of the same network functionaries he fathered, although I'm not sure he acknowledges paternity.

Not only are there too many network executives, they are usually too young, too inexperienced, and too given to taking their titles, their assigned duties, and their designated authority far too seriously. Most of them were "born and raised in the building." They've never written or directed or produced a show, but they haven't the least hesitation about telling professional and experienced program suppliers how to do all those things and more.

Obviously there are some networkers who don't deserve that sweeping indictment, or who do have legitimate credits, but not that many. Those few know enough to let the creative people do their work, helping when asked and getting out of the way otherwise. I am speaking here about projects that are commissioned, or ordered, by the networks. Most submissions by producers never get beyond the original presentation—not to pilot, not even to script. Many deserve to die early deaths, but uncounted others are killed at the entry-point by people who wouldn't recognize potential in a project if it leapt over their coffee tables and bit them.

There is another way network Entertainment divisions penalize themselves in putting too much responsibility in inexperienced hands. Young buyers of programs tend to be more comfortable with sellers their own age; the result is known as "graylisting," usually inadvertent but no less damaging to both parties. This practice is common enough to have become a matter of considerable concern to the creative guilds, whose older members have been its victims. They either don't get into the tent to present their wares in the first place, or their ideas are rejected out of generational bias. The television audience is the loser, and so is the medium itself. One might even speculate, not too idly, that the qualitative level of network programming has fallen as a result of this unfortunate behavior, all of which could be cured by placing more experienced practitioners in those network chairs.

I returned to NBC with very clear knowledge of all the foregoing, and with the strong opinion that Brandon Tartikoff, though just past thirty himself, was definitely an exception, a genuine product of Fred Silverman's renowned "golden gut." I've heard many times since that onlookers expected me to replace him as soon as I took over, but my intention was exactly the opposite. Even before reporting for duty myself, I phoned Brandon to tell him I hoped he would stay on. I had the strong conviction, from having dealt with him on a number of occasions, that he had the goods—particularly the programming instincts that are essential to that job.

At the same time, I was determined that in my administration, NBC would not be guilty of the network sins of the past. In the production community I was leaving, I had shared plenty of complaints about how networks behaved. A change in NBC's act would be well received by my former counterparts, I knew, a plus for NBC's own interest. I wanted the very best creative people to find NBC the most hospitable network, offering the most comfortable and pleasant working relationships. That had made the difference at MTM, and it should have the same results at NBC.

Yet I put most of my good intentions on the back burner as I got into my new duties. In addition to the low state of company morale, and the need for me to be a quick study in a number of unfamiliar areas, I soon learned the truth of what I had told Thornton Bradshaw at lunch. The job really was in New York, where NBC and its parent were headquartered. And benign though RCA was in the hands of Bradshaw, it still required ceremonial attention and various kinds of stroking, official and otherwise. There was no way I could do the job from California. In short, I was up to my ass in alligators I not only hadn't tamed, but hadn't yet met. In an effort to moonlight back into the program business as I began my weekly transcontinental commute, I took a second office in Burbank, where I managed to be most Fridays. On those days I would get to spend some time with Brandon.

It's a bit of a leap from knowing a guy as a customer to suddenly becoming his boss. But I'm not that hard to get along with, and Brandon managed a nice blend of deference and partnership. Though we were a generation apart, I don't remember a single instance when we didn't communicate easily and effectively. That's not to say I always told him everything I was thinking, and I know he would say the same. Sometimes our agendas differed, as did our jobs. But if he experienced any uneasiness, he hid it well. We both knew what his job was, and I'm sure he quickly realized I wasn't going to try to do it for him. He gracefully allowed me to participate in programming matters when I was inclined to, and as my corporate duties permitted.

Clearly we had one thing in common: We both had immense respect for good creative talent and wanted as much of it working for NBC as we could attract. That meant establishing a reputation for letting those people do what they were inspired to do, and not to arbitrarily impose network "improvement" on their output. As had happened at MTM, not only would the good people tend to stay with us, but they would spread the word that NBC was a warm and cozy company with which to do business. We agreed that hospitality would be our M.O., and over the next few years that policy produced real prime-time dividends.

The trade-off during that period was that I never suggested to Brandon, certainly not in any manner remotely close to a directive, that we reduce the division workforce. Because we were working well and cooperatively together, I went along with his belief that his numerous minions, officers and noncoms, were all essential to the mission of the Entertainment division. No one was invited to take a hike.

And by the time our comeback was underway in 1984, it would have been churlish not to let everyone stay awhile to savor our considerable accomplishment. For that matter, at the distance from which I observed the Entertainment division, I would have been hard-pressed to identify the more expendable members of the team—although I had some specific notions—and Brandon believed more than ever that all on board performed necessary functions.

Finally, in mid-1985, I acknowledged that a company-wide review of all costs was appropriate and overdue. It was barely launched when General Electric swallowed RCA whole, including NBC. With the new owners on the way in, our cost study slowed to a relative crawl, as did most activities that didn't simply execute our basic business duties.

Unlike Fred Silverman, Jack Welch, GE's CEO, never met a company that couldn't be improved by a bit of shrinkage—and more improved by a lot of shrinkage. Not long after GE took charge, with me barely out of sight, studies were undertaken in earnest, and bodies began flying out the windows. Predictably, the rationale for the downsizing was ascribed to the cost review the prior administration (that's me) had put in motion. And why not? There was no point in the new owner taking the rap for unpopular policies and practices until it had to—and it would provide plenty of opportunity for that soon enough. The irony was that none of the population reduction occurred in the swollen Entertainment division. Welch had quickly and correctly identified that area as the big profit producer, and he wasn't about to tamper with it at all.

So thanks to my temporizing with my original instinct to thin out the executive ranks in Burbank, compounded by GE understandably not having a clue when they arrived as to how television programs get commissioned and made, the bureaucracy lives on to this day. For similar reasons, that inefficient situation also persists at CBS and ABC, in spite of the fact that they, too, are now run by owners with very sharp pencils. Only the newcomer, Fox, is lean and mean. Fred Silverman never worked there.

One of the many men who headed Programming for NBC was David Levy, who had the job from 1959 to 1961. Today he's largely retired, but he remains active in Hollywood. He has published a couple of novels about television, *The Chameleons* and *The Network Jungle,* and wrote me a while back to ask if I'd compose something laudatory for the jacket of his latest effort. I was somewhat surprised that he'd expect a "blind" endorsement, and called him to say I couldn't do the blurb without first seeing the book.

Levy was quick to agree my point was well taken, and promised to forward the galleys. In the course of our conversation, he mentioned a couple of other people from whom he'd already secured quotes of praise. One of them was Jack Valenti, the hugely capable and respected president of the Motion Picture Association of America, and my longtime and cherished good friend.

In due course, the book arrived, and I read enough to know exactly what I'd want to say for public consumption. Something else in the publisher's packet caught my eye, and prompted me to fire off a letter to Valenti.

Dear Jack:

David Levy has written me a note asking for a line or two of praise for his new book, Potomac Jungle. *He hopes that my comments "would express positive and affirmative reactions to the novel."*

He mentions that you, among others, have already agreed to contribute your own approbation. And he encloses uncor-

rected proofs which do indeed have your puffery prominently represented on the back of the jacket.

Forgive me, Jack, but I'm guessing that you've never read Potomac Jungle. *And you probably never will and probably will never admit it.*

Is the renowned Valenti probity another casualty of our times? Say it ain't so.

Best,
Grant

Two days later, Jack was on the phone. "You got me! I haven't even seen Levy's book, but when he wrote I just didn't know how to say no. I certainly didn't have time to read the damned thing. What did you do?"

"Well, I certainly wasn't going to give him a blind rave like the one you gave him," I told him self-righteously.

"So you're turning him down?"

"No, I read enough to give him a quote he'll like, and which won't compromise my integrity the way you blatantly compromised yours."

"How the hell do you do that?"

It's a rare treat to one-up Valenti. Smugly, I read him my letter to David Levy:

Dear David:

Here's a quote about Potomac Jungle *you are certainly welcome to use if you wish:*

David Levy's pen has not lost its skill. Potomac Jungle *is every bit as gripping as* The Chameleons *and* The Network Jungle. *Page for page, just as spellbinding a read.*

Hope that works for you, David.

Best,
Grant

Jack loved it.

Among his many other attributes, Valenti is one of the most accomplished public speakers I know. His job requires him to make countless talks at luncheons, dinners, and industry gatherings of all kinds, and given his diverse duties as "the world's highest-paid lobbyist," I had always assumed he was just a natural orator who could almost phone in any lectern assignment. Hearing that, Jack was shocked to the point of being insulted.

I challenged him. "You mean you write all those speeches yourself?"

"Not only do I write every word of every speech, but I rewrite each one several times."

"How many times?"

It was my turn to be shocked. "Ten, maybe twelve times," he said, which explained why his speeches were invariably well written and well delivered.

Throughout the early years of my business life, I was terrified to get up and talk to more than three people at a time. Meetings were fine, but more formal events could induce something close to a panic attack. Colleagues would breeze through sales pitches or presentations to clients; I would change jobs to avoid them.

Over the years, very gradually, I have overcome my anxieties about speaking in public. Today I can acquit myself reasonably well at a podium, occasionally, when I've prepared properly, very well. I'll never be a match for Jack Valenti in that department, but I do share his compulsion to write my own speeches. If a group invites me to talk, I figure they want to hear my thoughts, not those of someone else, and if they're going to give me an award, they certainly deserve to be thanked in my own words.

During my last term of service at NBC, I had five opportunities to deliver to the annual affiliates convention the "chairman's message"—four at the Century Plaza Hotel in Los Angeles and my swan song on the island of Maui. I worked hard to give NBC's station partners encouraging but straightforward accounts of where we stood. That assignment got easier as our performance improved, and my talks reflected the company's changing condition.

My first such appearance, in May 1982, was the most difficult. The two-hundred-plus affiliates would be getting their first live look at me. If they didn't conclude that Bradshaw had picked the right horse, keeping them on board through a long and painful recovery period was going to be an impossible task. And after several years' slide into third place, they were not in the mood for platitudes.

I spent the first few minutes ticking off NBC's assets, which were largely our good people, who were equally sick of losing. I then devoted plenty of time to recognizing our considerable problems, because I wanted the affiliates to be sure I knew the extent of them. With nothing in the way of improvement to point to at the network, I drew shamelessly on my reputation as a programmer in order to end on a positive note.

Programming, with all its uncertainties and intangibles, is still closer to an exact science than it is to black magic. It is, after all, nothing more than the product of creative people. The better the creative people, the more likely the product will be good. In my twelve years at MTM, I learned that lesson over and over.

It's that MTM experience that makes me so sure that the theory is sound. I am frequently and inaccurately credited with having produced MTM's successful shows, a mistake I don't usually knock myself out to correct. In truth, I produced none of the MTM shows, which were fashioned by a collection of talented members of the creative community. . . .

Now, programming NBC and running an independent production company are two different-sized jobs, but the approach is exactly the same. If we can get our hands on more than our share of those "best creative people," we will inexorably improve our relative standing. There are only so many of those coveted creators, not enough to program three networks, and everyone we capture is one the competition must do without. Sad to say, NBC has not been their first port of call lately. It's just been too hard to have a hit on NBC.

Lastly, we have had the reputation of sometimes according creative people, or at least the fruits of their labors, insufficient respect. In its frantic attempts to compete in recent years, NBC has jerked around its schedule, moving programs too often and with usually negative results.

Those of us at 30 Rock or in Burbank need to know that you are with us, and that we are all pulling in the same direction. You've been promised a rose garden before, and you've gotten mostly weeds. If you believe, we'll meet here at the Century Plaza a year from now, and we'll talk about how far we've come, and how to go farther.

The affiliate convention wound up that night with the traditional star-studded banquet, with as much talent from NBC shows as we could cajole into showing up. For many of them it was a trip to the dentist, but most of them comported themselves in a manner that gave affiliates and their wives a feeling of being part of the NBC family.

The affiliates' comments to me were positive and encouraging. I might not have won their hearts completely yet, but it appeared I hadn't bombed. On the contrary, most seemed to be as happy as NBC's sorry circumstances permitted. I was gratified by their reaction, because it meant I could count on their patience and faith while we struggled to get our house (and theirs) in order.

I am very secure about some things and not terribly secure about others. I don't particularly care whether people love me (as opposed to like me), but I do care about the impression I make. And when I feel I have been unfairly judged, or misjudged, I tend to fret about it.

One recent Sunday morning, for example, browsing through *The New York Times,* I happened upon a piece about Roger and Michael King—the formidable brothers who run King World, the enormously successful company that syndicates *Oprah, Jeopardy,* and *Wheel of Fortune,* among other television activities. In an accompanying sidebar, Jim Coppersmith, president of WCVB-TV in Boston, a major buyer of King World programming, was quoted as saying of the Kings: "I like street people. They have a reverse chic style. They are not Grant Tinker, with the $2,000 suit, the 32-inch waist and the Gucci loafers. They are big healthy guys who look more like wrestlers. They're not like studio guys who come in their Armani shirts and have nicer tushes than their wives. I hope I never get into a barroom fight, but if I do, I hope it's with the King brothers on my side."

Whatever I was scheduled to do first on Monday morning gave way to the following:

Dear Jim:

Have we ever met?
    Since I don't think we have, here are a few facts about me:
    1. I have never bought or owned a $2,000 suit, or even come close.
    2. I have never bought or worn Gucci loafers.

3. I don't know an Armani shirt when I see one.
4. I haven't had a 32-inch waist, if I ever had one at all,
probably since you acquired a 32-inch mouth.

All I know about you is that you are into "big healthy guys"
and men's "tushes." Sounds like you will need the Kings in
that barroom fight you hope never to get into.

In the language of the street people you prefer: Go fuck
yourself.

Best,
Grant

A week later, Mr. Coppersmith responded. He had taken my
rude correspondence in good humor and wrote me a funny note
to prove it. But I was still glad I'd written him in the first place.

The year after my first affiliate outing was not spent quite so
frivolously. Everyone at NBC, from New York to Burbank,
leaned into the job, and there was plenty to lean into. During the
1981–82 television season, we did not have a single program in
the top twenty.

But the audience had finally found *Hill Street Blues,* and the
show, which won the prestigious Peabody Award and eight
Emmy Awards (a record for one season) in 1981, was generating
a lot of kudos for itself and for NBC. At the same time, Barbara
Mandrell told Brandon and me over lunch at the Bel Air Hotel
that for personal reasons she would have to stop doing her variety show, which was making our Saturday night presentable. It
was an unusual request, yet there was nothing to do but reluc-
tantly let her go.

While we had seen no ratings improvement yet, we were at
least managing NBC in a more efficient, businesslike manner.
The frantic churning of the program schedule had been stopped,
and the resulting stability had improved the bottom line somewhat. So there was a modicum of hope in the air as we returned
to the Century Plaza the following May. This time I brought to
the podium a little less gloom and a bit of good cheer.

I began with some impromptu comments about the fall schedule we had all seen that morning, which included *St. Elsewhere,*

Family Ties, Fame, Cheers, Hill Street, and *Remington Steele.* Most would take time to achieve appreciable ratings, but it was already apparent that we were moving in the direction of quality, as promised.

Next I shared with the affiliates excerpts from a couple of viewer letters I had recently received. The first gave new meaning to the expression *captive audience:*

> *As a lifer in California's Folsom Prison, I never knew I could feel sorry for anyone, but I must confess that your situation, i.e., those damnable ratings vs. your generally excellent programming, almost breaks my heart.*

The other letter was my favorite:

> *I'm an old man. I haven't liked anything on TV since* Perry Mason. *The kid who delivers my groceries told me to watch* Remington Steele, *because he knows I like mysteries. I did, and that kid's not so dumb. It's the best thing I've seen since* Perry Mason. *I thought I'd let you know, because by the time you get another show that I might like as well I'll probably be dead.*

The affiliates enjoyed those missives as much as I had, and I moved into my prepared material while the mood of the room was friendly:

> *I'd like to spend my few minutes picking up where I left off last year, when I talked about inertia and about plans to overcome it. This year, just up to a point, I want to talk in terms of momentum and achievement—for instance, our improved financial performance in 1982 and so far in 1983.*
>
> *That's not just good for us, it's good for you. It provides strength and resources. In prime time we are up, and the competition is down, in the demographic quality of our audience. We sell it, and so do you. Our audience is younger, another positive signpost pointing to our future growth and yours. But we want it all; we want quantity of audience as well as quality.*

Again, though, I was frank about deficiencies:

> *Let me say it straight out: We are satisfied with nothing. Pro-*
> *grams, people, policies, plans—all are subject to review and*
> *change, not capriciously and not thoughtlessly, but there are*
> *no sacred cows, nothing is set in concrete. We are a network*
> *in progress. I want to put the word* stability *in its proper*
> *lowercase place. It works for us, we don't work for it. . . .*
>   *Ours is a formidable task which does not lend itself to a*
> *quick fix. I say ours because I'm speaking on behalf of the*
> *NBC management team. . . . We are not a laid-back group of*
> *losers. Our company impatience with the state of things is a*
> *palpable, positive, motivating force—and that force is begin-*
> *ning to be felt.*

Some real evidence of that force would be seen a few months
later when we dominated the Emmy Awards show, winning a
total of thirty-three, more than ABC and CBS combined.

The telecast of the event turned out to be a mixed bag, however. Production of the program rotated annually among the
three networks, and it was our year. Steve Sohmer, NBC's vice
president of advertising and promotion, who deserves a great
deal of credit for his skillful support of our programs during our
recovery, overreached himself that night. As NBC won Emmy
after Emmy, the black tie audience at the Pasadena Civic Center
was mercilessly bombarded, via monitors, with self-serving and
self-congratulatory promotional announcements. The television
audience was seeing the same promos, which was standard practice, but piping them into the hall was bad form. Ultimately, a
good portion of the audience, all industry people, began to hiss
and boo each new announcement. It was criticism NBC deserved;
luckily it went unheard by the viewers at home. Moreover, the
live broadcast was co-hosted by Joan Rivers and Eddie Murphy,
and some of Joan's remarks were judged to be a tad raunchy for
the all-family audience. She comedied through herpes, prosti-
tutes, and homosexuals, and at one point allowed that Joan Col-
lins's character on *Dynasty* "has had more hands up her dress
than the Muppets." All this on the network that was trying to
head uptown.

I took a hit of my own that evening, one that proved yet again that no good deed goes unpunished. It had been pretty much my idea, the prior fall, to pick up *Taxi,* the very funny ensemble comedy that ABC decided had run out of gas. It was created and produced by four *Mary* alumni, aided and abetted by several other escapees from my erstwhile production company, altogether as talented a group as television ever assembled. Our hope was that *Taxi,* following *Cheers* at 9:30 Thursday night, would exhibit renewed strength on our network, but that hope was never realized during the season, and it was known by the time of the Emmy show that we would not be renewing it.

As luck would have it, the program's decline didn't prevent Judd Hirsch from winning the award for Outstanding Lead Actor in a Comedy Series. Not that he didn't deserve it—the son-of-a-bitch is a wonderful actor. He chose to make his acceptance speech in the form of a diatribe about NBC, and about me personally. My seat for the telecast was down in front, just below the stage level, so, during the Hirsch harangue, unavoidable reaction shots of me gave the world a good, long look at the network schmuck who had been so stupid and crass as to cancel *Taxi.*

I was steamed, but there was nothing to be done. I could only wait for Hirsch to wind down what seemed like an endless complaint. After the program was over, many people criticized him for his ingratitude toward the network that had given his show an additional year of life. But I didn't get any satisfaction until about a year later, when an American Airlines flight attendant handed me a note of apology, handwritten by Judd, who was sitting somewhere behind me. I didn't even turn around to acknowledge it, allowing myself my little retaliation, though unfortunately not one televised nationally.

The months just before my third affiliate convention had seen the departure of Bob Mulholland and the arrival of Larry Grossman. Larry acquitted himself admirably before the affiliates, as he does behind a desk.

NBC had survived a disastrous beginning of the 1983–84 season. Gone was every single one of the nine new shows we had selected and scheduled in the fall. Fortunately, the affiliate convention didn't come around until May, by which time they had all been replaced. In the intervening months, our recovery had begun. The growing strength of some of our second-year shows

—Brandon Tartikoff called them "sophomores"—more than off-set our fall transgressions. I gave the latter short shrift on the way to more philosophical matters:

> *Occasionally I see or hear comments which suggest that I personally embrace some kind of program elitism that is offended by what works today. People who hold that view have seen only the MTM successes. They were spared our failures, which looked exactly like most other failed programs.*
>
> *At MTM, the handful of programs we produced each season had a look often generously described as "quality." That was because we did the kind of program that interested us, because we attracted a group of creative people whose interests were similar to ours, and, most important, because we had the luxury of doing only a few series each year.*
>
> *At a network, any network, the mission is quite different. Instead of running a boutique which attracts only people with the same taste as ours, we're running a giant department store, which has everyone in the country as a potential customer. If we're doing our job well, we're appealing to a great diversity of tastes—not just our own. . . .*
>
> *To some critics, nothing is quality unless it's on PBS and used to be on the BBC. Others are a little less doctrinaire. Quality is truly in the eye of the beholder, and most of the people who are paid by newspapers to behold television have treated NBC kindly. Even though some do have difficulty understanding that we are a department store and not a boutique.*
>
> *I don't have that difficulty. Our job is to get all of America into our tent, and we're going to be doing that with programs that have great popular appeal. You've seen some of them this morning. They are well written, well produced, and will be, I think, well received.*

I closed, uncharacteristically, with a confident claim: "As we look toward fall, for the first time we have the horses. In short, we're ready."

That claim had become reality a year later, when the affiliates met again. In 1984–85 we were competitive all day and all night, and in the center ring—prime time—we were about to become the eight-hundred-pound gorilla. NBC was a real factor again, and it was great to be able to hold up our heads among our broadcasting peers.

The two principal peers were enjoying a different kind of excitement. Tom Murphy and Cap Cities had recently taken over ABC, and several interested parties were sniffing around CBS. In an interview in *U.S. News & World Report,* I had been quoted as saying, "I don't spend a lot of time thinking about network takeovers. . . . We at NBC, given our RCA parentage, are probably the least likely to be taken over." Events, of course, were to give ample evidence that I suffered from rampant myopia.

Murphy may momentarily have had some second thoughts about Cap Cities' acquisition as we opened the ratings gap between our second place and ABC's worsening third and took dead aim at CBS. By the end of the full 1984–85 season we would move to the head of the pack. From that vantage point, I could tell L. J. Davis, writing in *Channels* magazine, our recipe for success:

> *It's been my experience that if I can associate myself with good people, good producers, good executives to man the network barricades, then it really does work if I get out of the way and let them do their jobs. If you ask me what I do here all day, the answer is not very much.*
>
> *That's the beauty of delegating. I encourage people, I praise them, and if I think someone has a terrible idea, I gently try to dissuade them, I guess. Once in a while, I've actually been grown up enough to let them go ahead and do it anyway, knowing that the project would fall to earth, or feeling that it would. You have to let people have their enthusiasms, most of which are good, and you also have to let them fail.*

By the time the 1985 affiliates' convention rolled around, I was able to say:

> *We have really come a long way—not swiftly, but surely. A couple of verities are taking shape. The first is that our program and schedule strategy really works. That's the one that calls for recruiting the best creative people, making them comfortable in a supportive environment, putting the pro-*

grams they produce in time periods where they have a chance to succeed, promoting those programs with great patience until, almost inevitably, they do succeed.

The second verity has a vaguely familiar ring; it may have predated television. It is that nothing succeeds like success. If one daypart begins to work, it's going to have a beneficial effect on another daypart, and then both on a third. Or, one news program on another from the same division. Or, the station or network you turn off at night tends to be the one you turn on in the morning. A synergy throughout and across the schedule. Once it's born, it grows. Or, the parts grow together.

And finally, almost four years after sitting down to lunch with Thornton Bradshaw, I could risk a little predicting:

If I must get into the prediction business, let me do it in a way that certainly won't stop the presses. I have no trouble saying right out loud, not that we will be first (I'll leave that to others), but that we will be best. The best in ways that Nielsen and Arbitron don't measure. The best in ways that critics do remark on, the best in ways that will cause viewers in cable homes to continue coming back to NBC, the best in ways that already attract audiences advertisers most want to reach.

Of course, it will be an exciting day when NBC is finally number one, and not just in prime time—but literally, and profitably, from sign-on to sign-off. I don't have to sell the magic of that moment; all of you have waited for it longer than I have. But it will only be a ranking in a ratings war that's taken on an exaggerated life of its own.

It will not change what we, you and NBC, already are. And that is—the best. And we're going to get still better.

That's a prediction—going on a fact.

Would you like to try for best and first?

It has a nice ring.

Six months later General Electric would devour RCA—lock, stock, and NBC—in one calendar week. It would be many months before the takeover was legally complete, somewhat delaying the departure I had planned to coincide with the end of my five-year enlistment.

Among my duties during that interim period was the "selling" of our new parentage to those in the company who were not thrilled by the prospect. Since, at the time, I considered the change salutary, I talked it up with sincerity and enthusiasm. I was also trying to sell my recommendations about my successors to Jack Welch. I wouldn't realize until much later that he never seriously considered them.

But most of our energy during those months went into increasing NBC's lead over the competition, pouring it on. Our prime-time schedule was a powerhouse, boasting *Remington Steele, St. Elsewhere, The Cosby Show, Family Ties, Cheers, Night Court, Hill Street Blues, The A-Team, Miami Vice, Highway to Heaven, The Golden Girls, Hunter,* and *Facts of Life.* And *L.A. Law* and *Matlock* were warming up. We called it the Championship Season.

The fifth and last time I stood in front of the affiliate body was on Maui. We had changed the convention venue as a way of celebrating the robust good health of our network and the two-hundred-plus stations that comprised it. We traded the ill winds of yesterday for the balmy breezes of Hawaii—a well-earned upgrade. It was no secret that I would be leaving NBC (taking retirement at sixty, actually) in two or three months, as soon as the RCA-GE transition was complete.

I spared the affiliates a long harangue about expectations. NBC was flying in virtually all dayparts, and in the big ball game—prime time—we were dominant. Very little needed to be said, and my prepared text ran only a couple of pages.

> *First be best, then be first. I said that at last year's affiliate convention in the hope that it would come true. Thankfully for all of us, it has. For the first time in recent television history, NBC is the number-one network in prime time. I think we can all take pride in the way the battle was won. We stayed with our quality shows. We gave our audience a chance to find them, and, sure enough, they did. . . .*
>
> *With all this good news, we seem to be heavy on opportunities, yet we do have our challenges. We must avoid complacency. We must remember what it took to get us where we are*

now. With cable services, independent stations, videocassettes, and direct broadcast, the viewer now has more and better choices than ever before.

The competition is going to be stiffer. Our biggest challenge is to continue our quest for quality and innovation. Our goal remains the same: Provide the viewer information and entertainment of quality and diversity. Our current leadership in both ratings and technology uniquely positions us to meet the competitive challenges. Together we worked hard to be best. And now it is our challenge to stay first.

I made a few heartfelt remarks of thanks and good-bye, particularly brief because I suddenly found myself nearly overcome with emotion. I was presented with a couple of gifts, by far the most meaningful of which was a poem, full of praise and gratitude, wonderfully written by Eric Bremner, then president of King Broadcasting and chairman of the NBC affiliate board.

What was certainly a tremendous sense of accomplishment was matched by the realization that I wasn't going to be leading these troops anymore. The long-odds business challenge I'd taken on had become, in the doing, a very personal matter—to a degree I fully appreciated only at that moment. I got off in a hurry.

The easiest management decisions are the black and white ones, because they essentially make themselves. It's the gray ones, often involving conflicting interests and values, that are tough. I've always been most comfortable with a more collegial process, where everyone concerned has the opportunity to talk through the issue and make recommendations. That way, when the head guy has to call the ultimate shot, he's doing it with the best information available to him.

But sometimes there's simply no call for that kind of participatory democracy. Sometimes the boss has to go by his gut, hold his nose, and jump. Over time, and sometimes in a flash, a company becomes known by the choices it has made, and that reputation can be as important as numbers on the bottom line.

One day in my office, I listened for the first time to Howard Stern on our New York radio station, WNBC. While I was aware of his reputation as a "shock jock" and his success at attracting an ever-growing audience, it's a measure of my preoccupation with NBC Television that I had never before been part of that audience.

I had a particular reason for listening-in that afternoon. A man from Randolph, New Jersey, had written a long and thoughtful letter to Thornton Bradshaw, describing a car trip with his young children. He had switched on the radio to WNBC just in time to hear Howard Stern speculating about what size tampon might be required to outfit the Statue of Liberty. Over the next few minutes, before switching the station, he and his children were regaled with a discussion of lesbian lovemaking techniques. His question to Brad was whether this was the sort of program RCA thought its NBC subsidiary ought to be broadcasting.

Brad's practice was to send all NBC-related correspondence to us for response, and my office would forward it to Bud Rukeyser. NBC responded to every one of the thousands of pieces of viewer mail we received each year, and Corporate Communications would decide from whom the reply should come and who should receive copies. Many letters were prepared by the executives who signed them; others were written by Bud's staff.

The complaint about Howard Stern was sent for reply to the general manager of WNBC. Before he got around to answering it, another letter from the man in New Jersey wound up on Bud's desk. This one took us to task for our lack of response, which he assumed meant we didn't give a damn. Bud picked up the phone and called him, then told me that the man from Randolph not only sounded sensible, but had voiced concerns that many NBC executives had expressed among themselves. Clearly, it was time for me to tune in.

As I listened that day, I was appalled and embarrassed that our NBC-owned station was the forum for Howard Stern. The program was so foul in subject matter and language that a listener could only conclude that the FCC had thrown up its hands about monitoring content. I asked Bob Walsh to join me in my office. Bob had long experience in station management, and was (and is) a respected broadcaster and a solid citizen.

"Bob, what the hell are we doing with Howard Stern on WNBC?" I greeted him.

"I think he's the pits," Bob replied, "but our guys [his WNBC station people] think he's going to be huge, right through the roof. Right now, he's the difference between profit and loss at the station. I assumed you knew all about him."

"If that's the only way to make money," I said, "we shouldn't be in business. Let's get rid of him as fast as we can."

Though he was well aware that Stern's pastiche of sexual references was getting big ratings for WNBC, Walsh instantly agreed. "I'd like nothing better," he said, although he predicted that Stern would go right across the street to some competing station and get the same kind of numbers against us.

"Yeah, he probably will, but it's still an easy call. Let somebody else put that shit on the air. It just shouldn't be us."

And so we fired Howard Stern, who today thrives on a number of stations around the country, exactly as Bob predicted. For people inside and outside the company, letting Stern go sent a message about what kind of corporate citizen NBC wanted—and didn't want—to be.

Stern wasn't pleased to get the boot. To this day, he occasionally talks on the air about his firing from NBC, referring to me as the culprit. No doubt he thinks I simply made a bad business judgment, but I'm always thrilled when someone tells me Howard's again given me the credit.

I recalled that decision following the 1992 Los Angeles riots, when an uneasy relationship prevailed between the police and young African Americans in virtually every large city in the country. Warner Bros. Records chose that very delicate moment to release an album, entitled *Body Count,* featuring a rap singer named Ice-T. One cut, "Cop Killer," became instantly notorious:

> *I'm 'bout to bust some shots off*
> *I'm 'bout to dust some cops off*
>
> *Die, die, die, pig, die!!*

President Bush spoke out against the release of a record that celebrated the killing of police officers, and most Americans agreed with him. Parent company Time Warner was flooded with calls and letters of protest, and some sixty members of Congress signed a letter beseeching the company to withdraw the album from sale. Police associations threatened to boycott Time Warner products and services, and to sell the stock. As the din of outrage grew, the ACLU and a few other self-appointed guardians of our rights and liberties leapt to the defense on freedom of speech grounds.

As it happened, the chief executive officer of Time Warner was only a couple of months into the job of running the media colossus. The unfortunate health problems of Time Warner chairman Steve Ross, following a round of executive musical chairs, had combined to put Jerry Levin at the desk where this particular buck had stopped. Levin is considered a first-rate executive, and had stepped into Ross's shoes in exemplary fashion. Now, with a great chance to make a clear statement about Time Warner and its values, he didn't flinch. He made a statement, but it was the wrong one.

In his typically articulate fashion, Jerry wrote an op-ed piece for *The Wall Street Journal,* aggressive in its defense of continuing distribution of the album. It appeared less than a week into the still-spreading conflagration, and called the message of the lyrics "a shout of pain and protest," not an advocacy of cop-killing. He argued that the dissemination of Ice-T's words— "rooted in the reality of the streets" and "raw with rage and resentment"—was serving the cause of "intellectual and artistic freedom." He noted that "obviously, as with any freedom, there are limits," but he just as obviously felt that Time Warner's activity fell within those limits.

Only weeks later Jerry faced Time Warner's shareholders at their annual meeting, held in Beverly Hills, complete with pickets and protesters. Again he rationalized the company's stance, adding that the easier course would be to withdraw the album from sale, but that Time Warner chose to take the heat that came from doing what was right.

Again he spoke passionately about what he insisted was corporate responsibility. "For a company like ours to have any meaning, any significance," Time Warner could not do otherwise. To do so, he said, would break faith with their artists, journalists, readers, and viewers. He waved aside the point that "while the First Amendment protects our right to publish and distribute a broad range of views, it doesn't oblige us," saying, "We must be willing to go beyond what is safe, familiar, innocuous."

Jerry deserved an A for courage and an F for judgment. I'm sure I wasn't the only one who wanted to call and try to persuade him that he was charging up the wrong road, but I decided not to. He was getting plenty of gratuitous advice, and was beleaguered enough without even a well-meaning comment from me. More to the point, Time Warner business was not my business. It was, however, Jerry's business in the largest sense of the word. Reversing the company's decision would have made an unmistakably positive statement about Time Warner's corporate good citizenship. The First Amendment would live on, undamaged. Some opportunistic and enterprising company, one with less need for a spotless reputation and image, would wind up selling *Body Count.* No one wanting to hear "Cop Killer" would be deprived. Time Warner would lose a few dollars and, perhaps, a rap group, a pittance to pay for polishing up its image. (As a matter of fact, the group and Time Warner later parted company anyway, over a similar matter.)

In at least this instance, Jerry Levin missed a chance to demonstrate to the world that Time Warner's corporate standards were exemplary. In the same way that Howard Stern didn't reflect the NBC we wanted people to know and respect, Ice-T was simply an awful choice of voice to sing for Time Warner. I deplored Jerry's decision, but I think I understand what caused it. Being a CEO of a large company can lead to a startling loss of individuality if you let it. The result may be executive decisions that are more corporate than personal common sense. On such occasions, it's helpful for the guy in charge of the company to approach the problem as though he *were* the company. Jerry Levin might have considered the Ice-T case in terms of a simpler scenario: that it's *his* mom-and-pop record company—Levin & Sons—and he's running it out of the garage behind his house. All his neighbors take an interest in the product he makes and markets; it has high visibility right where he lives, among friends whose respect he seeks and enjoys. Somehow, I don't think Levin & Sons would have anything to do with "Cop Killer."

But it wasn't neighbor Jerry Levin making the judgment for Time Warner, it was the CEO of a media colossus. It's hard to think for all your employees and for thousands of shareholders. It's so hard that you're better off just thinking for yourself. That's why they gave you the job. Make the call the way Levin of Levin & Sons would make it.

It was late afternoon in mid-December 1985, and the lights from the Rockefeller Center Christmas tree were reflected in the windows of my sixth-floor office. John Petty, the chairman of Marine Midland Bank and a fellow member of the RCA board, was sitting across from me on my beige couch. He had called that morning and asked to meet with me, alone.

Mentioning the names of a couple of others who served with us on the board, he got right to the point: "We don't think the sale of RCA to GE should happen and we want to enlist your support in opposing it."

I was more than surprised. A few days earlier, on December 11, the RCA board, with my vote included, had already approved the merger.

"It doesn't have to be a done deal," John told me. "Things have moved much too quickly. We have concerns about the impact this will have on the people who work at RCA and NBC, and we have doubts about the price. If we're really pressed into selling the company, we ought to see if others might be interested in buying it, and how much it's worth to them."

And why had he come to see me?

"Four years ago, NBC was down and out, and now it's far and away the healthiest business RCA owns. Your record carries considerable weight with the board. If you speak out against the sale, others will join us." Implicit in John's presentation was criticism of RCA chairman Thornton Bradshaw, the man who had hired me to run NBC, whose engineering of the General Electric deal had clearly put some noses out of joint.

It had only been a couple of weeks earlier—it seemed an eternity—that Bradshaw had come down from his fifty-third-floor digs to have lunch in my dining room. Normally, when Brad and

I lunched alone, it was in his dining room at his invitation. On the rare occasions when I did the inviting, it meant I had something important—to me, at least—on my mind.

The subject that day was my job, more specifically how long I wanted to do it. I had been NBC's chairman for four and a half of the five years I had originally signed on to serve. I didn't have to review for the chairman of RCA how far we had come. NBC had been restored to heights beyond his and my most optimistic dreams. In the 1981–82 season, my first, we had been barely competitive in prime time, three rating points behind ABC and four behind CBS. Morale was terrible, the press had written us off, and 1981 pretax profits for the entire company had been $48 million—one-sixth of our competitors'. Now we were on the way to NBC's first clear-cut winning season ever, with a strong prime-time schedule that should make the network virtually failure-proof for years to come. Company profits would jump in 1986 to well over $400 million. Equally important to me, NBC now had the respect and admiration of our most important constituencies—affiliates, advertisers, viewers, the press, Emmy voters, and our own employees. The job was done. I reminded Brad of our understanding and told him it was my intention to leave at exactly the five-year mark, July 13, 1986.

He knew how much pleasure we were all deriving from our celebrated recovery, just as he was himself, and he was a bit surprised that I didn't want to hang around to enjoy it for a while. That was certainly tempting, but much more tempting was the thought of not having to commute between coasts just to spend weekends in Los Angeles. Nearly every week since my arrival in 1981, I flew to New York on Monday, spent Tuesday, Wednesday, and Thursday in my office at 30 Rockefeller Plaza, flew back to California Thursday night, and put in a full day Friday at NBC's West Coast headquarters in Burbank.

I was more than a little pooped (sometime later, the diagnosis of an Epstein-Barr condition would help explain why). In any case, I firmly believed, and told Brad, that NBC was sailing along in such great shape—with senior management so well prepared to provide my successor—that I'd be missed for about an hour. He made a pass at persuading me to extend my stay, but ultimately he reverted to the promise-keeper he was.

On my regular Thursday schedule, I flew that night to California, with mixed emotions about my decision. I knew that Bradshaw himself had one foot out the retirement door, and the symmetry of our situations seemed appropriate. The next day I was in Burbank enjoying what was usually the best day of my week. I was mostly an observer of the program process, participating if I was inclined or asked to, but without feeling the nagging pressure always hanging in the air in New York. There were plenty of phone calls to keep me involved with whatever was going on back there, but most of them were unremarkable. Late that day, so late that I picked it up myself, there came a call that would prove quite remarkable.

Bradshaw's secretary put her boss on the phone. It was after 9 P.M. in New York, way beyond Brad's normal Friday getaway time. Surprised, I greeted him with, "What the hell are you doing in the office?"

"Something's developed, unexpectedly. I know you got home late last night, but I wonder if I can ask you to fly back tomorrow. I'm calling a special meeting of the board for Sunday."

I told him I'd be there. Brad shared with me that he had had a drink the night before, while I was flying west, with GE's Jack Welch. Only later would I learn (from Ken Auletta in *Three Blind Mice*) that the meeting had been their second. Brad told me that Welch had broached the subject of GE buying RCA.

During my years as NBC chairman, I was aware of only two other instances of conversations Brad or others might have had about potential major changes in the corporate makeup of RCA. The first had involved Lew Wasserman and Sid Sheinberg, chairman and president, respectively, of MCA, accompanied by their head financial guy. On two successive days in mid-85, Bradshaw, Rick Miller, RCA's chief financial officer, and I had met with them in a suite high up in the Helmsley Palace Hotel. The subject was the possible purchase of MCA by RCA. Since I was not "corporate" RCA, my presence was explained partly by the growing importance of NBC to the parent, and partly by the fact that I knew Lew and Sid and had once worked at MCA myself.

At the time, there were specific government regulations that did not allow networks to be significantly in the production business, but that fact was not discussed. I think Brad felt that if Lew was sitting there, he must have known something we didn't about how to make those restraints go away—or at least was confident that would happen not too far down the road.

The second day's meeting was rather short, and Bradshaw later told me why. Bob Frederick, Brad's successor, was not participating, and it had been deemed appropriate that on the first evening, Bob and Sid, who had never met, should get together. They had done so, and afterward, according to Brad, Lew had asked Sid if he could work with Bob.

"Not for twenty minutes," was reported to have been Sid's answer. I can't vouch for the truth of that, but the meetings were rather summarily terminated. If it is an accurate account, it would be further evidence of Wasserman's high opinion of Sheinberg and of his judgment.

On a far less orchestrated occasion sometime later, Brad and I met at my house in Bel Air with Disney chairman Michael Eisner and Richard Rainwater, representing the Bass brothers, who held a considerable Disney stake. I felt the meeting had been almost more social than business, sort of a get-acquainted session. If Bradshaw had any follow-up contact with either of them, I am unaware of it.

But this was a very different situation. The overture from GE called for consideration by the full RCA board, and convening on Sunday gave the matter a clear sense of urgency. So on Saturday, December 7, I headed back to New York without great enthusiasm but with considerable curiosity. After a rare weekend night in my Dorset Hotel apartment, I walked over to the Park Avenue law offices of Wachtell, Lipton, Rosen and Katz. It was there, not to the RCA Building, that members of the board had been summoned.

Brad opened the lengthy session with a report on his meeting with Welch. He assured us that hostile takeovers were not Welch's style. Welch had given Bradshaw an "in the neighborhood" number of $61 a share, and our discussion had focused more on the question of whether the company should be sold than on how much it was worth. Brad's role was that of moderator, and there was no hint of his own reaction.

There were two principal non–board member speakers: Marty Lipton and Felix Rohatyn, both experienced in such heavyweight games. Each seemed to me to be advising us to consider the GE offer seriously, if not explicitly recommending a favorable response. That was particularly true of Felix, who (we later learned) had brought Brad and Jack together a month earlier, and whose investment banking firm, Lazard Frères, would obviously profit from a completed transaction. Marty Lipton spoke more about various scenarios that could result once a company was "in play."

There followed substantial discussion by the board. I listened mostly, asking only a couple of questions about how a change in parenthood from RCA to GE might affect NBC. All in all, my impression was that the attitude of most board members was favorable. We adjourned with an agreement to meet again on Wednesday, December 11, to reach a decision based on work to be done in the interim. Brad was authorized, along with RCA president Bob Frederick, to initiate further discussion and negotiation with General Electric.

On Wednesday, the boards of both companies met again, RCA's at 7 P.M. at Wachtell, Lipton, and each voted in favor of the deal. The agreed-upon price was $66.50 a share of stock, meaning GE paid just under $6.3 billion for all of RCA. In a hastily called Thursday morning press conference, held at GE's Manhattan offices on Lexington Avenue, Jack Welch and Thornton Bradshaw made what for a number of people was a historic announcement. Having originally gone to work for NBC in February 1949, I was one of those people.

The reaction inside NBC was generally positive. Jack Welch had gone out of his way to praise NBC's management, to point out GE's practice of letting its successful companies run themselves, and to observe that NBC would benefit from the deep pockets of its new owner.

The company had always been under the parentage of RCA —when General Sarnoff ran RCA and Bob Sarnoff ran NBC, somebody had dubbed the place "the father, the son and the wholly-owned subsidiary." So, unlike either of the other two network companies, which had operated independently, NBC's entire history was as part of a larger entity.

Even though RCA had never attempted to micromanage NBC (indeed, during Brad's tenure, they had given us complete autonomy), there seemed to be few regrets about the prospective change. Many NBC executives had run up against RCA's bureaucracy at one time or another, and they liked what GE represented: a well-managed company, with plenty of resources, that would let the broadcasters run broadcasting.

It was clear that Brad thought the deal should happen. Although he never shared all his thoughts with me, I do know that one of his concerns was his own choice of Bob Frederick as his successor. Bob had been appointed CEO of RCA only one year earlier, but Brad was already second-guessing himself.

I could only speculate about how a GE/NBC relationship would play out, but I had a picture of what lay ahead under RCA. Even then, NBC's burgeoning profits were disappearing upstairs, to be allocated to the support of troubled divisions of the corporation. I had little confidence that some of those divisions wouldn't simply go farther south over time, eating up more and more of NBC's profits in the years ahead.

I'm no seer, but it was easy to look down the road NBC was traveling and anticipate that there would be opportunities and industry changes which would require major investments. We had to be allowed to apply to NBC's own future some of the profits we were generating, and perhaps a well-heeled parent could provide additional help. Comparing the two large companies from an NBC point of view, which I considered my primary responsibility, brought me down on the side of General Electric.

John Petty had been unable to attend either RCA board meeting in which the GE offer was considered. He had learned Friday evening, December 6, about the Bradshaw-Welch conversation, but didn't catch up with Brad until 8:30 Saturday morning. He tried unsuccessfully to persuade the RCA chairman to go much more slowly. The company didn't have to be sold, Petty argued, but should the directors vote to sell it, the price GE was offering was woefully inadequate.

Petty then tried to reach other directors, but it was Saturday afternoon and they weren't available. He flew to Moscow, where he was scheduled to deliver a speech, and didn't return until late in the week, after the Wednesday meeting when the deal was approved. Some of the directors, he learned, had felt steamrollered, and while there had been no effective resistance, there was a certain amount of grumbling.

NBC's success gave me influence with the RCA board, John Petty said in my office. Working with the directors whose views he represented, it was not impossible that we could undo what appeared to be a fait accompli. Further, as a public expression of the board's feelings, the first step would be to vote Brad out as chairman and give Bob Frederick a chance to run RCA alone for a few months. That could all happen during the built-in delay that was going to happen anyway: Several Washington agencies and departments—the FCC, the SEC, and, because GE and RCA were involved, the Department of Defense—were going to be scrutinizing the deal. Approval wasn't going to be automatic.

I listened, then told John I saw no reason to change my vote. I said I was enthusiastic about the prospect of NBC's future under the wing of GE and, as politely as I could, declined to join in an effort to derail the deal. Still on my desk as Petty left my office was the memo I had sent to our employees on December 12:

> *To: THE NBC FAMILY*
>
> *From: Grant A. Tinker*
>
> *This morning's news about the RCA merger agreement with the General Electric Company is good news for all of us at NBC. It means that our parent company, which has always been supportive and will continue to be, will be even stronger in the future.*
>
> *The resources of the combined companies will not only enhance competition in the world marketplace, but will also strengthen NBC. In their message to RCA employees, Thornton Bradshaw and Bob Frederick point out that "GE has a long history of providing an environment in which businesses gain from being part of GE, but have the entrepreneurial freedom to grow rapidly and independently. GE has clearly demonstrated that it knows how to give its businesses —even its very large businesses—the type of independent environment in which they flourish."*
>
> *NBC's recent performance—in ratings, in profits, in prestige, and in every other measure of leadership—is one in which we can all take pride. That performance is well recognized by everyone in the management of RCA and GE.*
>
> *Today's announcement signals that an already bright future for the NBC family will now be even brighter.*

I said I was no seer.

It would be nine months between the announcement that GE had bought RCA and my departure from NBC the following September. Had GE not come along, I would have been out of there when my five years were up in July.

Jack Welch sought me out soon after the deal was struck, because Brad had told him of my plans to quit and return to California. Jack urged me to stay on longer, and in the air was a "tell me what it will take" message. He didn't know me, but he knew NBC was really humming and understandably didn't want anything to change, at least not until it had to. I can remember one meeting and at least one convivial dinner, during which we covered a wide range of topics. The possibility of my staying was one of them, but Jack is realist enough to acknowledge a dead horse when he sees one. He did invite me to join the GE board of directors after I left NBC, but, since my intention was to return to the world of television production, that would have created an immediate conflict of interest.

For my part, I told him, as forcefully as I could, that there was such depth of top management, and such capable succession among my immediate colleagues, that NBC would have no problem maintaining its leadership after I was gone. He listened, or seemed to. I talked about the people who constituted the Chairman's Council. A number were qualified to do my job, and I made two specific recommendations: Larry Grossman as chairman and CEO, and Ray Timothy as president and chief operating officer. I thought they would make an ideal team, each doing what he did best—Larry as Mr. Outside and Ray as Mr. Inside—and knew they would use Bob Walsh and Bob Butler importantly. Along with the rest of the group, it was a hell of a management team.

If Jack had chosen to accept my recommendations, the business and image embarrassments that were to befall NBC a few years later simply would not have happened. Not only did he reject my advice, but he chose a suicidal path. His belief, it would later become clear, was that NBC was "just another business," and GE knows how to run businesses. He was to discover that broadcasting, and particularly operating a network, is not just another business. That misjudgment would prove to be very expensive, and not only in dollars. It would tear holes in the fabric of a great institution.

But whatever his thoughts as I made my recommendations, he kept them to himself. He asked me to stay on past July during the transition, and he promised he would get to know Grossman, Timothy, Walsh, and Butler. In the following weeks, he invited all four, in turn, to his office, and no doubt formed an opinion about each. It's astounding to me that over the next couple of years they would all be encouraged to leave. Jack Welch is a man of proven management skills. But over time, and from a distance, I've concluded he has a blind spot. In the case of NBC, it became an Achilles' heel. I don't think he reads people well, which causes him to make some questionable choices of executives.

Bob Butler is today the chief financial officer of International Paper; he performed the same role for us at NBC, and before that was vice president and controller of RCA. He's a graduate of the Wharton School of Business. When he came back from his get-acquainted interview, he told us how Jack greeted him: "I've got a hundred guys like you."

Another special person in our management group was Gene McGuire, who headed Personnel and Labor Relations. Gene had been at NBC for twenty years, knew everybody, and had the respect of the entire company. He was perfectly cast for his job, a terrific negotiator with NBC's unions and, even with his ample girth, was worth his weight in gold. Jack inexcusably replaced him with an exceedingly ordinary ex-RCA functionary he had met and hugely overestimated during the transition.

The worst and most expensive manpower mistake Welch made didn't involve a bad guy, just bad casting. While he was still mulling over the matter of my successor, or at least seeming to, Jack called to say that he wanted me to meet Bob Wright, who "could be a candidate." At the time, Bob was running GE Financial Services. In spite of my protests to Jack that no outsider without broadcast experience could measure up to the NBC candidates I had strongly recommended, I agreed to have dinner at Wright's house in Southport.

On the appointed summer evening, I helicoptered up to Connecticut and landed at GE headquarters in Fairfield. Bob picked me up in his car, and we made small talk on the way to his attractive house, which looked out on Long Island Sound. I met his wife, Suzanne, who is charming, vivacious, and gracious; the Wright kids; and at least one dog. The evening was warm and Suzanne had gone to considerable trouble to lay on an outdoor lobster feast to which I didn't do justice. My thoughts weren't on food.

Being with the Wrights in their home precluded discussing the subject that hung in the air, which may be why the event was arranged in such domestic fashion. NBC did come up, of course, but only very generally. I do remember that in mentioning Tom Brokaw, Bob pronounced the second syllable to rhyme with "how." That may simply have indicated that he felt as ill at ease as I did. Despite Suzanne's hospitality, it was a relatively awkward meal.

My scheduled rendezvous with the helicopter kept the postdinner conversation mercifully short. With profuse thanks to my hostess for her kindness, I climbed into Bob's car for the return trip. There was more small talk, but I couldn't let the evening come and go without mentioning my reservations.

"Bob, I'm sure Jack has told you that I don't think you're the best choice to run NBC," I began. "I hope you won't take that quite the way it sounds; I don't know you well enough to have any opinion of Bob Wright, positive or negative. The problem for me is that we already have some wonderful candidates, a team of people in-house who can take over without dropping a stitch."

I stopped, waiting for Bob's response. None came. I glanced over at him, and he was looking straight ahead, both hands on the steering wheel. If any further words were said, other than my thanking him again and saying good-bye, I don't remember them. I climbed aboard the waiting copter and returned to New York.

I would not see Bob Wright again until well after the press

had reported his selection as NBC's president, when he and Welch and I did a baton-passing closed circuit on August 26 to the NBC affiliate stations. I reassured all concerned that NBC's future, under the leadership of Wright and the parentage of GE, was bright. It certainly was my devout wish, if not my total conviction. Jack talked about "independence," how GE left flourishing businesses alone, and how he would "stay with a winning team." I didn't yet understand that he was not to be taken literally.

After a small lunch in my dining room with Wright, Welch, and some of the Chairman's Council, Jack left, knowing I had invited about forty of our senior management people to meet Bob, up close and personal. For that, we moved to the large sixth-floor conference room next door. Though Bob and I had not discussed it, I assumed he would make some remarks just to say hello and let the gathered executives get a sense of him. My introduction was short, but I managed to sound upbeat about his arrival, and what it would mean to NBC. I concluded with, "I imagine Bob has a word or two he'd like to say."

An hour and thirty minutes later, Bob Wright brought to a close his opening address to the troops. I doubt that he's made as long a talk to them since. His remarks weren't tape-recorded, but the thrust went from generalities—*you've let program costs get out of hand and you failed to diversify*—to specifics—*your margins on the owned stations aren't high enough* and *NBC News has to evolve into a kind of wire service for the local stations.*

It seemed he just didn't want to stop, or didn't know how to get off. Eyes glazed over as he rambled on, telling people how to run a business they were running very well. And I didn't know how to step in and wind him down, but it was not an auspicious presidential beginning.

Finally, mercifully, it was over. The group dissolved and Bob left the building and headed home. About 6 o'clock, still bemused, I was in my office—now to be Bob's—doing whatever lame-duck chairmen do. Jack Welch was suddenly on the phone. "How did it go?"

"It went okay."

"C'mon, tell me the truth, how did he do?"

"Well, he did go on a bit."

"Goddamn it, I knew it! I knew I shouldn't have left!"

No permanent damage had been done. It probably took Bob Wright a little while to overcome the first impression his new minions drew from that inexplicable monologue, and for me, long gone, it's a funny memory. Over time, in many forums and situations, Bob would make a very different impression—that of a sharp, highly intelligent guy. For a while, I genuinely thought he was a good choice. Now I know he was a bad choice, and why.

The first months of 1986 had been spent enjoying our ever-widening lead over ABC and CBS while we waited for completion of the necessary governmental and due diligence formalities that would make the GE-RCA agreement a fact. It was a period of extreme courtesy among the parties and the principal players. There were meetings and dinners and phone calls and interviews, sorting-out and stock-taking, as everyone got used to the idea that the only parent NBC had ever known was dying at sixty years of age. Most people didn't realize that the real GE had not yet stood up.

I spent a couple of rainy days in Washington with Jack Welch. It's a town in which he is entirely comfortable, as he proved in visits with each of the five FCC commissioners on February 4, and with several congressmen the following day. My most vivid memory of those ritual calls is of the ratty raincoat Jack wore; it would have given Columbo pause. It made him seem all the more likable, just one of the guys.

Most of the work that was required to secure the necessary official blessings and complete the transition didn't require my participation. For me, it was business as usual. I continued my weekly commute, with Fridays and now an occasional full week in Burbank.

No one was getting more of a kick out of NBC's recovery than Brandon Tartikoff. Given his key role in bringing it off, that was to be expected. While we had never had the hint of a problem working together, I know Brandon looked forward to my departure. That was nothing more than human nature; he wanted to do his job without a program-oriented boss looking over his shoulder. By sticking to my retirement plan, I had done him a real favor. In the same session in which Jack Welch finally accepted my intention to leave as firm, he'd said, "Jesus, if you're going to leave, it's all the more essential that we don't lose Tartikoff."

It hadn't taken Jack long to spot programming, particularly in prime time, as just about the whole ball game. He knew that he could afford whatever it took to keep Brandon; no matter what it cost, it would be a pittance compared to what a successful schedule meant to NBC. One Thursday night, as I walked into the house at the end of a New York–to–Los Angeles run, Brandon called to share the status of his negotiations with Welch and to get my input. I have no idea where the deal wound up, but I do know from that conversation that the going price for Entertainment division presidents took a steep upward turn. And I'm sure the terms were significantly improved in the next few years —as was only fair to Brandon and smart of Jack.

But Jack wasn't smart enough. Schedule momentum and further good work by Brandon would keep the dollars coming for several years. But because he viewed NBC as just another business, instead of one he really didn't understand, Jack Welch would squander a lead that should have been unassailable. In locking up Brandon, he made sure he kept the best man for the job, but he would learn, when it was too late, that it wasn't a one-man job. It never occurred to me that the senior management of the company, the entire Chairman's Council, would be gone. To me, as chief executive, they had been essential; to Welch and Wright, they were an expendable layer, and that assessment was made clear to them in the form of financially attractive exit arrangements.

By the end of 1988, Walsh, Butler, Grossman, McGuire, Segelstein, and Rukeyser had all departed, and Timothy and Dunham were to follow. With them went the vast store of network television experience they embodied. My absence, by itself, would have entailed nothing more than some chair-changing, had not my immediate lieutenants followed me out the door. Brandon was left with no one on a senior level to talk to except Bob Wright, and Bob's training, experience, and instincts were in disciplines far from television programming.

The kind of attention senior management had paid to Brandon's job was subtle, but it was always in the air. The Chairman's Council, all of them stationed in New York, had been around the network track more than a few times. They didn't consider themselves program experts, but programming is the software of our business and they knew the business. Except in the spring, when pilots are being looked at and assessed, and executives from both coasts are in the same room, most of their contact with Brandon had been through me. In New York, anyone with an opinion about a show or its scheduling didn't hesitate to express it to me.

On my Fridays in Burbank, I might give Brandon my overview of his area and often the thinking of some of the New Yorkers. Without in any way denigrating his celebrated program skills and judgment, I have no doubt that this aggregate advice was an important plus. For his part, Brandon had respected the New York contingent and knew they talked his language. Their questions frequently caused him to think over some projected action one more time—never a bad idea. In GE's NBC, however, he would be left to do a single in a business that requires constant collegial interchange.

Of course, back in 1986, I had no way of knowing what was to transpire. I swallowed my disappointment that Jack Welch hadn't taken my advice regarding succession, and rationalized the choice of Bob Wright. He would have all that highly qualified support, I thought, and he would bring the fresh eye of one who, not having been too long among the trees, would be able to see the forest, particularly the part not yet explored. There would be judgments and investments to make, new opportunities; if NBC, as constituted, was in a declining business, its bets should be hedged in other program services and technologies coming on line. I was right that Bob would see the future clearly, but I never expected him (or Jack) to let NBC's basic business suffer such a disastrous fall.

I know Brandon prized his new autonomy, and I'm sure it was institutionalized by a Welch-to-Wright programming dictum: Leave the kid alone. The hardest part of the climb from number three to number one had already been accomplished: developing a schedule of appealing programs of quality and then having the patience to sit, week after week for several years, watching them take a beating from entrenched hits on the other networks. We had suffered through that for far too long. Now NBC was the leader, and would be able to use its own established hits to attract viewers to its new programs.

That's how the next generation of winners gets created, and the leading network is always in the best position to get it done.

NBC had most of the top-ten shows and was so far out in front of its competition—in first place most nights and not worse than second any night—that continued success seemed inevitable. Momentum and the lead time realities of the business would carry the company to several more hugely profitable years, but NBC was not storing up nuts for the winter. The building blocks of current hits, which eventually tire and leave the air, must be continuously supplemented by promising new programs, or the advantage is lost. If your new programs fail at the same time your building blocks are crumbling, call the coroner.

As old age caught up with *Hill Street Blues, St. Elsewhere, Family Ties, Bill Cosby, Golden Girls,* and other high-rated shows, NBC failed to develop and nurture a roster of new ones to replace them. ABC and CBS caught up and passed NBC, and Brandon, his own once-lustrous batting average significantly lowered, left to become chairman of Paramount Pictures before the worst of the stuff hit the fan.

What had gone wrong?

The "it's just another business" approach of General Electric had led to the willful, systematic displacement of the senior executives who had managed NBC to the top of a business GE did not yet understand. It also accelerated the deterioration of NBC into a company that is seen to have no higher purpose than making a buck.

For example, GE regarded Broadcast Standards as a costly frill, a relic of the profligacy of the past. That department, responsible for working with (and sometimes fighting with) producers to assure that NBC's program service was what NBC wanted it to be, became a victim of cost-cutting. Programs were broadcast without the usual standards supervision. As a direct result, the network suffered a few well-publicized exploitative embarrassments—*Devil Worship: Exposing Satan's Underground* was one that any functioning Standards department would have rejected—and some less-publicized sales problems. The cost-cutting measure was actually cost-producing; sponsors were shunning some shows because of their content. When that became painfully clear to management, the Broadcast Standards unit was reconstituted.

The lowering of programming standards was further evidence that one of NBC's enduring strengths, its tradition as America's first broadcasting network, was being ignored. Five years after GE took over, NBC was criticized in the trade press for some tasteless and misleading promos. The response from the NBC vice president in charge: "Where do we draw the line? We just keep moving it."

GE decided to sell off the sixty-year-old NBC Radio Network for cash, although CBS and ABC continue to maintain profitable radio operations. What really put the just-another-business stamp on the transaction was GE's willingness to allow the purchaser, Westwood One, to continue to identify the service as "NBC Radio News" long after NBC had any involvement with it. Selling the company's good name was apparently no problem.

GE believes good managers don't wait for something to go wrong before they make changes. An article of faith in the company's operating philosophy, much praised by business schools for its pro-active approach to change, is "If it ain't broke, fix it." In mismanaging NBC, surely as different a business as there is, that became "If it ain't broke, break it."

For several weeks before I left NBC, I fielded a number of phone calls from people with ideas about my immediate future. After crossing off those inquiries that didn't seem worthwhile or substantial, I had a list of seventeen I felt were worth following up. During the two months following my departure, I met and talked with most of those who had been kind enough to call; many wanted me to return to production, either as an employee of some kind or as a partner.

One call was from a member of the Gannett board of directors (and a former NBC chairman), Julian Goodman, inviting me to sit down with that media giant's CEO, Al Neuharth. I told Julian I'd be happy to do so, but not until I was out of the RCA Building for the last time. And that's the way we did it. On the very day I made my final exit through the doors of 30 Rockefeller Plaza, I walked directly over to the Waldorf Towers, where Gannett maintained a suite for its singular chairman.

I had met several of Al's people at NBC affiliate functions, but never the man himself. With him that day were his two senior lieutenants, John Curley and Doug McCorkindale, as well as Goodman, serving as introducer. Curley was Gannett's president and Al's eventual successor; McCorkindale was vice chairman and chief financial officer. As I would come to learn over the next several years, when Al was in a meeting largely populated by his own staff, he talked and they listened.

Many subsequent get-togethers would confirm that pattern. Al was definitely in charge, conversation was about matters he wanted covered, and in the order he chose. John Curley usually made intelligent comments and suggestions and more or less spoke Al's language, if deferentially. He read Al well and could alter his tone and participation to match the mood of the boss. John is bright and has a mind of his own, but in Neuharth's presence, he knew how bright to be—and when.

Doug McCorkindale was a different story. He's no dummy either, but on occasion, with Al, he behaved that way. Almost every time I saw them together, Doug would find a reason to disagree with Neuharth, or to make a suggestion he knew would produce a flash of the anger Al could manufacture at will. Invariably, Al's reply would start: "For Christ's sake, Doug . . ." It was as though each was playing a scripted part. Ultimately, having seen this interplay any number of times, I concluded that McCorkindale yanked Al's chain purposely and perversely, knowing that a Neuharth explosion would inevitably result. After the storm, Al would wind down quickly and proceed with the business at hand, and Doug would calmly settle back in his chair. One had the feeling that Doug considered the exchange no worse than a draw, and that he believed he had brought to the meeting a constructive ingredient. It was a bizarre ritual, to say the least.

Our initial meeting was short and largely social. Once Julian Goodman made the introductions, in his characteristically self-important manner, Al and I chatted almost as though we were alone. As I might have guessed, he thought Gannett should be in the program business. The company already owned scores of newspapers, a bunch of radio and television stations, and was the leading outdoor advertising company. The apple of Al's eye was *USA Today,* an idea of his that had become a reality, despite doubts and derision from all sides, thanks to his enormous drive and commitment. As Neuharth spoke of his interest in yet another business, it was clear that he was a man who liked to finish what he started. That was important to me, as was my impression that Al was a man I could deal with.

After that meeting, I flew back to California. My weekly coast-to-coast commutes had normally been on American Airlines, but this time, schlepping five years' worth of accumulated mementos, I used one of the GE jets. The only thing I left in New York was a bunch of suits hanging in the closet at the Dorset Hotel. To me they symbolized the big-city life I was eagerly leaving. I called Bud Rukeyser at 4:30 in the afternoon from the airport, where I was about to leave for Los Angeles, and asked him to help me get rid of the suits.

"Meaning what?" Bud asked. "Give them to charity?"

"No. Find someone they'll fit and give them to him."

Bud told me later that he hung up the phone and turned to Gene McGuire, NBC's head of Personnel and Labor Relations. "What the hell was that all about?" Gene wanted to know.

"Tinker's left twenty suits at the Dorset, and I'm supposed to do a Cinderella search. Whoever fits gets the suits."

McGuire leapt from his chair. "This is exactly the incentive I need to lose some weight," he said. "I've got the key to the Dorset apartment and I'm going right over there to try them on." He dashed out, visions of a lifetime supply of tailor-made suits dancing in his head.

An hour later, McGuire, a forty-six-regular, was back. "The good news is there are twenty Carroll & Co. suits hanging in the closet," he said. "The bad news is I couldn't button anything."

McGuire and Rukeyser agreed that making a general announcement about the availability of the chairman's clothes would be in questionable taste, and set about looking for likely candidates. Eventually the suits were awarded to a young San Francisco executive with only a peripheral NBC connection but exactly the right build.

Over the next two months I had meetings at my house or at lunch with other people who had contacted me about life after NBC. It was the first time I didn't have an office to go to, and I hated it. That was no doubt one reason I rapidly passed over the various other opportunities to take the partnership vows with Gannett. In addition to my positive feelings about Neuharth, I knew Gannett was a substantial, healthy media company well able to underwrite a television production enterprise.

At our second meeting, held at my house in Los Angeles with the same cast minus Goodman, Al had offered two additional considerations. "I'll tell you exactly why we should look good to you," he said. "We don't know anything about your business and we're located in the East. That's a combination that guarantees we won't be around looking over your shoulder all the time."

Neuharth, Curley, McCorkindale, and I had one additional meeting before the partnership agreement jelled. It was our third get-together, the second at my house in Bel Air. With hindsight, it's the one I wish we had skipped. We had talked for more than two hours, and it was time for a break. Al and I left the others and walked outside. Standing by the pool, he sprang the question. "You read *USA Today*," he said. "Do you think there's a television show in the newspaper?"

A simple "no" at that point would have saved all of us a lot of grief and Gannett a lot of money. "There probably is," I told him, "but it's not the kind of work I know much about. Let me think about it."

A couple of weeks later I remembered a conversation I had had with Steve Friedman, the smart and volatile executive producer of the *Today* show, as I was leaving NBC. The message was clear. "I need another challenge," he told me. "I'm not going to be in this job forever, and I can't go on getting up at four in the morning. When you're doing whatever you're going to be doing, don't forget I'm here."

It was, for Steve, the right time to be looking around. The *Today* show, which had fallen behind ABC's *Good Morning, America* in the Nielsens for a couple of years, was solidly back in the lead. Even when his show was in second place, Steve had stayed in the media spotlight by saying disparaging things about his competition, always in a quotable way. "CBS would be brain dead, if it had a brain," was typical. Steve was no doubt aware that his fame as the savior of *Today* could diminish if the ratings went bad again. In the job market, it was time to strike while Friedman was hot.

From my standpoint, Steve seemed the ideal choice to pump up the *USA Today* show Neuharth clearly wanted. None of my experience had been in this sort of reality programming, but all of Steve's had, and his *Today* show track record was excellent. Around the time I signed the partnership agreement that created GTG Entertainment (the initials were a combination of Grant Tinker and Gannett), I told Al, "I've thought of a guy who's probably perfect casting to do the show you asked me about."

Perfect was hardly the word, but that realization came later. We eventually signed Steve to a contract for more money than he (or I, for that matter) had made at NBC, and called him president of GTG East. Gannett's headquarters are in two thirty-story towers in Rosslyn, Virginia, just outside Washington, so our *USA Today* program was going to require an East Coast staff. The idea was that the resources of the newspaper would be made available, that segments of the program would originate from the newsroom, and that the show would translate the strengths of *USA Today* into a daily television show.

That *USA Today* project was an afterthought. My purpose in entering the partnership was to develop and produce situation comedies and dramatic series for network television, and we were going to need a place in California to do it. At the point where discussions with Gannett had progressed to where we essentially had a deal, we still hadn't talked about a home base. Naturally, I had thought about it.

At MTM, I'd never had to worry about production facilities. After the first season of Mary's show, MTM took up residence at CBS Studio Center in Studio City, which was being renovated under the able direction of Bob Norvet. As we got bigger, CBS fixed up soundstages and we filled them. The lot was small, with about fourteen stages and assorted office and support buildings, and very efficient. I recalled the great convenience of commandeering additional stages as MTM shows proliferated through the seventies.

Now, with GTG's needs in mind, I became aware that the Laird Studios in Culver City were going to be sold. The facility had been built by Thomas Ince in 1917 and through the years, under many different names, had been home to Cecil B. DeMille, RKO Pictures, David O. Selznick, Howard Hughes, and Desilu. In all my years in Los Angeles, I'd never been there, and one gray, rainy Saturday afternoon in October 1986 I went over to have a look.

In a golf cart that had seen better days, I was piloted around puddled potholes to twelve soundstages, a number of support buildings, and some bungalows that served as office space. The last stop was the lot's signature building, an antebellum structure rather grandly called The Mansion. Like the rest of the studio, it was badly in need of some loving care. The owner had encountered financial difficulties serious enough to have the property scheduled for auction, and the entire lot was held together with spit and baling wire. I marveled that it was a going operation, but at the same time, there was something magnetic about it. The place had real restoration possibilities, all of which were later realized. With Gannett's approval, Brown, Kraft, our accounting firm, did the necessary homework to be ready for the approaching auction date. We determined that $32 million would be our prudent top bid given the considerable fix-up costs that would necessarily follow acquisition.

We and Gannett had kept our interest secret, and no one knew that our man at the auction, Sid Tessler of Brown, Kraft, was representing GTG. There were a number of other interested parties present, the most prominent being the formidable team of Marvin Davis and Aaron Spelling. At the time, Marvin had a sizable investment in Aaron's production company, which apparently was looking, as I was, for a lot to call home.

For some reason, the auction itself was videotaped. In an underlit, amateur fashion, the tape shows Davis and Spelling seated side-by-side in the first row of prospective buyers. Sid Tessler cannot be seen at all; he was on the other side of Davis, entirely obscured by Marvin's considerable presence. The auction proceeded with dispatch. After Sid's bid of $24 million, Marvin looked at Aaron to see if he was interested in staying in. The tape shows Aaron shaking his head slightly, clearly indicating "no." Our bid prevailed, at a level much lower than we expected. We had thought Marvin Davis would blow us away.

One of the very significant contributors to our Gannett adventure was Alan Levine, then a partner in the law firm of Armstrong, Hirsch and Levine. Acting on my behalf, he presided at the birth of GTG, which proved to be barely a warm-up for the next task. Whole forests were felled to put on paper my simple understanding with Al Neuharth to go into business with Gannett. My prospective partner had plenty of legal representation in its own right, and Alan wrestled with all concerned for several months before our marriage was put in writing to everyone's satisfaction.

Buying the studio became a federal case, too. Alan and several of his associates had a second chance to discover that, at a media colossus like Gannett, the business affairs people never use one piece of paper where five will do. It was ironic but appropriate that all the homework done on the real estate part of our deal would later be put to use by Alan a second time. In 1989, Sony bought Columbia Pictures, acquiring Culver City's largest studio in the process, the one most industry folk have trouble remembering is no longer MGM. Alan Levine was involved, still wearing his attorney hat, in that much more complicated matter. When all the smoke finally cleared, someone—probably Sony

Pictures chairman Peter Guber—had the good sense to invite Alan to become the president of the newly formed company. In that role, a couple of years later, the same Alan Levine would buy the Culver Studios from Gannett, completing a sequence that converted my lawyer into my landlord.

The studio was our home base, and we would spend another $40 million of Gannett's money vastly improving the lot, building two state-of-the-art stages to house multiple-camera comedies, and acquiring additional acreage across the street for a planned new office building. (That last project never came to pass under our ownership, but when Sony bought the lot in 1991, they announced their intention to use the extra parcel in a similar fashion.)

By 1989, after we had accomplished the transformation, people who returned to the studio to make television shows and movies often expressed their amazement at how different the place looked and what a great production facility it now was. The eventual Sony purchase price was $80 million, so Gannett made out very well on at least the real estate part of our venture together.

Al Neuharth was to keep his promise not to second-guess me for the entire time he remained at Gannett. There were a few occasions when McCorkindale got a little inquisitive, but never to a degree he could be arrested for. After all, we were playing with Gannett's money, and that was Doug's department. From time to time, particularly when we were restoring and improving the grounds and studios, various Gannetteers would visit us on the Culver lot. The capital expenditures involved in building soundstages and remodeling office space were considerable, and Gannett had every right to be interested.

The first few members of the GTG family moved onto the lot in early 1987. We worked out of a couple of trailers for many months as we planned and executed the restoration, scrambling for space as creative people signed on. The fine studio management group we had inherited was headed by Jack Kindberg, who had run the studio for Laird. For several years he had been renting out soundstages and services, managing the business while keeping the place together with Band-Aids. Jack had two very good lieutenants, Bob Sirchia and Jan Kelly.

Bob was a resident of Culver City and was to prove immensely helpful with the town fathers, a crowd that seemed to think the only thing better than slow growth was no growth. We couldn't drive a nail or paint a sign, much less undertake more significant improvements, without seeking permission for each and every activity from the municipal bureaucracy. I felt the city should be happy with our plans to greatly improve an enterprise they were proud to have in Culver City. After all, the official city seal still bore the motto coined more than a half-century earlier: "The Heart of Screenland." When we changed the name from Laird to The Culver Studios, I thought it would buy us some goodwill from the city powers. They were pleased to hear about it, but I never perceived any change in their attitude or behavior toward us.

At the time we acquired our studio, it was the home of several independent production companies owned and run by some of the most talented producer/directors in town. Blake Edwards, Norman Jewison, and Bud Yorkin had offices on the lot, and Blake especially used the stages for his film projects. I had known all three and admired their work for many years, and Yorkin was a close friend. He occupied The Mansion's prime space, run-down though it was, a circumstance that put our long friendship to a severe test.

I had first visited Bud's office when it became known we had bought the lot and would soon move in. He asked where my own office would be. "I have no idea," I told him. "We'll be working out of a trailer until we fix up the place." In the early weeks, there was a series of long meetings with architects and assorted planners, all of whom did work that resulted in a first-class home for GTG. Not too long into the process, I began to think about where I, the resident big cheese, should be located. Late one afternoon I picked up the phone and called Yorkin. "Why don't you buy me a drink?"

"Come on over."

Seated on a sofa in Bud's office, I thanked him for his thoughtfulness the day before. He had arranged for his son David to provide me with some street route information that would make my daily drive to and from the studio quicker and easier.

"Cut the shit," Bud interrupted. "I know why you're here. You want this space for your office."

From me, sheepishly: "Yeah, you're right. There isn't another location in the whole place that works for me. I'm really sorry."

"Don't worry about it. I figured you'd get around to throwing me out sooner or later."

Whatever may have been his private reaction, to my face Bud took this rude behavior from a friend in the best possible spirit. That's probably why I had the gall to evict him. He moved his activities into a building in Beverly Hills, continues to be a good friend, and has never mentioned the matter since. Needless to say, neither have I.

The support we got from Al Neuharth during this start-up period, and for the entire duration of his tenure at Gannett, was total. My view of him may be more benign than that of his subordinates, because he can't have been easy to work for. But he was unfailingly courteous to me, even on those infrequent occasions when we found ourselves in disagreement. I think Al is a fight-and-make-up kind of guy, and the trick is to use all that's good about him and just roll with the rest. It's true that Al the doer—the risk-taker and visionary who built a media empire —sometimes blends into Al the actor. Most often, though, the two Als work well together.

One of my early opportunities to see the blend in action was at a meeting in his Gannett office, called to discuss *USA Today: The Television Show* and how it would relate to his pride and joy, the national newspaper. Al's white-on-white office at the top of the Gannett tower was big enough to accommodate Little League batting practice. With me were Steve Friedman and Bob Jacobs, whose assignment was to sell the show to television stations around the country, a job he did brilliantly. Neuharth's team that day, a Greek chorus without singing parts, were the usual suspects: John Curley, Doug McCorkindale, and John Quinn, the editor of *USA Today* and executive vice president of news for Gannett. We sat around a conference table within shouting distance of an enormous fireplace containing a conflagration that could have warmed the entire Continental Army. Al started the meeting in his chair but soon was on his feet, circling the table. Most of the time he was doing the talking; when he wasn't, he was impatiently jingling the coins in his pocket, waiting for one of us to finish making a point. His own people said virtually nothing.

From the moment, months before, that he had first raised the possibility of GTG doing a television version of *USA Today,* Al's position had been perfectly clear: We'd produce the show, but Gannett would retain authority over it. *USA Today* was a valuable Gannett franchise, a Neuharth-invented one at that, and the program was going to be produced and broadcast from their corporate headquarters. It was to me an easily justified exception to GTG's agreed-upon television autonomy.

For the first few minutes, the conversation was entirely civil. We were still in the honeymoon stage of our marriage, and Al presented his views in a positive and polite manner. So did we. Even Steve, who had once kicked in the screen of a television monitor at NBC to express his unhappiness with the equipment, was on his best behavior.

When Al made one of his less inspired suggestions, I couldn't resist shaking up the orderly atmosphere. Maybe it was the sight of the three Gannett executives just sitting in silence while their boss held forth, or maybe I just wanted to see what would happen. "That's horseshit, Al," I volunteered. Neuharth's head snapped around in surprise and he fixed me with a glare. His subordinates shifted uneasily. Then, as if he knew I had talked back more for the territorial benefit of my team than to be rude, he took only the briefest beat before quietly resuming. I would come to learn that Neuharth is selectively adversarial, and this was a fine example of how he picks his spots. Sometimes he'll pass up a challenge or a potential skirmish just for the surprise value. But don't count on it, and don't think he ever accepts half an answer to a whole question.

A meeting with him was always memorable. One, held on the lot, was devoted to discussing my recommendation that Gannett purchase some available property across a side street from the studio. The property would give us room for additional office space to support stage use. Al was all for it; Doug McCorkindale was not. Doug is a brilliant financial executive, much admired on Wall Street, who saw part of his job as being a counterweight to some of Al's expensive predilections. As Doug spoke forcefully about why this particular seven-figure expenditure shouldn't be made, Al was doing his Al thing. While the rest of us sat around the table, he paced and jingled. His constant movement shifted everyone's attention from the speaker to him.

Suddenly, he stopped pacing and planted himself right in back of McCorkindale. He stood stock still, perhaps six inches from Doug's back, his face and the sound of the jingling coins well expressing his impatience and irritation to the rest of us. Doug manfully continued, but it was apparent to him that we were all watching Neuharth, whom he couldn't see. Finally, Al had heard enough. "For Christ's sake, Doug," he bellowed, "I don't want to listen to any more of this and I don't want Grant to have to listen to it either." Switching to the Socratic method, he asked: "Doesn't Gannett already own a lot of real estate?" Doug nodded yes. "We ever lose money on any of it?" Al persisted, with the zeal of a prosecutor who already knows the answer. "No," replied the witness. Case closed.

Other than that one time, I never saw a Gannetteer truly argue with Al or even voice a notion that might derail the superchief's train of thought. Once, in fact, that reticence became a health hazard to an entire roomful of people.

It was another meeting in Al's office. I was having some trouble breathing and my eyes felt dry, almost stinging. I dismissed the symptoms as typical minor health disorders caused by spending too much time on airplanes, part of my bi-coastal existence. But an hour later I was still in distress. As the meeting wound down, I noticed others were suffering similarly, and finally I said something about it. Instantly everyone present acknowledged the very same difficulties. The cause turned out to be a mostly closed damper in the chimney of Neuharth's Bunyanesque fireplace. Al's staff, all regular visitors to his office, had sat through this entire airless meeting without daring to interrupt him. It wasn't the last time I would see otherwise strong Gannett executives transformed into wax figures by Al's presence.

I was never privy to internal Gannett numbers, but one didn't have to be an insider to know that Al Neuharth was an expensive CEO to maintain. Certainly many of his colleagues and fellow directors muttered about his high living behind his back. But the man delivered, and Gannett prospered and grew under his aggressive and bold leadership. One would think his lieutenants and board members would have judged him principally on his record, but he was no sooner retired and out of his office than the negative opinions surfaced.

The depth of their antipathy was remarkable, and surprising

for an outsider to behold. Obviously, there were a great many people who had hidden their true feelings about Al during all the years they worked under his supervision. They may have chafed, but they stayed the Neuharth course. Despite their unspoken complaints during his stewardship, they apparently recognized the value of what he was building for them.

One thing he didn't build for them—more accurately, *we* didn't—was a viable production company. There are several reasons why GTG failed as a company, and most of them stem from misjudgments of mine.

One of the more significant areas of our GTG failure, certainly the most publicized, was *USA Today: The Television Show* (later titled *USA Today on TV*), our effort to create an electronic cousin of "the nation's newspaper." Had I not caught the ball Al Neuharth had casually tossed me in my backyard one morning, that expensive, embarrassing misadventure never would have happened. I should have let it fall to earth, or into the swimming pool, because it concerned a kind of television I knew nothing about, either as a producer or as a marketer.

The appointment of Steve Friedman as executive producer, which looked so good on paper, turned out less well in the doing. Steve spent most of a year hiring a staff, telling the press his show was going to be "television of the nineties," and throwing around a great deal of Gannett's money. The show was produced from Gannett's headquarters building in Rosslyn, Virginia. All the necessary equipment was purchased, not rented, and all of it was top of the line. "The best that money can buy" was Steve's mantra when showing visitors through his state-of-the-art control room, usually followed by a high five with one of his acolytes. At one early stage, he insisted that a structural pillar in the thirty-story tower be removed, because it was interfering with the sight lines in his studio. As the owner of the Washington Redskins once said about his coach, George Allen, "The man had an unlimited expense account, and he exceeded it."

Unfortunately, when the show went on the air in September 1988, everyone was disappointed—the press, the stations, and, particularly, Gannett. One of the Gannett requirements had been that *USA Today on TV* have four separate sections, just like the paper, and that each section have its own anchor. In retrospect, that was a heavy burden for a half-hour show to bear, and the quick cuts and frenetic pacing made it worse. Nothing was on camera long enough to make an impression, and, to viewers, the program must have looked like a VCR on fast-forward.

For several months after the disastrous premiere (on which a segment on "A Day in the Life of Miss America" flew by in forty-five seconds), Gannett scrupulously kept hands off, despite what surely must have been some agonized meetings in Rosslyn. By October, we had brought in Jim Bellows, an experienced news professional, to help Steve give the show some editorial direction. By early 1989, Jim was running *USA Today on TV* and Steve was back in New York. We had hired Jim for his editorial skills, which were considerable, but we forced him into the de facto role of executive producer. The show's ratings were at their peak on his watch, but there were two problems, only one of which we knew about at the time. The program was wildly over budget, and badly needed controlling. The problem we didn't know about until later was that the editorial changes Bellows had made ran counter to what Gannett wanted. Our thought in January 1989, just four months after the show premiered, was to let Jim do the job he had been hired to do, and bring in an executive producer to put the program house in order. We gave Gannett a couple of specific suggestions, including Jerry Nachman, an experienced television news producer who was then a columnist (and later the editor) at the *New York Post*.

Gannett had other ideas. By that time they had concluded that we didn't know what the hell we were doing. Without any discussion with us, they brought in as executive producer a man from their Oklahoma City station, which prompted Bellows to quit, and then replaced him a few months later with another Gannetteer with no experience in national television.

Gannett had gone from hands-off to total control. Not only was GTG no longer in charge of the show that bore our "produced by" credit, we were shut out of the process. The problems we had created then grew worse as a bunch of newspaper mavens tried to make a television show "more like the paper." Throughout the summer, with *USA Today on TV* clearly in extremis, we tried vainly to convince Gannett that someone experienced in the production of nationally syndicated television should be brought in to help.

But they had stopped listening to us. Our Gannett partners insisted on doing it all themselves, with the predictable result. One possible explanation: Al Neuharth, who had fathered the partnership with GTG and the creation of *USA Today on TV,* was gone. Gannett was now in the hands of people who had their own doubts about Al, never were fans of his expensive television venture, and preferred to get the company back to its newspaper roots. In this scenario, saving *USA Today on TV* was never a priority. The show was scrubbed in January 1990.

In the discussions we had before we became partners, and in many conversations after GTG was created, Al Neuharth had not once mentioned the word *retirement.* His decision to leave the chairmanship to run the company's foundation came as a complete surprise to me. His energy and youthful appearance had given no clue about his plans, and it simply never occurred to me that he would not be around as long as we were. GTG itself, and *USA Today on TV* in particular, had been his brain-children, and his departure left them orphans.

While I was never an expert about the syndication market-place or how to produce that kind of show, I *was* supposed to be well versed in the business of making and selling prime-time network television programs. It was my intention as I left NBC in late 1986, my halo glowing brightly, to repeat the MTM performance somewhere else. The attention I got from various suitors, all seeking to be involved with my return to production, had been more than gratifying. It was apparently stupefying, as well.

Somehow, the euphoria of the moment was enough to make Grant a dull boy. I failed to take enough notice of the changes, economic and otherwise, that had occurred since the beginning of MTM in 1970. Those changes were not a secret; I just hadn't stopped to consider their significance.

Probably the most important error was in not acknowledging the power now exercised by agents and lawyers, as compared with their lesser role fifteen years earlier. In dealing with the original MTM talent who created Mary's show and with the many others who followed, there was seldom any problem arising from the failure to make a deal. They all had agents and lawyers, of course, but more to handle the details and reduce everything to writing—after the company and the talent had a pretty good idea of the basic arrangement.

That's something of an exaggeration, but it suggests the climate of those earlier times. In the years after I left MTM, those who represented creative people, particularly the ones in greatest demand, had come into a good deal more power. Where once talent had gone underrewarded, to the advantage of the employing production company, now the too-few "best creative people" were overpriced. Through their smarts and their clout, agents representing the most sought-after writer/producers made outrageous multimillion-dollar deals for them, usually with the large studios. And the performing artists, especially the stars, were compensated in matching proportion.

Beginning in the eighties, as a result, the deal came first, the show came second. Where in earlier years the production companies had wielded all the clout, now the pendulum had swung too far. The inmates had taken over the asylum. And the customer networks, which even in good times had railed against ever-rising production costs, were complicit. With ABC, CBS, and NBC in bitter competition for an audience that was steadily becoming more fractionalized, it was easy for program suppliers to divide and conquer them. They played one against another to make outsized deals the networks could not afford—and could not afford to pass up.

Into this very changed business returned a former practitioner who had spent almost six years breathing the rarified air in which chairmen exist. I hadn't been totally out to lunch about the *business* of programs, but I had certainly spent much more time attending to the larger business of a broadcasting company. Now, when I looked into the cost of making contract deals with the kind of talent I had become accustomed to having at MTM, I discovered those people commanded fees to which I had not become accustomed. Fuck that, I reasoned.

Right at that early stage, something else occurred to cloud my judgment. Larry Tisch, who had just achieved control of CBS, came twice to my house in Bel Air to talk about the task of trying to do for his company what we had done for NBC. I hesitate to say that he asked me to run CBS, because our conversations weren't that specific, partly because Larry was new to the territory and didn't speak the language of the business yet. Suffice to report that he picked my brain for clues about the NBC experience and wound up asking, "How can you help us?"

"I don't know, Larry, but let me think about it."

He was back at the house a couple of weeks later, by which time I had thought about it in a most self-serving way. To be fair to myself, I did consider that my suggestion would work to the benefit of CBS, in the same way MTM had made a positive contribution to CBS in the seventies. I told Larry I would be going back into the production business and would be happy to talk about a multiseries deal that would guarantee CBS first crack at the programs my new company would produce. He wasn't too familiar with such arrangements, but he reacted with seeming enthusiasm and said he'd get back to me.

He did so in the form of a phone call from Bill Paley, still chairman of the company he had founded, and at the time seemingly still active in its affairs. I had known Bill somewhat in the seventies, when MTM was an appreciated supplier of CBS programs. Mary and I had dinner with him a couple of times, during which he would flirt with her and suffer my presence agreeably enough. He was an immensely attractive, egocentric man whom I enjoyed, to some extent, for his unapologetic "let 'em eat cake" style. Of course, I was never a CBS employee. In the eighties, while in New York with NBC, I would see more often, and up close, an aging bear of a man determined to leave behind a museum dedicated to the industry in which he had spent his business life.

Paley invited me to join him for breakfast at the Beverly Hills Hotel. A couple of mornings later, Bill's valet (maybe he was a steward) admitted me to a large suite on the second floor of that venerable hostelry. The chairman was fully dressed and waiting for me. Soon there arrived enough breakfast for six stevedores, much of which Bill consumed as we talked.

I was there well over an hour, generally talking television ("the good old days") and specifically talking about the kind of bargain we might strike. This was not Paley's normal line of work, even when he had been more active in the company, but he understood the concept well enough. The breakfast is far more memorable to me for its three, maybe four, sudden interruptions, when Bill leapt from his chair, excused himself, and disappeared around the corner into an adjoining bathroom. Without bothering to close the door, he would relieve himself noisily and at length. Each time, he returned and sat down, muttering, "Sorry.

The doctor has me on some damned diuretic thing. I'm going every twenty minutes." I already knew that.

Eventually we agreed to an arrangement that called for CBS to buy and GTG to deliver ten television series over five years, or as soon thereafter as could be managed by the parties. On its face, I thought it was a good deal for all concerned. It meant that I would not have to worry about selling; GTG's time could be spent entirely on developing and producing programs. CBS would have, in effect, exclusive call on the quality product I expected us to turn out.

The deal Bill Paley and I made never had the anticipated results. I certainly can't duck my share of the blame, but it's also fair to say that the network's Entertainment division people hated the deal from day one and, through program development nit-picking and business affairs hardball, would have managed to fudge it to death, whatever the level of product we turned out.

A good axiom might be: Don't make a deal at the very top of a company when the worker bees will be the implementers. To do so may make a good deal in theory become no deal in practice. CBS was inclined to find fault with projects we brought them even before we got out of our cars in their parking lot. At the same time we were inhibited about taking our wares to other networks. Ultimately, I sent a legal letter asking out of the remaining commitments, which was most of them; CBS was only too happy to comply.

With a couple of program exceptions, we were the authors of our own shortcomings. Shocked by the fees those "best creative people" (my miracle workers at MTM and again at NBC) were now commanding, I chose a bad course. I should have bitten the bullet, taken on a few established creator/writers, and paid them the huge bucks. Instead, I opted to winnow out from a raft of considerably less experienced talent about fifteen relative newcomers at much more reasonable prices. It was my misguided conceit that we could grow our own successful writers and producers, as we had in the halcyon days of MTM. Alas, that was the business then, and this was the business now. We did indeed find some exceedingly talented people, many of whom have gone on or will go on to do good and successful work. While they were at GTG, they only did good work. Audiences aren't quick to take note of good work, and networks don't give them much time to do so. On balance, I would say that for the most part, GTG chose too many beginners and too few proven winners.

There were two shows we turned out, both for CBS, that I think had more promise than the network had faith. One was an 8 o'clock hour called *TV 101*, set in a fictional high school and spotlighting the students and teacher of a communications class. Created and produced by the talented Karl Schaefer, one of our young writer recruits, it was worthwhile material. I think CBS, then a network without the courage of any convictions, would have done well to promote and patiently support that show until it was discovered by a sufficient audience. The cast was attractive and effective, but the network lost faith before that could happen.

I liked even better *WIOU*, a 10 o'clock hour about a contemporary television station and its news department. John Eisendrath and Katherine Pratt crafted this effort, based on their own experiences in the local CBS station newsroom in Chicago. The ensemble cast was uniformly accomplished, and the material was a mix of drama and humor that I love—reminiscent, for me, of *Hill Street Blues* and *St. Elsewhere,* but obviously without the life-and-death story opportunities of those shows. CBS took a harder view, and *WIOU* didn't make it through a full season.

Again, I thought the network was too quick to pull the trigger. At the time, the CBS schedule was in trouble most of the week, and in my opinion *WIOU* rather classed up the joint. It was the kind of literate program I would have been inclined to give more time to find its audience were I back at NBC participating in such judgments. On the other hand, Steven Bochco's assessment of the show, which I foolishly sought, was that it was "a case of style over substance." What does he know, anyway?

Most of GTG's other efforts weren't good enough, although nobody failed for lack of trying. Had I chosen to pay the big bucks for a couple of creative superstars, we might have turned out product that got on and stayed on. There is an incalculable bonus that goes with accomplishing that: The promising, less experienced writers can be part of the staffs of the resulting shows, working with and learning from the pros who already know how it's done. *Then* they go on to shows of their own, their chances of success vastly heightened by that experience.

The Gannett money that went into buying and restoring the

studio itself always figured to be a pretty safe investment. It ultimately was—and then some. But there came a time when, Neuharth having retired, our underwriting partner lost confidence in our adventure together. I know John Curley and Doug McCorkindale had no resistance from the Gannett board to the decision to bail out. From their standpoint, we were not performing well enough in a business that in fact might no longer be a business at all.

In the few years since our divorce, I have become more and more convinced that no company this side of a major studio, or a company underwritten or partially owned by a network, should expect to make a living by producing and selling television programs to networks. The deficits are just too big and postnetwork syndication too uncertain. Even when all goes well, the money simply takes too long to come back. The business only makes sense for big companies with deep pockets and multiple divisions, with interacting activities that can take profitable advantage of every ancillary opportunity.

The parting from Gannett was amicable. John Curley, now CEO, and I exchanged relatively warm letters lamenting our mutual fate, but leaving no doubt that the marriage was over. Some months later, before Gannett sold the lot itself, Doug McCorkindale paid a visit to Jack Kindberg, still running the studio in his low-key, effective fashion. That done, Doug came up to my office, and we spent a pleasant hour just schmoozing about past and current events. A couple of years later, Sony bought the Culver Studios. Though I kept my office on the Culver lot, I did so as a rent-paying tenant, not as the landlord.

There's no question Al Neuharth was missed at GTG after his Gannett retirement. He had created our partnership, and when he was gone, no one in management had any interest in our continuing to be part of the Gannett family. It's also true that at the time the partnership was dissolved, in early 1990, we had little to show for our efforts. But I thought then, and think now, that an equally important reason for the unhappiness of the post-Neuharth Gannett management was the fact that GTG had been Al's baby.

After he left, we had no advocate on the Gannett board; when he was still chairman, I know there were times he came to our defense. That was true during the worst of GTG times, when our entertainment shows were not succeeding and *USA Today on TV* was an expensive failure. Several board members, including Meredith Brokaw, questioned the wisdom of the company's investment in us. The fact that Meredith had begun to look askance at the venture made a particular impression on Al, who knew the Brokaws were my friends. "Isn't it about time to stop the bleeding?" she had asked her colleagues. She was surely fulfilling her board member obligations responsibly, but when Al told me about it, it became even clearer that the Tinker-Gannett union was headed for divorce court.

Indeed, Meredith's feelings were not exclusive to her, and eventually probably belonged to every member of the board. It did not surprise me to learn that one who had taken his negative opinion of GTG outside the boardroom was Julian Goodman. Perhaps he was a bit embarrassed to have played a part in getting Tinker and Gannett together in the first place. Whatever his reason, I would have preferred that he express his thoughts to me instead of running around knocking me to others, as some of them have reported.

The only bit of good news about the unhappy end of GTG was our timing. Our kind of independent production had become a nonbusiness, fraught with huge episode deficits, in which even a company with better luck than ours can succeed its way into the poorhouse. In spite of our best efforts to pump up a viable production company, we inadvertently did Gannett a long-run financial favor by failing.

From the day we met through the day he stopped being Gannett's chairman, Al Neuharth was a stand-up guy who played it straight with me. Like Bob Kintner at NBC, no one ever had to guess what Al was thinking. And, like Bob, he was a leader.

Jack Welch is a charismatic leader, and no sophisticated observer would bet he won't achieve his stated goal: to make GE the "highest-valued corporation in the world."

Jack's a persuasive guy, and his ability to get people to see things his way is based on much more than likability. He's so believable that it's easy to get carried along when he's doing the talking, and sometimes he seems to carry himself along. He probably thinks he meant it back in 1986 when he said publicly that GE doesn't tamper with winning businesses. And he may even think he hasn't done so. But as a direct result of not heeding his own words—"I will stay with a winning team"—Jack has seen the NBC he inherited reduced to something considerably less.

There may have been a portent of the managed failure to come in remarks Jack made to about a hundred NBC executives gathered at the Sheraton Bonaventure Hotel in Fort Lauderdale, Florida. It was March 1987, six months after my departure from NBC, and the first time Welch had addressed that group, which he did in an informal Sunday evening after-dinner talk.

Here's some of what he told them:

> *There is no question that you are leaders responsible for a vision of what you want. And your ability to communicate that vision—to rally a team of people around that vision of what you're after—is all you are paid for. If you can't do that, if you can't capture what you want, and you can't communicate it and get a team to follow it, you're not worth the powder to blow you to hell.*
>
> *Now what about NBC with General Electric, versus NBC*

with RCA? Because there are some who say we've had a change—a revolution. . . . But are you better off or worse off in this new deal? I'd say a little bit of both. I'd say for the good people, it's a dynamite deal. For the turkeys, it's a little marginal. . . .

And for those of you who aren't good, who aren't winners, and who aren't striving to differentiate, don't get on the NBC boat. Because if you can't demonstrate your performance and your differentiation, and your people can't—ain't no game for you! It was a deal in the other place where you could hide. So very clearly, we are out to provide the winners with more opportunity, to chase and search for those that are hiding under the umbrella, and rid ourselves of those.

There's a lot of win for some people—and there's some lose for others. There'll be more rigor, there'll be more demands, there'll be more capital, there will be more speed, there'll be more differentiation. But there'll be a hell of a lot more expectation. Lots of expectation, lots of delivery.

As for NBC, my view is obvious. I mean, you're clearly making us all look smart. We bought RCA; NBC is hitting a home run, we all look smart, people writing nice articles about us, how clever we are. We're just a turn away from bad ratings, and we wouldn't be as clever, and we know that. More important, we're in a business that we like—a game we like to play in. . . .

We used to have seven to eight to nine layers from the president to the plant floor. We now have no businesses with more than five. We'll have everyone with close to four by the end of next year. Layers are the bane of a corporation. You ought to think about that at NBC. Layers not only cost cost, they screw up communications to a factor of ten.

We want a team that recognizes that the world is changing. We don't want NBC to be in the dink while it changes. We want to be on top while it changes. You can change with time, you don't have to panic, you don't have to be crude. You don't have to be anything but sensitive. But you've got to change. Your world is changing. We're going to demand from you earnings growth every year. And don't give us any shrugs about that—those are the rules of the road.

We want the highest quality, and the absolute lowest cost

*in the game. And don't you dare listen to that Dan Rather
blabber about cost and quality! The Japanese have proven it
long ago—that cost and quality don't go together. . . . And
high-cost/high-quality have been a loser since day one. So
you get to be the lowest-cost/highest-quality guys and ladies
in town. And win the ball game on that basis.*

*Demonstrate leadership. Take charge of your destiny.
Don't leave it in our hands. We want your culture. We don't
know how to run your business. Our game is for you to win.
We've got resources, a playing field. You take charge of your
destiny.*

*If you don't, we will. But we don't know how to do it. You
know how to do it. . . . No one wants you to stay on top more
than we do. We live off your success. We want to be number
one more than anything in the world.*

*We want to be the most valued corporation in existence.
We're out to do it. You are a visible, highly important part of
it. We are so lucky you've done so well. We are grateful for
what you've done. And we are a pain in the ass and want you
to do a hell of a lot better for the next years ahead. I think of
no team that can do it better than this.*

If I had been in that room, as part of the NBC team that had
taken the company from the depths to the heights, I would have
found Jack's remarks anything but a pep talk. On the contrary,
they were insulting, condescending, and more than a little
threatening. He was happy—"clever"—to have acquired the
crown jewel among the RCA businesses, but he was quick to
dump on the parent company he had bought for $6 billion just a
year earlier. And he showed contempt for some of the very people
who had polished NBC to a high luster—the "turkeys" who
would now be an endangered species.

In the room that night were the eight executives who had
comprised my own Chairman's Council, who would all be gone
in a couple of years. Each received generous payouts, which
means that General Electric spent a lot of money to ensure
NBC's abysmal performance to come. Bob Wright, untutored and
without a lifetime of broadcasting behind him, was expected to
fill the void. It was a kamikaze assignment.

Jack's promise that night to supply more capital has led NBC into a variety of expensive ventures, with mixed results. While the primary business of the company, television broadcasting, has fallen into disrepair, NBC has purchased a television station in Miami; started a cable channel, CNBC, and is birthing another; bought minority interests in a wide variety of programming services here and abroad; and lost an estimated $100 million on the misconceived 1992 Olympic Triplecast.

The Triplecast was a costly example of what happens when broadcasting decisions are made by nonbroadcasters. NBC had already paid hundreds of millions of dollars for the right to present 160 hours of coverage during the two weeks of the Olympics. The Triplecast, on three cable channels, competed directly against that coverage—and viewers were asked to pay for it. Not surprisingly, hardly anyone did.

CNBC was designed to compete against an older cable service, the Financial News Network, but despite the resources of GE, cable operators resisted giving it channel space. In order to attract enough circulation to make CNBC viable, NBC was forced to buy out FNN at what Wall Street considered an exorbitant price. Other than its stock ticker, CNBC has failed to develop any discernible persona, and in prime time is indifferently, sometimes pruriently, programmed. I've wondered whether Jack ever watches it and what he thinks of it.

Under its GE owners, much of the energy of NBC has understandably been directed to the new technologies. Not so understandably, network broadcasting, the business that made NBC a national institution, was left on automatic pilot. Jack Welch may have wanted to duplicate the Japanese highest-quality/lowest-cost model with his American network, but his NBC management team became committed to running the company at lowest-cost—and frequently ignored highest-quality. Leadership in broadcasting is derived from a combination of elements—high ratings, quality programs, the best news organization—not all of which can be measured in dollars-and-cents terms. If all your major decisions are made on the basis of cost, if your only management horizon is the bottom line, you can bet your peacock you'll have a second-rate network. Even in the best of times for ABC, CBS, and NBC, which these clearly are not, there's always been a battle between what should be done for the bottom line and what should be done. With network audiences now only two thirds what they used to be, the bottom line is almost always the winner.

Starting in 1993, viewers in Los Angeles could see this first-hand. KNBC-TV, which NBC owns, moved *Meet the Press,* the longest-running public affairs show in all of television and a fixture since 1947, to the impossible hour of 7 A.M. Sunday. They did so in order to clear the 8 to 9:30 period for a local "news" show consisting of soft features, many repeated from prior broadcasts, assorted fluff pieces, and distinctly nonurgent talk between the two anchors. Barely a smidgeon of hard news in the whole ninety minutes, but because it's local, the station apparently makes a little more money.

Exiling *Meet the Press* to 7 A.M. does more than deprive many viewers in the country's second-largest market of exposure to the information and opinion it offers on national issues affecting their lives. It also disparages a show that has a proud tradition, an institution valued as special to NBC for more than forty-five years. Fortunately (but not accidentally), Angelenos get their information fixes from ABC and CBS, which see fit to air *This Week with David Brinkley* and *Face the Nation* when people are available to watch them.

I called Tim Russert one day to register my complaint about the cavalier scheduling. Tim, an ex-colleague, not only hosts the show and runs the Washington bureau of NBC News, but is one of those people who can get things done. Except this one. "Grant," he said, "of course I hate that L.A. scheduling. I've tried everything I can think of to have it changed to a later time. I just can't do it." In microcosm, the Los Angeles Sunday morning schedule illustrates what's wrong with GE owning NBC. Their attitude is: Never mind doing the right thing. We can make a few more bucks with the local show. The ironic capper is that GE is a *Meet the Press* sponsor! Under the current ownership, the king isn't just in the counting house; the king *is* the counting house.

In Fort Lauderdale, after urging his NBC audience to "take charge of your own destiny," Jack Welch had added, "If you don't, we will. *But we don't know how to do it.*" Subsequently, by trying to do what he didn't know how to do, Jack distinguished GE's stewardship from that of the new owners of NBC's counterparts. Even as the business of being a network, any network, began to decline, NBC made the trip south faster than its competitors.

At ABC, the arrival of Cap Cities was accompanied by the most salutary bonus possible: The new owners were broadcasters when they came through the door. At the top, Tom Murphy and Dan Burke had impeccable credentials derived from long and successful management of television stations. In taking control of a larger arena, including important news and prime-time programs and people, they also knew what they *didn't* know. They moved quickly to get up to speed in the less familiar areas, making many trips to Los Angeles to steep themselves in what the folks in the Entertainment division do.

At CBS, the learning process took more time. I thought Larry Tisch, in the early days of his CEOship, might hurl CBS into the drink also. Larry knows a lot about a lot of things, and he may have temporarily believed that broadcasting was one of them. At the time, it wasn't, and with the good counsel of his trusted and able lieutenant, Jay Kriegel, he made sure he was never without an experienced broadcasting hand to run what CBS calls, appropriately, its Broadcast Group.

When Gene Jankowski, who had been president of the Group for eleven years, exited in 1988, Tisch moved Howard Stringer, the president of CBS News, into his job. Howard has spent his entire working life at CBS, and came to his new responsibilities with a solid background in management and production. In turn, Howard's own divisional aides, also trained up in the business, are fluent in the programming language spoken in the Entertainment division. That's a key operational asset for CBS, just as the NBC Chairman's Council was for me. Over time, Larry obviously became confident and comfortable with Howard's management skills, and the fortunes of CBS have greatly improved under his capable leadership. And then in 1993, Howard pulled off one of broadcasting's great executive feats.

Johnny Carson, after an amazing thirty-year run, had finally announced in May of 1991 his decision to retire the next year as undefeated champion of late-night television. *The Tonight Show with Johnny Carson* was an institution—far and away the most successful, most watched, most profitable long-running program in television history. The late-night time period on NBC had earlier inhabitants: Jerry Lester (with *Broadway Open House* in 1950) was the first, followed by Steve Allen (the first *Tonight* show) in 1954 and Jack Paar in 1957. But Carson had taken it to a new level, fought off so many challengers from the other networks and been on top for so long that many viewers had no memory of late-night television B.C.

Moreover, *Tonight's* success delivered enough audience for NBC to open up the 12:30 A.M. time period for David Letterman, whose own distinctive show we had premiered just after I returned to NBC in 1981. He had been lighting up the post-*Tonight* hour for more than a decade. Letterman proved that a good show could make a post-Carson hour viable, leading NBC to extend the late-night franchise for yet another half-hour with Bob Costas's *Later* show. It was an invincible, moneymaking block of time, all based on Carson's dominance, and it was an NBC exclusive.

No one who saw the last two Carson shows in May 1992 will forget the poignancy of Bette Midler singing, right to his naked face, "You Made Me Love You," and Johnny's own moving good-bye on his final night. There wasn't a dry eye in anyone's house. The people who should have been crying the hardest were the executive decision-makers at NBC, although they didn't yet know it. With the considerable advance planning time given them by Carson's early retirement announcement, they fretted and fiddled and agonized over the matter of choosing his successor. What seemed to me (and to many others) an "automatic" decision proved to be one that NBC had all kinds of trouble making. Finally, only days before the deadline and Johnny's imminent departure, network management made the call—and they made it wrong.

Jay Leno, an accomplished stand-up comic, had been the designated guest host on *Tonight,* and had done a creditable job. He had to be a candidate to replace Carson on a regular basis; at the very least, NBC owed him the courtesy of seeming to consider him seriously. The other obvious candidate was Letterman.

NBC's ultimate choice of Leno was, to many of us looking on, a bonehead decision; it would prove to be a mistake of monstrous proportions and repercussions. I can make an educated guess at part of the network's rationale.

They saw Leno as a proven commodity behind the *Tonight* desk, and certainly Letterman was bringing up the rear nicely. To move Dave up to Johnny's role presented at least the possibility of failure; one school of thought was that he would be too hip for the larger 11:30 audience, that the comedy that played so well with his young fans wouldn't work with the more demographically diverse viewers in the earlier time period. If he were to fail as Carson's replacement, NBC would be blowing two hours of solid programming. The safe course, they probably thought, was to bring Jay in for Johnny and leave Dave where he was doing just fine.

At the time, I thought NBC had come down on the wrong side of the question, mostly because there was no upside to their decision. Jay Leno was a serviceable replacement host, but all he had ever really done was keep the chair warm for Johnny. He lacks a crucial quality; in the jargon of the business, he has no sex appeal. Carson has it in spades, and so does Letterman.

At dinner a few nights before his own final show, I had a chance to ask Carson his opinion of NBC's choice. Characteristically, he was very clear in his response, saying not only that the network had blown it, but that David had been paying his dues for ten years and deserved the shot. I asked how NBC had reacted to his opinion, and was stunned by his answer: "They never asked me." For three decades this man had been performing magnificently in a singular job that now needed filling, and no one thought to consult him about his successor. I'm tempted to comment that the omission typifies what has been wrong with the management of NBC under its current owners, but perhaps I just did.

I don't think even Johnny anticipated Letterman's extreme reaction to the network's choice, however. I know I didn't. Dave had been typically laid-back, publicly at least, while NBC had dithered and vacillated. But it would turn out that Letterman cared, and cared a lot. Moreover, the network executives, who, at the very least, owed him a personal visit of explanation, were far too cavalier in notifying him. Despite hearing the decision almost when the rest of the world did, David's public comments were mild and unemotional.

Some weeks later Howard Stringer invited me to breakfast, as he sometimes does when he's in Los Angeles. Howard, among a number of attributes, is bright, articulate, and amusing. We bantered about a wide range of industry topics, and then he shared a confidence with me: "I'm going to make a run at David Letterman."

My surprise quickly gave way to an appreciation of the enormous potential of such a coup, assuming Howard could pull it off. For years CBS had been trying, without success, to put a dent in NBC's late-night supremacy; Pat Sajak had been the latest to find Carson too tough to handle. With one audacious move, it was now at least possible that Letterman would derail the entire NBC late-night train. Privately, though, I thought the odds against the success of Howard's mission were long. I couldn't imagine that NBC would let David get away, whatever the cost to keep him. I didn't yet know, of course, the extent of his disenchantment with his longtime employer.

Months later Letterman jumped ship, with huge attendant publicity and national interest. CBS had stepped up to a very expensive contract for Dave, and sprang for a lot more to refurbish the old Ed Sullivan Theater on Broadway to provide a gleaming new home for their new star. Finally, Stringer and his colleagues put on a full-court press to persuade CBS affiliates, many with very profitable syndicated shows playing at 11:30 P.M., to return to the network fold.

From Letterman's first night on CBS, his show has been a winner and, as it shines, the competition sinks slowly in the west. Howard Stringer's accomplishment—call it "The Stealing of Late Night"—would produce a tremendous swing in CBS's fortunes. The long-range impact in both dollars and industry prestige is far beyond that of the most successful prime-time show, even a *Cosby*. The only comparable masterstroke in broadcasting history was Bill Paley's theft of NBC's biggest radio stars, back in the forties.

I think it's fair to say that NBC, alone among the three major networks, has had the culture and business philosophy of the parent imposed on it. GE said all the right things but didn't do them. Mostly, it meddled and mandated. The result was analogous to the water skier who lets go of the tow rope. As NBC ran out of the momentum supplied by GE's predecessors, everything sank—audience, profit, image, and morale.

Bob Wright became a victim of the culture he grew up in. In a business that didn't always behave like other businesses, a business with which he was largely unfamiliar, GE's obsession with delayering left him with fourteen direct reports—and a nearly total absence of broadcast experience at the senior-management level. Out in Burbank, Brandon Tartikoff soldiered on alone, outmanned, outgunned, and finally overcome. Actually, as he fled, he tossed the live grenade of NBC's program schedule to Warren Littlefield, the new head of the Entertainment division, but the results had long since been determined.

NBC's implosion was heard around the television world. CBS and ABC and Fox were delighted beneficiaries, and all their fortunes improved. And though NBC is a relatively small piece of the GE pie, it did not go unnoticed in Fairfield, Connecticut, that their cash cow at 30 Rockefeller Plaza was lying down and breathing hard. Jack Welch's high marks for his accomplishments at General Electric will surely not change as a result of NBC's reversals. But as the principal author of those reversals, he has to be embarrassed, and he should be. I left him an NBC that was the 1927 New York Yankees, and some good advice about how to keep it that way.

My observation of GE's management of NBC has led to some thoughts about the ownership of broadcasting entities. Maximizing profit is an honorable goal, and American companies are devoted to achieving it. For most business people, it's the reason for coming to work. For broadcasters, it's a prescription for being second-rate.

My ideal world would require bottom line–fixated companies and individuals seeking to participate in broadcasting ownership to play by different rules. Those rules would obligate anyone wanting the unique and priceless franchise of immediate access to American homes to recognize the public service component of their responsibilities. Being a broadcaster, not just a businessman, ought to be required. Trying to squeeze every last buck from the enterprise wouldn't do it anymore; the inevitable result of that—to borrow from Jack Welch's rhetoric—is low cost/low quality. People who care more about money than programs are going to produce a kind of television that too often aims low and still misses the target.

Wonderful programs, entertainment and news, sprout and flourish only in an environment where high quality is encouraged and recognized. Just as the young Gary Goldberg was inspired to do his best work by the creative standards of his peers at MTM, so did Ed Murrow and Bob Kintner and (today) Roone Arledge create an atmosphere where memorable broadcast journalism could live. High standards produce high quality.

Where the focus is solely on money, public service becomes a nonstarter. The result can be seen every evening in local newscasts that are short on news, filled with murders and mayhem, fires and felonies, and singularly lacking in useful information for the viewer. Anyone claiming to be a broadcaster should be committed to giving something back to the community, spilling a little on the way to the bank. The spillage would be in the form of broadcast public service to the community being served, a job that too frequently these days goes undone.

For those who simply can't buy that "give something back" philosophy, whether as outright owners or as shareholders, I would advise their investment in other, more traditional businesses, enterprises dedicated to wringing every last dollar of profit out of their efforts. To be clear, I'm not advocating altruism; operating a television station or a network can be a very good business, indeed, if done well. I'm talking about taking a little less profit—not taking a loss. Those who can't get the job done, and done well enough to live by this code of company good citizenship, should be in another business anyway.

One of the events that's supposed to mark the arrival of the new century is the debut of "the electronic superhighway." This five-hundred-channel cornucopia of interactive programming, pay-per-view services, and on-line data will, according to its most optimistic cheerleaders, hasten the extinction of what they call the network dinosaurs. There will be no further need for the inflexibility of traditional network schedules. However programs get into the home, by wire or by satellite, viewers will be able to do their own scheduling, selecting whatever they want to see (or interact with) from a dazzling array of possibilities, and having it on the screen whenever they choose.

Maybe. There's certainly no question that technological advances will continue to change how television is presented and viewed, but don't count the old networks out just yet. At this stage, hardware is king. Discussion about what actually might be transmitted over the superhighway has remained vague; for now, the focus of tomorrow's highway superintendents is on how they'll deliver all the myriad services the fast-moving technology will make possible. Recently we have begun to hear doubts and questions about those services: Is the average viewer ready to interact? Does he even want to? Will there be any significant traffic on the electronic highway? Who will program five hundred channels? With what?

I've already owned up to having no credentials as a seer, but forty-some years in broadcasting have given me a pretty clear idea about why there's a television set in everyone's home, and why it's on for seven hours each day. For most American families, watching television is their primary leisure-time activity. They like what they see, or at least prefer it to doing something else. It's an enjoyable part of their daily routine—and it's always been a totally passive one. Once you turn on the set and select the channel, all you have to do is watch it.

Moreover, even in the much more limited thirty- to seventy-channel universe now generally available, most of us seek out the same six or eight. That suggests we may not be terribly responsive to the five hundred alternatives promised by the hardware enthusiasts—less so if couch potatoes come to believe that "interactive" means work. Trying to turn television viewing from a passive exercise into audience participation is going to take some doing. Fully realized use and appreciation of the new services on the superhighway, if they are ever to be achieved, will surely have to wait for a new generation of viewers. In the same way that older folks struggle to master computers while kids take to them with ease and speed, the proposed television of the future can't possibly attain its potential until people start growing up with it.

I'm not going to be around long enough to care whether there will ever be five hundred viable channels, but I do have some thoughts about the next few years:

• Programming will get worse. The financial pressures on the networks will continue to put a premium on low-risk, low-cost programming. For a while, newsmagazines provided one solution, but in early 1994 the glut of these shows appeared to have exceeded the public's appetite. Although tabloid television, under the cover of "reality programming," continues to thrive in syndication, the newsmagazine genre seems to have reached the saturation point on network prime time. But don't hold your breath waiting for the next *Hill Street Blues*. (Someday, such high-cost, high-quality efforts will be back, but at direct cost to the audience.) That kind of program was risky and hard to find even when network license fees covered most of the production cost, and the syndication business was still good. Today, no production company in its right mind will accept the prospect of a weekly deficit of hundreds of thousands of dollars with little prospect of ultimately making some money on the back end. Networks have always been "department stores," offering an array of programming of all shapes and sizes, from which we selected merchandise we liked. The assortment is already more limited, and the quality line is nearly out of stock.

• A significant number of the new channels will be specialty shops. Those not dedicated to movies on demand or sports or shopping services will be given over to special interest fare— anything from auto racing to zoology. Some of this niche programming surely has a market, but all-family viewing it's not.

• You're going to pay for what you get. Unlike networks we have known, the new delivery systems will have no public service obligations, no reason to present a balanced and diverse schedule, and will be able to price their product at market rates. And big movies, major sports events, and many of the proposed new services will be pay-per-view.

• They don't deserve it anymore, but the networks will continue to take the bulk of the blame for what's wrong with television. For most of the lives of our lawmakers in Washington, the networks *were* television, and old habits die hard. These days, sex and violence on the tube come mostly from cable movies, the local news, and a few syndicated shows. Network programs, by comparison, are generally bland if not blameless, but when Congress needs a villain as the centerpiece for a hearing, the networks will be it.

• Networks are not dinosaurs and will not become extinct. They have a distribution system in place that's the envy of all the new technologies, and the strongest among them will continue to make money. With all their problems—costs that are too high, competition from dozens (soon to be hundreds) of other channels that didn't used to exist, and a difficult economic climate—they still capture more than half of the prime-time audience every night. Other companies are even trying to *start* networks, so the Jurassic age is not right around the corner. Just last May, in an aggressive display of confidence in the future of network broadcasting, Rupert Murdoch invested $500 million to bring twelve CBS, ABC, and NBC affiliates to Fox.

As an erstwhile networker, I'm not unhappy about that. There was always a special excitement about being part of an event that could move the entire country at once. No niche programmer will ever match the thrill I enjoyed when one of our NBC shows became a national favorite, or when we moved from worst to first with an array of programs we could all be proud of.

As I look back at the last forty years, I think my greatest good luck was my timing; I just happened on the scene as television was beginning to flex its muscles, getting ready to take center stage. Once we all got past the wondrous miracle of having pictures with sound delivered to our living rooms, we judged television by its programs, not by how they arrived.

Now we're entering a new era of indeterminate duration, one that may bring back Marshall McLuhan's famous phrase, but with a twist. The medium will indeed be the message, because programming will take a backseat to how we get the programs. The name of the game will be delivery, and what's delivered is more likely to be of special interest than special.

Somewhere down the road, enterprising producers will find a way to underwrite elaborate, expensive shows—tomorrow's *Hill Street* and *Cheers*—by getting viewers to pay for what fiber optics, direct broadcast satellites, and other new delivery services will have on the menu. Whatever the means, whatever the cost, that's when the good times will begin again for the people who produce the shows. The tail of affordability will no longer be wagging the dog of creativity. It's not likely that I will be among the producers who inherit that return to the way it used to be, but I will envy them. If they get just half as much enjoyment from their work as we did in television's first four decades, they're going to have a hell of a lot of fun.

INDEX